I SAW A LIGHT AND CAME HERE

I SAW A LIGHT AND CAME HERE

Children's Experiences of Reincarnation

by

ERLENDUR HARALDSSON, Ph.D., AND JAMES G. MATLOCK, Ph.D.

www.whitecrowbooks.com

Pay particular attention to phenomena at the beginning and at the end of life. They may tell us what was before and what may follow.

~ KARLIS OSIS

CONTENTS

PART 2 BY JIM MATLOCK

ACKNOWLEDGEMENTS

Grants and support are gratefully acknowledged from the Division of Perceptual Studies (Prof. Ian Stevenson) at the University of Virginia, Institute of Borderline Areas of Psychology in Freiburg, The Druze Heritage Foundation (Mr. Salim Kheireddine) in London/Beirut, The Bial Foundation in Oporto, The Helen Abadzi Fund in USA, The Tate Fund of the Society for Psychical Research, and the University of Iceland.

For invaluable assistance in field work I thank the late Godwin Samararatne, the late Hector Samararatne, Tissa Jayawardane, the late A. B. Ratnayake, Rohana Bodhinarayana, Vimala Periyannanpillai, A. W. Ranasinghe, Prof. P. D. Premasiri of Peradeniya University, Mrs. Shanez Fernando and Terence Amarasekara, Majd Abu-Izzeddin, and Dr. Marwan Gharzeddin and the late Prof. Sami Makarem of the American University of Beirut (AUB). Special thanks to Duminda Ratnayake and Purnima Ekanayake who have kept in touch over the years.

Erlendur Haraldsson

I am indebted to Guy Lyon Playfair and Suzuco Hashizume, custodian of the files of the late Hernani Guimarães Andrade, for assistance in compiling the data on his cases tabulated in Chapter 26, and to several other colleagues, case subjects, and witnesses in relation to individual case summaries. Antonia Mills discussed with me her cases of Nathan and Toran (Titu) Singh. Jim B. Tucker put me in touch with Cyndi Hammons, who graciously answered my many questions about the memories and experiences of her son Ryan, enabling me to add details to Jim's account of the case in *Return to Life*. Mridula Sharma spent considerable time going over her own case, which was investigated by Ian Stevenson and Satwant Pasricha in the 1970s, but never reported by them. Satwant gave me permission to use her interview transcripts, which Jim Tucker sent me from the files at the University of Virginia. Kuldip Kumar Dhiman shared with me transcripts of his more recent interview with Mridula, and supplied the photograph of the house in which Mridula recalls having lived in her previous life.

"Katherine Mitchell" welcomed me into her home, put me in contact with other witnesses, and went to considerable effort to track down death certificates, birth certificates, and other documents related to her father and her son "Craig." I reported Craig's case at greater length at the Third Annual Meeting of the Lithuanian Society for the Study of Religions in Vilnius in in October, 2015. Two other cases are entirely new. I am grateful to Patricia and Steven Stein for sharing with me Steve's childhood memories of having died at the Alamo, and to Ronni Tepp-Rodriguez, Bianca Rodriguez, and Derek Moscinski, for their memories of Cruz Rodriguez and his apparent return as Cruz Moscinski. I learned about these last three cases through Facebook. Chapter 29, on suicide cases, is revised from a post in my Facebook group, Signs of Reincarnation. My analysis of the Carl Edon case in Chapter 30 also originally appeared as post for the Facebook group.

Jim Matlock

FOREWORD

In 1961, Ian Stevenson, then Chairman of the Department of Psychiatry at the University of Virginia, made a research trip to India after hearing about a few children who said they remembered a past life. Once there, he was surprised to find not just a few, but over twenty such cases.

So began a new field of study. Stevenson learned of more children who had talked about past lives and, once he began looking for them, hundreds more. He quickly saw that the details the children gave could often be verified to match ones belonging to the life and death of one particular deceased person. He published dozens of papers on the phenomenon, along with numerous books. When *JAMA*, the Journal of the American Medical Association, reviewed one of his books, the reviewer wrote that "in regard to reincarnation he has painstakingly and unemotionally collected a detailed series of cases ... in which the evidence is difficult to explain on any other grounds."

I had the good fortune in the late 1990s to join Stevenson in this research at the University of Virginia. I learned a great deal from him and from the work of other researchers who had followed him in this area. One was Erlendur Haraldsson. Along with studying some cases with Stevenson, Erlendur has independently investigated many more. Focusing on cases in Sri Lanka and Lebanon, he has demonstrated the same dogged attention to detail that Stevenson did, as he has worked to determine exactly what the children said and what the previous person did or did not do.

Erlendur has also moved beyond the study of individual cases to explore aspects of the phenomenon that no one had previously investigated.

He has done extensive psychological testing of children in both Sri Lanka and Lebanon, comparing those who reported memories of past lives with others who did not, and his findings are significant. He was also the first to systematically interview the child study group once they had grown into adulthood. Again, his findings are significant.

Jim Matlock is an anthropologist by training with a longstanding interest in parapsychology. He notes that he was often comfortably ensconced in his armchair while Erlendur was traveling to various parts of the world investigating cases, but that doesn't mean Jim wasn't working. Among numerous other papers, he wrote what was essentially the definitive review of this research, a 1990 paper in the *Advances in Parapsychological Research* series [Matlock, J. G. (1990). Past life memory case studies. In S. Krippner (Ed.), *Advances in Parapsychological Research* (Vol. 6, pp. 187-267). Jefferson, NC: McFarland.]

With the present book, Erlendur and Jim have produced an important contribution to the field. We get impressive individual case reports from both of them, such as the case of Duminda, a little boy in Sri Lanka who made the unlikely claim to have been a senior Buddhist monk who nonetheless enjoyed a red car, a moneybag, and a radio. Rejecting a journalist's quick identification of a deceased man whose life was a very imprecise match for the boy's statements, Erlendur worked until he found a monk from the temple that Duminda named who had in fact owned the items Duminda remembered.

Erlendur and Jim also consider the trends in the cases, along with examining the phenomenon in a broader context. Jim explores factors such as cultural patterns and particular kinds of cases, including ones involving children who speak in a foreign language or remember lives cut short by suicide, and Erlendur shares his studies in areas such as deathbed visions, near-death experiences, and mediumship. In the end, they have produced an essential work that, as Erlendur says, suggests that life is circular—as life is followed by death is followed by life—but also a spiral, as humanity's development gradually moves along a slow but sure path of progress.

~ Jim B. Tucker, M.D.

INTRODUCTION TO PART I

Children who insist that they have lived before and claim to remember incidents from an earlier life have been found in most parts of the world. This book presents some of the research to test if there is any basis for such claims. Written sources show that belief in reincarnation has existed for millennia. Do these alleged childhood memories offer any support for this ancient belief? This book tries to answer that question.

The book is divided into two parts. Part 1 is written by Erlendur Haraldsson and Part 2 by Jim Matlock. I, Erlendur, primarily describe my investigations of children who insist they remember or are assumed to remember episodes from an earlier life. I have investigated around one hundred such cases in Sri Lanka, Lebanon, India and Iceland. I have interviewed the children, their parents, and other witnesses who talk about their past life. I give detailed descriptions of a number of these cases and of my findings in general. I also write about the consequences of the "circular/spiral" model of life, namely the age-old concept of reincarnation.

I have conducted psychological studies to find out how such children may differ from children with no claimed memories. They do in several respects. I also have conducted longitudinal studies to examine how these childhood memories may fade away from childhood to adulthood, or diminish over that period.

Jim, with a doctoral degree in anthropology, has conducted little field research on reincarnation cases but is exceptionally well read about studies conducted around the globe. Jim writes about cases that have been investigated in various parts of the world and about the various aspects of such cases. He has also through social media developed contacts with a large number of people who are interested in or have "reincarnation experiences" as he likes to call them. An attentive reader may find that our views or emphases may differ slightly on some points, which adds to the value of our book. Let us see if that turns out to be the case. My first chapter is about a Sri Lankan girl who starts to speak about her memories at an early age. I describe this as a remarkable case in my attempt to verify her memories.

I

I SAW A LIGHT AND CAME HERE

One of our most memorable cases is that of a girl named Purnima Ekanayake, who was nine years old when I first met her at her home in Bakamuna in northern Sri Lanka. At this time she was still speaking about her previous life, which is unusual for a child of that age, having begun to do so when she was as young as three. Purnima seemed well adjusted and happy in her family, and communicated freely. She already understood some English and took a keen interest in my conversations with her parents, sometimes correcting what they told me about her.

Purnima, a charming young girl who according to her mother enjoyed wearing beautiful dresses, recounted her memories with great clarity. Her case turned out to have some particularly interesting features, one being that she had memories not only of the events leading to her death in her previous existence, but also experiences in the 'intermission' period between that death and her rebirth. She bore prominent birthmarks on her chest corresponding to the wounds suffered in her fatal accident as well as manifesting some psychological features I have observed in other children with similar memories. In school she excelled, and was top of her class of 33.

Although she began speaking of her past life in 1990, it was not until three years later that Purnima's parents began to take what she was telling them seriously. In Table 1-1 you will find statements which, according to her parents, she made before her previous family was traced. These statements are based on several interviews I carried out with her parents, spread over three years. Purnima herself also made these statements to me, although unfortunately her parents did not record them in writing before attempting to verify them.

Let us look at a few of them.

Table 1.1. Statements Made by Purnima (According to her Parents)
Before First Contact with her Alleged Previous Family

	Statement	Status
1.	I died in a traffic accident and came here.	+
2.	My family was making incense and had no other job.	+
3.	We were making Ambiga incense.	+
4.	We were making Geta Pichcha incense.	+
5.	The incense factory is near a brick factory and near a pond.	+
6.	First only our family worked and then two people were employed.	?
7.	We had two vans.	+
8.	We had a car.	+
9.	I was the best manufacturer of incense sticks.	?
10.	In the earlier life I was married to a sister-in-law, Kusumi.	+
11.	The owner of the incense factory, [I] had two wives.	+
12.	My previous father was bad (present father is good).	?
13.	Previous father was not a teacher as present father is.	+
14.	I had two younger brothers (who were better than present brothers)	+
15.	My mother's name was Simona.	+
16.	Simona was very fair (in skin color).	-
17.	I attended Rahula School.	+
18.	Rahula School had a two storey building (not like in Bakamuna).	-
19.	My father said, you need not go to school, you can make money making incense.	-

20.   I studied only up to the 5th grade.   +

+ Statement verified. (14)

- Statement did not fit and was wrong. (3)

? Impossible to ascertain; may or may not be right. (3)

I died in a traffic accident. As a small child Purnima repeatedly said: "People who drive over people in the street are bad persons." Sometimes she would ask her mother: "Do you not also think that persons who cause accidents are bad people?" These were the first indirect statements referring to a previous life. She also told about a fatal accident with a "big vehicle." Her mother thinks that this statement first came about (or she started to pay attention to it) as a traffic accident occurred near their home. Purnima's mother was upset about the accident. Then Purnima tried to soothe her by saying: "Do not think about this accident. I came to you after such an accident." She told her mother how she closed her eyes after the accident and then she came "here." Her mother asked if she had been taken to a hospital. "No" she replied. She added: "A heap of iron was on my body."

1. Purnima remembered a life as a male incense-maker who died when a bus drove over him. She remembered the name of the brands they were making and many other details that were verified. Here she is in a festive dress with Erlendur and his interpreter Mr. Ratnayake.

5

Purnima said that after the accident she floated in semi-darkness for a few days. She saw people mourning for her and crying, and saw her body until and including the funeral. There were many people like her floating around. Then she saw some light, went there and came "here" (to Bakamuna).

She spoke of her family being incense makers. They were making Ambiga and Geta Pichcha incense. Purnima's parents thought that she might be speaking of Ambiga because a jeweler firm of that name was advertising on television. Her mother assumed she was mixing something up. They also thought that she might be speaking of Geta Pichcha as there are "geta pichcha" flowers (a variety of jasmine) in their garden. Purnima also stated that all her family and some outsiders were working for them making incense sticks. She used to walk around with her hands behind her back imitating how she had examined how they were doing their work. We checked the shops in Bakamuna and found only two brands of incense made in Kandy and one from India; no Ambiga or Geta Pichcha incense.

In the earlier life I was married to a sister-in-law, Kusumi. She had been a man in her previous life. Further statements will be listed and discussed below. Soon after her birth Purnima's mother noticed a large cluster of light-colored birthmarks to the left side of her chest, and on her lower ribs. Birthmarks or birth defects can be important features in children who speak of previous-life memories. A child may explain birthmarks on his or her body as resulting from wounds inflicted in a previous life. In his two-volume work on birthmark and birth defects, Ian Stevenson (1997a, 1997b) gives a detailed description of 225 such cases.

However, birthmark cases are relatively rare. Among the 64 cases I investigated in Sri Lanka there were three children who associated birthmarks on their body with injuries inflicted on them in their previous life, or talked about accidents and injuries in a previous life which were later found to correspond to birthmarks on their body. One of them was Purnima.

How Purnima's Previous Family was Found

Purnima saw a television program on the famous Kelaniya temple that is close to Colombo and some 145 miles away from Bakamuna, where she lived. She said that she recognized the temple. She was then four years old. A little later her father, who is principal of the secondary school in Bakamuna, and her mother, who is also a teacher, took a group of school children to Kelaniya temple, a major place of pilgrimage among Buddhists in Sri Lanka. Purnima was allowed to join the group. In Kelaniya she said that she had lived on the other side of the river, which flows at the side of the temple compound.

In January 1993 W. G. Sumanasiri was appointed a teacher at her father's school in Bakamuna. He spent the weekends in Kelaniya, where he had married. Purnima's father and Mr. Sumanasiri decided that he would make inquiries across the Kelaniya River.

Purnima's father gave Mr. Sumanasiri the following statements to check: She had lived on the other side of the river from the Kelaniya temple; she had been making Ambiga and Gita Pichcha incense sticks, and had a fatal accident with a big vehicle, and was selling incense sticks on a bicycle. Mr. Sumanasiri and his brother-in-law took the hand-driven ferry across the river as there was some distance to the next bridge. They inquired if there were incense makers in the area. There were three. One of them named his brands Ambiga and Geta Pichcha. He was L. A. Wijisiri. His brother-in-law and associate, Jinadasa Perera, had died in an accident with a bus as he was taking incense to the market on a bicycle in September 1985. This was about two years prior to Purnima's birth.

Shortly afterwards, Purnima, her parents, Mr. Sumanasiri and his brother-in-law made an unannounced visit to the Wijisiri family after spending a night at Sumanasiri's home in Kelaniya. There, Purnima's mother told me that Purnima whispered to her ear: "This incense dealer (she) had two wives. This is a secret. Don't give them my address. They might trouble me."

When the group came to Mr. Wijisiri's house he was not in but he arrived a short while later. His two daughters were at home and Purnima met them first. When Wijisiri came walking towards the house Purnima told those around her: "This is Wijisiri, he is coming. He is my brother-in-law." He heard her say this just as he was entering the house. When Purnima said that she had come to see her brother-in-law and sister, he was puzzled and did not realize that she was talking about a previous life. Mr. Wijisiri wanted to send them away saying that those they were asking for were not here. Then, when he thought about it and the little girl started to ask about various kinds of packets and such things, then only was he inclined to believe her story. She alone spoke; no one else said anything. This is how Wijisiri remembered her visit. This account was confirmed by Purnima's father.

Purnima said to Wijisiri that she used to sell these incense sticks. She asked: "Have you changed the outer cover of the packets?" Wijisiri used to change the color and design every two years or so. She seemed to realize that the packets looked different from the time Jinadasa was working with Wijisiri. Then she spoke about the various packets and about an accident Wijisiri experienced many years ago (since that time he could not bend his knee). Also that Jinadasa (she) had applied medicine to his knee after the accident. She asked about Jinadasa's friends, like Somasiri and Padmasiri. Padmasiri is Wijisiri's brother who had gone with him on business on the day Jinadasa met with his accident. They had left home together and then split and went to different places. She mentioned their names. These were the things that convinced Wijisiri.

Purnima also asked about her mother and her (Jinadasa's) previous sister, who is Wijisiri's wife. The sister was abroad working in Saudi Arabia, and the mother was absent at her ancestral home. Then Purnima showed her birthmark. She said: "This is the mark I received when I was hit by a bus." Purnima also mentioned the place of Jinadasa's accident, Nugegoda, and that they had moved their home and factory to a somewhat different location from the time she was with them. These facts were correct.

From Wijisiri's family I learned that Jinadasa had in fact had two wives. After several years of living together he had disagreements with his first wife (Wijisiri's sister). He went to south Sri Lanka, became acquainted with a lady by the name of Nanda, and left his former family. In the town of Weligama he lived for five years with Nanda and produced incense with a friend, M. Somasiri, who gave us valuable information. (Jinadasa legally married neither of his wives. According to Sinhalese tradition a man and woman who live together are referred to as husband and wife). During a visit to Colombo, Jinadasa learned of Wijisiri's accident, which made him bed-ridden for several months. He then went to him to offer help. A few days later he met with his accident.

Did Purnima say anything that was wrong and that did not fit with Jinadasa's life? She had said that two vans and a car had belonged to her (Jinadasa). This was a family business so that was correct but formally the vehicles had belonged to Wijisiri. This is the essence of Wijisiri's account of his first meeting with Purnima.

We had been told that Purnima had recognized an old co-worker, Somasiri. He told us that he had come to see her at her first visit. He stood there amongst a group of persons. Then she pointed to him and said: "This is my friend." When Purnima's father asked who that man was, she answered: "This is Somasiri, my friend." Apparently she also recognized Jinadasa's younger sister, Violet. She and Somasiri told us that she had pointed to her and said: "This is my younger sister." These were the only names that Somasiri and Violet heard her say during the first visit.

Purnima's Knowledge of Incense-Making

Did Purnima know how incense is made? Yes, she said and gave a detailed reply. There are two ways to make it. One is with cow dung, the other is from ash from firewood (charcoal). A paste is made, and then a thin stick is cut from bamboo and some gum is applied on the bamboo stick. Then the stick is rolled over the paste and something is applied to obtain a nice smell. As far as she can remember they made their incense from charcoal powder. What is charcoal made from and how is it produced? "When firewood is burnt you get charcoal."

We asked Purnima's parents, if they knew how incense is made. The father had heard that it is made from cow-dung, and learned now for the first time that it can be made from firewood. Her mother knew even less. Godwin Samararatne, my interpreter, had never heard how incense is made. We later asked Wijisiri to describe to us and show us how they make their incense. Wijisiri did it the way that Purnima had described.

Further Verification of Purnima's Statements

Of the 20 statements listed in Table 1-1, 14 fit the life of Jinadasa (1-5, 7, 8, 10, 11, 13-15, 17, and 20), three are indeterminate (6, 9, 12), and three statements (16, 18, 19) are incorrect. During five visits in 1996 to 1999 numerous witnesses were interviewed, some of them several times.

Let us first consider the incorrect items. Jinadasa had attended Rahula School, we learned independently from his mother and younger sister. However, our inquiries revealed that this school did not have a two-storied building until the 1980s. It was correct that Jinadasa attended school only up to 5th grade, however, he was doing odd jobs until his sister married Wijisiri. Then he took up incense making and two years later "married" Wijisiri's sister. Hence the statement that Jinadasa's father had told him to leave school to earn money by making incense cannot be true. The statement of Jinadasa's mother being very fair, was not correct at the time we met her, and, that she was before seems unlikely.

Some of the correct items have already been described. Regarding item 5: Within 200 yards from Jinadasa's old residence is a pond. The old factory, which was some 100-150 yards down the road, had been demolished and close to it, a neighbor told us, there used to be a brick-making facility, and another is still close by. Item 13: Jinadasa's father had been a poor farmer (hence not a teacher). Item 14: Jinadasa, indeed, had two younger brothers (and two sisters).

The indeterminate items: Items 9 and 12 (best maker of incense sticks, and his father was a bad man) we had no ability to check. Items 6: First our family worked, then two people were employed. This was primarily a family business but soon they employed people who worked in the factory or in their homes. We could not ascertain when exactly they started to employ people, but gradually up to 30 persons came to work for them in the time of Jinadasa who was an industrious and popular man.

Most specific are items 3 and 4 stating that the family was making the brands Ambiga and Geta Pichcha. According to Wijisiri this is correct and they showed us packages of both brands. Since the time of Jinadasa the family has started to make two additional brands.

After the two families met, Purnima made some interesting intimate statements about his life with his first wife that she could hardly have learned from anyone. Unfortunately we found no way to verify them.

More on Purnima's Birthmarks

We have already mentioned that Purnima was born with prominent birthmarks on her lower chest, left of the midline (see photo 2). Her mother noticed them when she was washing Purnima as a baby. In a light-hearted way she said to her husband that these marks might be the result of an accident in a previous life. However, it was only when they met Jinadasa's family that the birthmarks became significant. Prior to the contact with that family Purnima never spoke about details of her injuries, nor do her parents remember that she associated her birthmarks with her accident. It was not until during Purnima's visit to Wijisiri that she mentioned that the bus wheels had run over her chest. Then she pointed across the left side of her chest where she has her birthmarks. Someone in Wijisiri's family then mentioned that Jinadasa had been injured on the left side of his trunk. Purnima's birthmarks were at the same location. The case was then considered confirmed by both families.

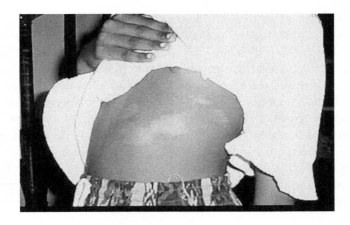

2. Post-mortem report on Jinadasa showed that Purnima's birthmarks corresponded to Jinadasa's fatal injuries in the bus accident.

Jinadasa died immediately after the accident. His brother, Chandradasa, was called into the mortuary to identify his brother and so was his sister. Chandradasa told us he saw massive injuries from the lower ribs on the left side and up and obliquely across the body, caused by the wheels of the bus. Sitriyavati, his sister, identified Jinadasa by his face. His body had then been covered by a sheet.

None of the persons involved in this case had seen the post-mortem report. After obtaining permission from the Magistrate Court of Gangodavilla, which handled Jinadasa's case, I obtained the post-mortem report from the physician, Dr. Kariyawasam, who conducted the examination. It gives a detailed description and a sketch of injuries. They had been massive, particularly on the left side of the chest, where several ribs had been broken.

The post-mortem report thus describes the internal injuries:

1. Fracture of the ribs, 1 and 2, 8, 9, and 10, laterally on the left. 1 to 5 anteriorly and 6 anteriorly and laterally, and 7 laterally. 8 and 9 anteriorly and posteriorly. 10 and 11 anteriorly.
2. The liver was ruptured.

3. The spleen was ruptured.
4. Lungs were penetrated by broken ribs.

Externally there was a "grazed abrasion 23"x10" running obliquely from the right shoulder across the chest to the (left) lower abdomen." There were lesser injuries on the legs and face.

Let us summarize the major points of this case. First the strong points. The two families lived far apart, and were complete strangers. A third party traced the person that matched Purnima's statements. Fourteen of seventeen statements that could be checked-were found to match the life of Jinadasa, who had died two years before Purnima was born. Purnima's cluster of birthmarks fell within the area of fatal injuries suffered by Jinadasa. Her birthmarks are on the left side of the chest where most of the ribs broke, and where he is likely to have felt the most pain. Also, Purnima has knowledge of incense making that is highly unusual for a child. She said she remembered it from her previous life.

The principal weakness of the case is that no record was made of Purnima's statements before the case was solved, and this occurred three years before I started her investigation. Still, the case of Purnima Ekanayake is of unusual strength and quality.

This case also has the rare feature that Purnima spoke of memories of her life between death and birth (Haraldsson, 2000). I have found this only in one other Sri Lankan case: that of Duminda Ratnayake (Haraldsson, 1999).

Purnima displayed prominently some psychological characteristics that distinguish children speaking of previous-life memories from ordinary children. She was highly gifted, had excellent vocabulary and memory, showed some tendency for dissociation, and was less suggestible than most children. She was a demanding child for her parents, argumentative and independent-minded, perfectionistic, much concerned with neatness and cleanliness, and at times hot tempered and boastful; in short, a vivid and memorable personality. Purnima is now studying for an M. A. degree. We keep in touch from time to time.

Channel 4 (producer Laura Granditer) made a documentary about Purnima in the year 2000 that was broadcast in the United Kingdom.

2

TOO GOOD TO BE TRUE?

I n Lebanon I found this truly exceptional case that is perhaps better
verified than any other I have investigated. Lebanon differs greatly from Sri Lanka in religion, race, culture and climate. For half a
century this Mediterranean country had been marred by civil wars
and political conflicts.

One night in July 1982 three men attacked the Druze Centre in
Lebanon, killed two guards at the gate and invaded the main building
where they shot Fuad Asaad Khaddage. He was the manager of Dar
El Taifeh, the religious and cultural Centre for the Druze, and a com-
panion for Sheikh Al Aql, the spiritual leader of the Druze community.
Fuad was one of his three heavily-armed bodyguards whenever Sheikh
Al Aql left the Centre.

Who the intruders were never became known but nine years later a
boy was born in a village 24 km away from Beirut. He was only a year
and a half when he began using words that his parents did not expect
a child of his age to know. He would tell his mother, "I am not small,
I am big. I carry two pistols. I carry four hand-grenades. I am 'qabadai' (a fearless strong person). Don't be scared by the hand-grenades.
I know how to handle them. I have a lot of weapons. My children are
young and I want to go and see them." Nazih described how he had
died. "Armed people came and shot at us. I also shot at them and killed
one. We were shot and later taken by an ambulance."

13

Nazih also used to tell his mother. "My wife is prettier than you. Her eyes and mouth are more beautiful." This may in fact have been the first statement that made his mother think that he was talking about a previous life. Later we learned that Nazih also said this to most of his six sisters who are older than he is. When he was around four he saw a young woman that worked in a store across the street. His mother and sister Mirna remember him saying that she looked like his previous wife and had the same beautiful eyes. He liked her a lot and went as far as to ask her to marry him!

Nazih wanted to go to his previous home to fetch some papers for money that he had lent to people so that he could get the money back. Furthermore, he wanted to bring his father to his house and show him his weapons. He told him that he, like his father, had children and deeds for a house. He often talked about a friend who was mute and had only one hand (or he may have said that there was something wrong with his hand). Nazih said his friend could hold a gun in one hand and work it, getting it ready to shoot. He referred to him as "my friend the mute."

Nazih often insisted that his parents take him to his previous home so that he could see his children and do other things already mentioned. Nazih's mother did not recall that he had specified where he had lived. Sometimes he would threaten them: "If you don't take me there I am going to walk."

Not only did Nazih's previous life memories puzzle his family; he also had some behavioral characteristics that are unusual for a child of his age, apart from his fearless, firm behavior. When he sees a cigarette box he, on occasion, wants to get it and smoke from a cigarette. If someone has a whisky, he wants it too. This was particularly the case during the period when he spoke most about his previous life, which was until the alleged previous family was identified.

Nazih was eight years old when I and my Lebanese assistant and interpreter, Majd Abu-Izzedin, first met him at his home in Baalchmay in May 2000. We learned about his case from the family of another child. We had difficulties finding Nazih's home on the Beirut-Damascus highway, and stopped at a shop to ask where Nazih's father lived for we had his name. When the shopkeeper learned that we wanted to speak to his son, Nazih, he seemed in no doubt what the errand might be: "What has he done now? He is a naughty boy."

Nazih was a slim and handsome boy, alert and attentive, but did not seem much interested in us. His mother told us that he is no longer spontaneously speaking of his previous life. He will only do so when asked and only remembers bits of what he was talking about earlier. This is in line with the general tendency of children who around the age of five to six either stop speaking of their previous life or do so much less than before, and then seem to have forgotten most or much of their former memories. Nazih's forgetting seems not to have started until after he met the previous family. He still remembers the fearful events that led to his death, and still speaks of being a brave, fearless person.

We met Nazih's father, Sabir Al-Danaf, a mason by profession, half a year later. He told us that he had been more ready to listen to Nazih's talk about the previous life than his mother. He did not encourage Nazih, but he listened to him. "Besides, his mother feared that he might go away to the previous family," he said. This is a common fear among mothers. Nazih insisted that his parents take him to Qaberchamoun, a small town that is about 17 km away. "My home (house) is in Qaberchamoun," he told his father.

When Nazih was two and a half years old, he drew a map of his previous house and also of an intersection near his house. Unfortunately these drawings no longer exist. Nazih's father tried for a long time to put off bringing Nazih to his previous home in spite of his persistent requests. Independently his sisters and brother told us that he had wanted to go and see his children and get his weapons and other things. For a detailed list of Nazih's statements, see Table 2-1.

Table 2-1. Statements by Nazih Al-Danaf Before his First Contact with the Alleged Previous Family

Statement	Informant[a]									Sum	Verification[b]			
	Fa	Mo	Da	Sa	Bi	Ma	Ma	Ha	Wa		Na	Ads	Ma	Ka
1. I carry two pistols.	x	x	x	x	x	x	x	x	x	9	x	x	x	
2. I carry four grenades. I know how to handle them.	x	x	x	x	x	x	x	x	x	9	x	x	x	
3. I am a fearless strong person, a "qabadai."	x	x	x	x	x	x	x	x	x	9	x	x	x	x
4. I am big; I am not small.	x		x	x	x	x	x	x	x	8	x	x	x	
5. I want to go and see them.	x		x	x	x	x	x	x	x	8	x	x	x	x
6. I have a mute friend.	x		x	x	x	x	x	x	x	8	x	x	x	x
7. I have a lot of weapons. I want to bring them here.	x		x	x	x		x	x	x	7	x	x	x	x

#	Sentence							No.			
8.	My wife is prettier than you. Her eyes and mouth are prettier.	x	x	x	x	x	x	7			
9.	I have a house. I will show you where it is.	x	x	x	x	x	x	7	x	x	x
10.	My friend, the mute, can hold a gun in one hand and work it.	x	x	x			x	6	x	x	x
11.	Armed people came and shot at us.		x	x	x	x	x	5	x	x	
12.	I have a map of, and papers concerning this house.		x	x	x	x	x	5	x	x	
13.	I shot at them.			x	x	x	x	4			
14.	There is a cave near my house.			x	x	x	x	4			x
15.	Something is wrong with one hand of my mute friend.			x		x	x	3			

	Statement					
16.	I killed one.	x	x	x		
17.	We were (shot and) taken by an ambulance.	x	x	x	3	x	x	x
18.	I lived in a house with two stories.	x	x	x	3	x	x	x
19.	My house was like a villa with trees around it.	x	x	x	3	x	x	x
20.	I have papers for money I lent to people. I went to get them.	x	x		2	x	x	x
21.	They gave me a shot of anesthesia in my arm in the ambulance.	x	x		2			
22.	Take me to my house in Qaberchamoun.	x			1	x	x	x
23.	I had a red car.	x			1	x	x	x

a *Informant:* Fa = father; Mo = mother; Da = Dareen; Sa = Sabrine; Ba = Baha; Mi = Mirna; Ma = Manal; Ha = Hanan; Wa = Waheeda

b *Verification:* Na = Najidyah; Ad = Adeeb; Ms = Mosleh; Ka = Kamal

Tracing Nazih's Previous Family

Finally, Nazih's parents agreed to drive Nazih to Qaberchamoun. They were accompanied by his sisters Sabrine and Hanan and his brother Baha. When they arrived at the intersection in Qaberchamoun where six roads converge, Sabir stopped the car and asked Nazih where to go. Nazih pointed to a road to the left downward, and told him to continue on that road until they come to a road that forks off upward. "My house is there."

The road to the left that started downward levelled off and became flat. Sabir drove on, perhaps 100 to 120 meters, until he came to the first road upward. He drove up the very steep road and had to stop a few car-lengths up the gravel road. A man was washing the stairs of his house with a water hose and the road had become too wet and slippery for the car. Here Nazih ran out of the car while his father backed the car down to the flat road and parked it. Then he walked up the road to find Nazih while his wife and daughters remained near the car.

Sabir asked the man washing the stairs if anyone around had died in the war (been "martyred?") Yes, a young man had been martyred nearby. Sabir went to that house and asked if somebody had died in the circumstances that Nazih had described. The man who had lived in this house had died in a bomb-blast so that did not fit. Sabir went further up the road to look for Nazih and found him. Nazih had also been looking for the right house. Nazih asked: "Take me to where I can see the white villa on the other side of the valley; I used to see it from my house." Then they walked down the steep road.

The women who stayed with the car saw a young man who was washing a car only a few meters below where they originally had to stop their car on the steep road. They started speaking to him. This is how he, Kamal Khaddage, described their first meeting:

"I was washing my car and watering at the entrance to our house. A car came up the road, stopped at the next house above and on the other side of the road. A young boy sprang out of the car. Then the car backed down and parked on the level road below at the corner of our lot. A man [Nazih's father] left the car and walked up the road to follow the boy. The women saw me and walked towards me. They asked if I knew someone who had been shot; they did not know his name but he had carried handguns, hand-grenades, and had owned a red car."

Kamal was surprised. The boy seemed to remember the life of his father, Fuad Khaddage, who had died many years ago. He asked about the age of the boy and Nazih's mother told him he was around seven. The visitors said more about the person whose life the boy seemed to remember but Kamal did not remember further details. What they did tell him fitted his father. He then shouted to his mother, who was working in a field close by. At this time Nazih and his father joined the group.

Najdiyah Khaddage, Kamal's mother and the widow of Fuad, the alleged previous personality, described her first meeting with Nazih. "When Nazih came here I was picking olives in our garden some distance away. My children yelled at me that there was a boy who said that he was their father, and they wanted me to come and see if he would recognize me. I went to them and told Nazih's mother that my husband died in the war. When he saw me, he looked like he knew me, and looked up and down at me. Kamal then said to him: Is she your previous wife or not? Nazih smiled."

3. Nazih Al-Danaff recalls being a bodyguard of an important Druze religious leader and being shot during an invasion of the Druze Centre in Beirut. He made many statements that were witnessed by many witnesses and later verified. He led the way to the place where he had lived and answered, correctly, sharp questions from his previous family. An exceptional case.

Najdiyah told us that she wanted to be sure of him, sure that he was her previous husband. She asked: "Who built the foundation of this gate at the entrance of this house?" Nazih replied: "A man from the Faraj family." This was correct. Najdiyah invited them into the house. Nazih went by himself to a room and pointed to a cupboard: 'Here I used to put my pistols,' he said, and pointed to the right side of the cupboard. 'Here I used to put the weapons' [used slab in Arabic which means unspecific kinds of weapons], and he pointed to the left side of the cupboard. He asked where they were and Najdiyah explained to him that they had been stolen. Fuad had kept his arms in this cupboard in the way Nazih described.

Najdiyah decided to test Nazih's memories with more questions. She asked him if she had had any accident when they were living at the house in Ainab. They had lived in Ainab, which is nearby, when they were building this house, and it was not fully completed when Fuad died. (See below). He replied that she had fallen and dislocated her shoulder. This had happened in the morning and Asaad, Fuad's father, was with them. Nazih said that she had skidded on plastic nylon while picking pinecones for her children to play with. Najdiyah said that Nazih mentioned that at the time he had told her: "After I come back home from work in the afternoon I will take you to the doctor," which he did. He said that a cast was put on her shoulder that she had on for some time. Najdiyah said that everything that Nazih had told her was correct.

Najdiyah also asked Nazih if he remembered how their young daughter Fairuz got seriously sick. He replied: "She was poisoned from my medication and I took her to the hospital." Fairuz had in fact eaten Fuad's medication pills that were in his jacket. She was four years old at the time, and had become very sick.

According to Najdiyah, Nazih also reminded her of some incidents in their life: "Do you remember when we were going up from Beirut in the car and the car stopped and twice the Israeli soldiers fixed it for us?" That was true. The Israeli soldiers had charged the car battery twice. This had happened during the Israeli invasion of Lebanon.

He told her of another incident: "One night I came home drunk. You locked the door and I slept outside the house on a rocking sofa." This was true; she had been scared, so she locked the door.

Nazih told her that there had been a barrel in the garden where he used to teach her to shoot. "Where is it now?" he asked. She told him it was still in the garden. They went out to the garden and found a rusty barrel. "This is it," Nazih said, and that was also correct.

Najdiyah showed Nazih a photograph of Fuad and asked him: "Who is this?" He replied: "This is me. I was big but now I am small."

Najdiyah was much impressed and so were her children. They told us that they all believed that Nazih was Fuad reborn. This was the only way they could understand how Nazih was able to reveal such knowledge of their father's life. Since that time the families occasionally visit one another. We observed affectionate embraces between Nazih and the family as we parted.

Further Verifications

Shortly afterwards, Nazih visited Fuad's brother, Sheikh Adeeb, who lives in the village Kfermatta outside Beirut. He was a senior executive of the Middle East Airlines. This is his account of their meeting:

"Nazih and his family came to my house and asked for me. I was at a Druze prayer house and left immediately to find my house full of people. I saw a boy running towards me who said: 'Here comes my brother Adeeb', and hugged me. It was wintertime and Nazih said: 'How do you go out like this [not warmly dressed], put something on your ears." Then he told me: "I am your brother Fuad.' I looked at him and said: 'What is the proof that you are my brother Fuad.' He said that he once gave me a handgun. I asked, what kind? 'I gave you a Checki 16', he replied. Fuad had given this handgun to him around 1980. I hugged him and was 100% sure that he was my brother." The Checki 16 is considered a precious item and is not common in Lebanon. "Fuad liked guns a lot," Adeeb added.

Sheikh Adeeb asked Nazih about his original house where he had lived with his first wife. Nazih asked him to go out so he could show him the house. They walked down the same street, and Nazih said: "This is the house of my father and this [he pointed to the next house] is my first house." This was absolutely correct. Inside the latter house, Nazih said, he had made one wooden ladder that still stands there. Adeeb affirms that he remembers that Fuad made this wooden ladder. Fuad's previous wife still lives in the house. Adeeb asked him afterwards about the woman that they met in the house. Nazih replied that it was his first wife. Adeeb felt sure that no one would have told Nazih who had lived in these two houses as he was visiting Kfarmatta for the first time in his life.

Adeeb showed Nazih a photo of three men and asked him who they were. Nazih pointed at each of them and disclosed who they were— Adeeb, Ibrahim and Fuad; their brother Ibrahim had lost his life in the civil war. Adeeb showed him one more picture and Nazih told him that this was their father, which was correct. Sheikh Adeeb showed us these photographs.

Nazih asked where their father was. Adeeb told him he had died, but he had been alive when Fuad died. Adeeb told us that the first meeting with Nazih was very emotional; people were crying and hugging, as it brought back so many memories.

Later Sheikh Adeeb visited Nazih at his home in Baalchmay. He took a handgun with him and asked Nazih if it was the gun that he gave to him. "No," Nazih replied, and that was correct. The story of the Checki 16 handgun completely convinced Adeeb that Nazih was indeed his brother Fuad reborn. Nobody would have known about Fuad giving this handgun to him, except perhaps his wife. By the time we met him he had sold the gun.

Table 2.2. List of Nazih's Additional Statements and Recognitions at his First Meetings with the Alleged Previous Family

Place of Meeting	Statements, Questions, Recognitions	Answers, Comments
Najdiyah's home	Nazih asked Najdriyah:	
	1. Do you remember when we were going up from Beruit, the car broke down and twice Israeli soldiers charged the battery for us?	Yes. (correct)
	2. Do you remember that one night I came home drunk and you locked the door and I slept outside on a rocking sofa?	Yes. (correct)
	3. Where is the barrel where I taught you to shoot?	It is in the garden. (correct)
	Najdruyah asked Nazih:	
	4. Who built the foundations of this gate?	A man of the Faraj family. (correct)
	5. Did she have an accident when they lived in Ainab?	She fell and dislocated her shoulder. (correct)
	6. Does he remember how their young daughter got seriously sick?	She was poisoned by taking medications and I took her to the hospital. (correct)
	Other events at Najdiyah's home	
	7. Nazih showed Fuad's family in which cupboard he had kept his arms.	Correct.

Adeeb's home	8. Nazih said to Fuad's brother, Adeeb, as they met: Here comes my brother Adeeb. I am your brother, Fuad.	Correct.
	Adeeb asked Nazih:	
	9. What is the proof that you are my brother?	I once gave you a pistol. (correct)
	10. What kind of pistol?	It was a Checki 16. (correct)
	11. Where was the house of your father and your first house?	Nazih stepped out and showed him both houses. (correct)
	Other events at Adeeb's home	
	12. Inside Faud's first house Nazih pointed to a ladder and said he had made it.	Correct.
	13. Nazih recognized Fuad's first wife and referred to her as Im (mother of) Nazih.	Fuad's oldest son was named Nazih. (correct)
	14. Adeeb showed Nazih a photo of three men.	Nazih pointed correctly to each of them and gave their names as Adeeb, Ibrahim and Fuad.
Nazih's home	15. Adeeb brought a pistol to Nazih to test him.	Nazih correctly stated: This is not the pistol I gave you.

Major Events in the Life of Fuad Asaad Khaddage

Fuad was born 1925 in Kfermatta, which is a few kilometers away from Qaberchamoun. He divorced his first wife after they had eight children and married Najdiyah with whom he had five children. The oldest was 8 years old when he died. After compulsory schooling, Fuad started to work at the Druze Orphanage in Abey, and then at the Druze Center in Beirut, where he was employed for 30 years. The center consists of an imposing building with assembly halls for religious meetings and funerals, offices for their religious leaders, smaller buildings, a burial site and a shrine. Fuad was the manager of the center, responsible for all paperwork besides being one of the bodyguards for Sheikh Al Aql.

This is how Adeeb described his brother Fuad: "He was a brave person, fearless, who liked people and they liked him. He was very honest, spoke gently and nicely to people and had a sweet tongue as they say here. He did not have enemies." We also interviewed his cousin

Sheikh Mosleh who described him as follows: "Fuad was brave, over-excited, took risks, liked weapons a lot, was 'qabadai' which means a brave, courageous and honest man. Fuad did not take part in the war. He liked to show off with his pistols, but never used them. He also worked for a very important person, Sheikh Al Aql and that he apparently enjoyed." Sheikh Mosleh's daughter Wafa added: "He used to like any kind of show off."

Table 2.3. A Brief Chronology and Some Characteristics of the Case of Nazih Al-Danaf

Year of birth of Fuad A. Khaddage	1925
Date of death	July 2, 1982
Age at death	57 years
Mode of death	Shooting / murder
Date of birth of Nazih Al-Danaf	February 29, 1992
Age in years when first speaks of memories	2-2.5 years
Age in years at first meeting with alleged previous family	5-6 years
Interval between death of Fuad and birth of Nazih	8 years
Number of statements made by Nazih	31
Statements fitting Fuad Khaddage	25
Statements not fitting Fuad Khaddage	1
Unverifiable/unfalsifiable statements	5
First investigation of case by EH and MA1	May, 2000
Further visits to sites	January, March, 2001

Verification of Nazih's Statements

We have 23 statements uttered by Nazih before his first visit to Qaberchamoun. There were many witnesses to Nazih's statements because he had six sisters and one brother, all of whom were older than he. These witnesses agree that he used to talk a lot about his previous life until he met his alleged previous family. Then he became more relaxed and spoke much less about it. All the witnesses heard him talk about carrying pistols and hand-grenades and being a brave person ('qabadai'). That fits Fuad perfectly as those who knew him describe him; also the statement that he had many children and the very specific statement that he had a mute friend. Sheikh Adeeb told us he knew him well; he disappeared before the civil war was over. Fuad's wife and his son Kamal knew about his mute friend but never met him.

Conclusion

Table 2-1 lists Nazih's 23 statements. 17 fit the life of Fuad but 5 are uncheckable, for instance, that his previous wife was prettier than his mother. Perhaps she was, and maybe more likely than not; middle-aged Najdiyah's features are still strikingly feminine. A wedding photograph shows her as a beautiful woman. One statement may not be correct, namely, that he received a shot of anesthesia in his arm as the ambulance brought him to the hospital. We obtained his post mortem report from the hospital. Fuad died from gunshot wounds in the head fired at less than one half meter and must have died instantly, the report states. Why would he have been given an injection? Unlikely but perhaps he had.

Almost never do we find that all of a child's statements can be verified. With Nazih we have 17 statements that are potentially verifiable. They all fit the life of Fuad. That is truly remarkable. Equally remarkable is the fact that Nazih correctly answered all of Najdiyah's and Sheikh Adeeb's many penetrating questions (see Table 2-2). Also remarkable are his recognitions of Adeeb and Fuad's first wife and persons on the photographs if they are correctly described to us. Also remarkable is the fact that Nazih was able to find his way to Fuad Khaddage's home.

We investigated this case as thoroughly as possible during three journeys to Lebanon in 2000 and 2001. All major witnesses were interviewed on more than one occasion several months apart to test the consistency of their testimony. With my interpreter, Majd Abu-Izzeddin, I visited Nazih's home seven times to interview his parents, six older sisters and brother, interviewing each witness separately and whenever possible alone. The witnesses were cooperative. Our impression was that they were honest and open about their observations and did not try to embellish the case.

We left no stone unturned in investigating this case for it seemed "too good to be true." The testimony was overwhelming. This case does not have birthmarks, phobias or intermission memories, but no case that I have investigated equals it in how perfectly they remembered statements that fit the facts in the life of the previous personality. It is a truly remarkable case (Haraldsson and Abu-Izzeddin, 2002).

3

I WAS A MONK IN MY PREVIOUS LIFE

With Godwin Samararatne I found three young boys in Sri Lanka who insisted that they had been Buddhist monks in their previous lives. Two came from Buddhist families and one was Roman Catholic. The behaviors that these children displayed made their cases particularly interesting, apart from their alleged memories. They all showed behavior that is appropriate and even ideal for monks. At the age of two to three years they began to demonstrate a keen and active interest in Buddhism. They aspired to live like Buddhist monks and their behavior seemed to correspond to these aspirations; two of them expressed a desire to join a Buddhist order. Their behavior caused considerable concern and distress to their parents.

Buddhism is the predominant religion in Sri Lanka, accepted by two-thirds of the population. There are also Hindus (16%), Muslims (8%), and Christians (7%). I have found reincarnation cases in all of these communities and so did Stevenson before me.

The concept of reincarnation is an important doctrine in Theravada and Mahayana Buddhism, with monasticism playing an important role in both traditions. In Sri Lankan Theravada Buddhism, children may enter monastic orders as early as 8-10 years. However, among the Buddhists of Sri Lanka, there is no tradition of searching for child novices through indication that they may have been monks in a previous life, as is found in Tibetan Mahayana Buddhism. Occasionally, but very rarely, in fact, children may speak at an early age of memories of having been a monk in a previous life, and express a desire to become a monk again. Their alleged memories and monk-specific behavior may therefore lead them into monastic orders.

Duminda Ratnayake

Duminda was born on June 16, 1984, of Sinhalese Buddhist parents some 16 miles from Kandy. At the age of three he started to speak about a life as a chief-monk at the Asgiriya Monastery in Kandy and often expressed his wish to visit that temple. The Asgiriya Monastery is one of the largest monasteries in Sri Lanka, and its monks share with the Malvatta Monastery the privilege of guarding the Temple of the Tooth, one of the foremost places of pilgrimage in Theravada Buddhism.

We learned about the case in September 1988 and interviewed the principal witnesses to the boy's statements: his mother, grandfather and grandmother. They all had heard him say that he had lived in the Asgiriya Monastery, had owned a red car, had taught other monks, had suffered a sudden pain in his chest, had fallen on the floor and been brought to a hospital where he died. He liked to recite stanzas (short religious statements) in Pali, the ancient language of Sinhalese Buddhism that is used and learned only by monks. This would be a case of xenoglossy (speaking a language that the person has not learned) as Duminda had never learned Pali. Duminda mentioned no personal names. He uttered these things repeatedly over a period of more than two years. You will find a list of his statements in Table 3-1.

Table 3-1. Statements Made by Duminda Ratnayake

	Statement	Status
1.	He had been a senior monk (nayake-hamduruvo, loku-hamduruvo, lokusadhu) at the Asgiriya Temple.	+
2.	He had a pain in the chest and fell and was brought to a hospital and died. (Used the word *apawathwuna*, which is only used for the death of a monk).	+
3.	He had owned a red car.	+

4.	He had been teaching the apprentice monks.	+
5.	He had an elephant.	+
6.	He had friends in the Malvatta Temple and used to visit it.	+
7.	He longed for the money-bag which he had in Asgiriya.	+
8.	He longed for his radio in Asgiriya.	+
+ Statement verified. (8)		

Duminda showed behavioral features unusual for a boy of his age. He wanted to carry his clothes in the fashion of a monk, wanted to be called 'Podi Sadhu' (little monk), went every morning and evening to a chapel (vihara) close to his house, visited the temple regularly, plucked flowers to bring there and placed them down in the typical Buddhist fashion. Cleanliness was very important to him. He did not want to play with other children but wanted to become a monk and wear a monk's robe, which his mother only seldom allowed him to do. And he liked to recite Pali stanzas in the way that monks do.

Table 3-2. Some of Durminda's Behavioral Traits

1.	Often talks about wanting to go to the Asgiriya Temple.
2.	Expresses early a wish to visit the local temple in Thundeniya.
3.	Wants to visit the Malvatta Temple.
4.	Wears and treats his clothes like a monk.
5.	Likes and shows great cleanliness.
6.	Goes to vihara (place of worship) every morning and evening.
7.	Requests a monk's robe and fan.
8.	Wants to wear a monk's robe (only seldom allowed).
9.	Wants his family to call him "podi sadhu" (little monk).
10.	Wants to become a monk.
11.	Tried to build a vihara at home in the fashion that children build toy structures, e.g., houses.
12.	Plucks flowers and takes to vihara 2-3 times per day on Poya-day (Buddhist monthly holiday), as monks do.
13.	Does not like killing insects or perceived wrongdoings to anyone.
14.	Knows a few stanzas in Pali and recites them holding the fan in front of his face, as monks do.
15.	Once when his mother wanted to help wash his hands he told her, "You should not touch my hands." (Women are not supposed to touch a monk's hands).

16.	When taken to Asgiriya temple he did not want to sit down until brought a white cloth to sit on (as is the tradition for monks).
17.	Does not like to play with other children.
18.	Displays calmness, serenity and detachment rarely found in children of his age.

Duminda's mother sought advice from a monk, Ven. Jinorasa, residing in a nearby temple. He tried to question Duminda, who did not answer, perhaps because he was shy. He asked for a monk's fan and the monk gave him one. He took the fan, held it in the typical fashion in front of his face and recited one of the Buddhist stanzas. On a later visit, the boy told the monk that he had been a monk in the Asgiriya Monastery, that he wanted to see the monastery and his car, and that he had had a room in the monastery with some belongings. This is about all that the monk learned from him.

Whenever Duminda visited the nearby temple he would go straight to the stupa to worship, and seemed to be very religiously oriented. As we questioned the Ven. Jinorasa, he remarked that he did not believe that the boy's parents could have taught him this behavior. In the end the monk advised Duminda's mother to take her son to the Asgiriya Monastery.

4. Duminda Ratnayake insisted that he had been a senior monk in the Asgeriya temple in Kandy. As a child he wanted to wear a monk's robe, and he carried his clothes in the way monks do. He was very pious,

30

wanted his family to call him "little monk", wanted to become a monk and could recite some stanzas in the ancient Buddhist language of Pali. He showed serenity, calmness and detachment rarely found in children but considered ideal characteristics for Buddhist monks.

In October 1987, Duminda was taken to Asgiriya by his mother and grandparents. A journalist from the newspaper *Island* learned about the case and was present during Duminda's visit. The boy's mother had ambivalent feelings about the visit as she feared that the boy might later leave her to become a monk.

In November 1989, we visited Duminda's family again. Duminda's mother reported the same statements as on our earlier visit. The boy had come up with one new statement when the death of the mahanayaka (chief-monk) of the Malvatta Monastery was announced over the radio. Spontaneously he said that he had known him. His mother further told us that before the boy had started to talk about a previous life he had wanted to carry a piece of cloth around his shoulder as monks carry their robes. He then asked for a robe and a monk's fan. Once when she helped him wash his hands, he made the remark that she should not touch his hands (women are not supposed to touch a monk's hands). He had also protested about her calling him 'son'; he wanted to be called 'podi sadhu' (small monk). When he was brought to pre-school he protested and did not want to go there because some girls had touched him.

Duminda's grandfather listened to our interview with his mother. When she left to prepare refreshments, he told us that two items had not been reported. Duminda's most frequent statements were that he had lived in Asgiriya, had been a teacher (preacher), and that he missed his red car, and—this was new—that he missed his money bag and radio. When we asked Duminda's mother about the money bag and the radio, she confirmed that he had mentioned them but was somewhat embarrassed, because these items are not considered appropriate for a monk to have.

We visited again in June 1990. Not much had changed. Duminda was adjusting well to school. His calm detachment and dignity were evident when we compared his behavior with his brothers, who, like normal healthy boys, would never be quiet or still for long.

There existed no ties of any kind between any member of Duminda's family and the Asgiriya monastery. They had not visited the monastery until they took the boy there, and the name Asgiriya had never come up at his home as far as they could remember. The family had no relative or neighbor who was a monk.

The Search for a Personality Matching Duminda's Statements

The journalist from the *Island* newspaper who first reported on the case, quickly concluded that the boy had been referring to Ven. Ratanapala, a senior monk who had died of a heart attack in 1975 in Galatera, outside of Asgiriya. We learned from three monks who had known the Ven. Ratanapala that he had not owned a car or an elephant and had no personal income, hence no money bag, did not preach, hence did not use the fan, and had no connection with the Malvatta Monastery. Besides, he had been known for his interest in politics. This excluded him as a candidate whose life may have corresponded to Duminda's statements.

We had to find out which monks had income from the temple (money bag), connections with the Malvatta Monastery and the Temple of the Tooth, had frequent occasion to visit these places, and had friends there. Which monks had preached sermons and exhorted laymen to recite the Buddhist precepts, thus using a monk's fan? Which monks travelled and often used a red car, had a heart condition, fell down, and died in a hospital? Which monks owned a radio and an elephant? Not until the 1920s had the chief monk (mahanayaka) owned a car, and it wasn't until the 1980s that other monks other than the mahanayaka owned cars. The same can be said about possessing money bags; nowadays a few of them may have some personal income, but this is quite a recent development.

We obtained the names of all the mahanayakas in Asgiriya from the beginning of the 1920s (when the first car came to Asgiriya) to 1975, when the present mahanayaka took office. We gathered this information from mainly from the Ven. Piyaratana, who knew no details about Duminda's statements. To cut a long story short, the life of mahanayaka Gunnepana Saranankara (1921-1929) fitted all of Duminda's statements. One statement fitted the life of three mahanayakas, and one none at all. All indications were that Duminda was remembering the life of the Ven. Gunnepana. The case was solved.

In the early 1990s, BBC Wales (producer Jeffrey Iverson) made a documentary on cases of rebirth. Duminda's case was included. He was asked to recite some stanzas, which he did, and they were, with one exception, recognized by the monks that were present. It turned out that this stanza was inscribed in a rather obscure place in the Asgiriya temple.

At age 21, Duminda disrobed and left the monastery on good terms with his chief monk. In the monastery he had become quite knowledgeable about computers, and found work with a company that installed security cameras. Later he studied computer science at Colombo University. Now he works as a computer scientist for a major institution in Sri Lanka. He is married and has a child. We stay in touch by email and he has been helpful in making inquiries for me. He is keen to serve his country and has campaigned against drinking by young people.

Sandika Tharanga

Sandika was born in May 1979 of middle-class Roman Catholic parents in one of the suburbs of Colombo. At the age of three he started to talk about a previous life as a monk in a monastery which he did not further identify. He frequently spoke of the chief monk who lived in the monastery. One day when he was going to attend an almsgiving with some other monks, he heard a big noise, shot, or explosion. This is the last thing he remembers. Almsgiving is a common religious ceremony where monks are invited for a midday meal by lay-people.

Sandika had a great fear of firecrackers and sudden noises. When he heard sounds of explosions he instinctively placed his hands in fear on the left side of his chest. His parents' explanation was that this fearful behavior was caused by a shot he had received in his chest, which had led to his death in the previous life. There is a small dark birthmark on his chest slightly to the left of the midline, and we were told it was more prominent when he was younger. His parents know of no monk in the area who has died from a gunshot wound. Sandika further stated that four or five monks had lived in his monastery. A list of his statements are given in Table 3-3. Sandika's statements bring to mind that Sri Lanka has had periods of violent political turmoil, particularly the Insurgency of 1971, in which a number of monks were killed.

Table 3.3. Sandika's Statements about his Previous Life as
Reported by his Mother

	Statement	Status
1.	The chief monk lived at the temple.	?
2.	The chief monk had a big bowl.	?
3.	One day he went away for almsgiving with some other monks.	?
4.	Then there was an explosion with much noise.	?
5.	There was a little monk (child monk) in the temple.	?
6.	Four or five monks lived in the temple.	?
7.	There was a jack-fruit tree there.	?
8.	The temple where he lived was close to his present home.	?
9.	He had a brother who was of fair complexion.	?
10.	His younger brother wore no shirt.	?
? Impossible to ascertain; may or may not be right. (10)		

What most impressed Sandika's Roman Catholic parents was not so much that he spoke of a previous life, but his unusual behavioral traits and exemplary behavior as well as his interests, which differed radically from the religious life and background of his family. The family did not force him to go to church, since he only wanted to visit temples.

Like many children who speak of a previous life, Sandika told his mother that she was not his real mother. He asked to be taken to his monastery and to his previous mother's place. He would also at certain times pick flowers and place them on his bed as long as there was no altar or shrine room in the house for him to place them. Placing flowers on an altar is common practice among Buddhists. Furthermore, he chanted religious stanzas (in Pali, his parents thought) and worshipped as Buddhists do. What verses or stanzas he chanted his parents did not know as they had not paid much attention to it or understood the words. Sandika had stopped chanting when we first met him.

Table 3.4. Prominent Behavioral Traits of Sandika,
as Reported by his Mother

1.	Asks to be taken to his previous temple.
2.	Expressed a wish to visit the temple to see the chief monk.
3.	Asks to be taken to his previous mother's place.
4.	Picks flowers to place on a bed or chair before worshipping.

5.	Wanted a Buddha image in the house for his worship.
6.	Requests family to give alms to monks.
7.	On Poya day (full moon, important public Buddhist holiday in Sri Lanka) requests his father to take him to the temple.
8.	Requests family to invite monks for alms-giving, which they did.
9.	Does not eat meat.
10.	In school, gets especially high marks on Buddhism (91 out of 100 possible).
11.	His main interests are visiting temples and doing his schoolwork.
12.	Displays fear of fire crackers and sudden noises, then places his hand on the left side of his chest, as if in defense.
13.	Is particularly clean in everything he does.
14.	Requests his parents not to cut his hair (as his hair was always cut in the previous life when he was a monk, and he does not want that now).
15.	His family became more sympathetic to Buddhism because of his behavior.

As a child he stammered but he chanted without stammering, according to his mother. From the age of three, Sandika would worship two to three times a day. At the age of six he was still offering flowers to a picture of Lord Buddha, which at his request was put up for him. Later he was given a small statue of the Buddha. A small shelf was placed on the wall in one room to serve as an altar for Sandika. When we visited the family in April 1996, there was one image of the Buddha displayed in a prominent place in the house. Only recently had Sandika placed another statue elsewhere in the house.

We first met Sandika when he was nine years of age. At this time his memories were fading, as is generally the case with children that old. His main interests were visiting temples and his school work. He had been very religious from the time he started to speak of his previous life, and tried in vain to convert his parents to Buddhism. He was eager to find the monastery where he had lived. At his request, Sandika's father took him to 6-7 temples in their wider area when he was 3-4 years old, in the hope that he would find his temple. He did not recognize any of them as his old monastery.

One day his mother took the boy to a temple some two miles away where there lived a pious monk and told him about the boy. The monk plucked some flowers, gave them to him, and observed what he did. He climbed the steps to the vihara (shrine room) and worshipped there, which is an appropriate response for a devout Buddhist. After Sandika was taken to some temples and became acquainted with the monk, he gradually stopped talking about his previous life unless he was asked to do so.

Sandika requested his family to give alms to monks and get monks to have a ceremony in their house (common in Buddhist households), which in the end they did. On full moon day he requested his father to take him to a temple, in line with Buddhist tradition. Already as a small child he abstained from eating meat. He showed unusual concern for cleanliness and was a very pious, gentle and obedient boy. Through his pious behavior his parents became more sympathetic to Buddhism than they had been previously, as they were deeply impressed by their son. He became an outstanding pupil after entering school. His highest grades were in his favorite subject, Buddhism. He also attended from an early age the optional Buddhist Sunday School.

In 1988 the mother was still afraid that he might want to become a monk. Sandika, however, has never expressed that desire. When we met him in 1996 he was still deeply interested in Buddhism, would often visit temples, but had no intention of becoming a monk. He received a scholarship for outstanding school performance and continued to be a very gentle and modest boy. In a class of 40 he had always been among the top three, and had recently been admitted to Ananda College, the most prestigious Buddhist college in Sri Lanka, where he planned to study mathematics and science.

Sandika was 26 years old when I interviewed him in 2005 for my longitudinal study (see Chapter 12). By that time he had forgotten all his past-life memories a long time ago. He only knew about them because his parents had told him. He had completed his studies, become an engineer, had a fine position, and was still single and apparently very happy with his life.

Gamage Ruvan Tharanga Perera

Ruvan, as we shall refer to him, was born in August 1987 and was eight years old when we met him and his parents at their home in the Kalutara District. Ruvan's parents were co-operative. He was quiet in our presence, but attentive.

According to his father, Ruvan started to speak of a previous life when he was 2 years old. He stated that he had been a monk living in the Pitumpe Monastery. The name Pitumpe was unknown to his parents. Ruvan said that this monastery was in Padukka, which is some 20 miles to the south of their home. Ruvan also stated that there was a monkey in the temple. Two weeks later he added that the monkey was made of clay. It was found that Pitumpe monastery did exist and there was in that temple a monkey made of clay. This was seen as evidence that Ruvan had lived in this monastery.

His mother stated that Ruvan had been talking about a Pitumpe monastery almost from the time he started to speak, and was keen to become a monk. He did not ask for toys, only for pictures of the Buddha, which he collected lovingly. Furthermore, he showed some unusual behavior that still persisted; Ruvan sits in a lotus position when they go to the temple, although no one had taught him to do so; he wants to wear a robe like a monk and knows how to put it on; he knows how to hold a fan when chanting. He does not want to eat at night and discourages his family from doing so (monks have no meals from noon until next morning); and he does not eat fish or meat (a few monks do not); he recites the Buddha's first sermon; he can read the book of chants (Gatha pota); and he wants the family to perform a puja (prayer-like ceremony of worship with recitations and flowers and incense) in the evening, and scolds them for not doing so. He does not like to sleep with his mother, telling her that monks do not sleep with women. Once when his father brought some liquor into the house with some friends, he protested vehemently.

Ruvan would chant stanzas in Pali which his parents recognized from hearing it in the temple and sometimes on radio and television. Ruvan may have learned the stanzas by listening to radio or television but his parents reject that explanation.

Table 3.5. Ruvan's Statements as Reported in *Lankadeepa* Newspaper

Statement		Status
1.	I lived as a monk in the Pitumpe Temple in Padukka.	+
2.	There was a statue of a monkey in the temple.	+
3.	There were six monks living in the temple.	about
4.	I led the flower offering ceremonies in the temple.	+
5.	I organized religious processions in the temple.	+
6.	I motivated many people towards meritorious living.	+
7.	My father and mother were very much devoted to religion.	+
8.	There were frescoes and wall-paintings in the temple.	+

+ Statement verified. (8)
- Statement did not fit and was wrong. (0)
? Impossible to ascertain; may or may not be right. (0)

Our inquiries revealed that Ruvan's parents had shown little interest in what Ruvan was saying and tried to keep the case a family secret. Had it not been for a journalist who learned accidentally about Ruvan from a woman neighbor, the case might never have become public. The reporter interviewed Ruvan and his parents, and published a report in the newspaper Lankadeepa on November 3, 1993, when Ruvan was six years old. In this report some of Ruvan's statements were published (see Table 3-3). This is important as they were published before attempts were made to learn whether his statements regarding the Pitumpe monastery could be verified.

A monk in the Pitumpe monastery and some laymen associated with the temple read the report in *Lankadeepa*. They made the 20-mile trip to visit Ruvan and question him about his alleged previous-life memories, and tested if he recognized any of them. Some in the group became convinced that Ruvan was the previous abbot of the monastery reborn, the Ven. Pannasekhara (1902-1986). They were impressed with Ruvan's monk-like demeanor and the way he carried his robes. The newspaper report had also described how he had been organizing and leading religious ceremonies and processions and that could only refer to a senior monk or abbot. However, the incumbent monk and former disciple of the abbot remained skeptical, because Ruvan did not recognize him, or know the former abbot's name. Sometime later more monks and relatives of the late chief monk arrived. Ruvan did not recognize any of them and hence they remained skeptical. He told them that he was the reincarnation of a lesser monk who attended the chief monk. One monk began to wonder if Ruvan was referring to the life of a young monk from Pitumpe, the Ven. Nanavasa, who died around 1986. More about him later.

A next-door neighbor, Mrs Wijeman, knew Ruvan from his birth. According to her, he started at the age of two to speak of a life as a monk but she no longer remembered details of his statements. She was primarily impressed with his monk-like behavior, serenity and peacefulness, his wish to dress like a monk, and how he frequented the shrine room in her house to sit there quietly alone. She told us that Ruvan's father had a drinking problem and the family had little interest in religion. Through Ruvan's influence, his father in due time stopped drinking and the family even became vegetarians. This was later confirmed by Ruvan's mother.

Another neighbor, Mrs Ranjani, knew Ruvan from early childhood. He had talked about having lived in Pitumpe as a monk. Mrs Ranjani was a teacher in a Montessori school that Ruvan was later admitted to. He was a very good pupil. It was there his monk-like behavior became more evident. He did not play with the other children. When he was asked to draw he would always draw incidents in the life of the Buddha. He wanted to dress like a monk, and expressed a wish to become a monk. He only wanted to eat vegetarian food.

Sometimes Ruvan would insist that the other children in his class stand as a mark of respect, as when a monk is brought in a procession to preach a sermon. He would get them to imitate that they were beating drums, then he would walk into the classroom and sit cross-legged on a chair laid with white cloth (monks always sit on white cloth). He would take a large leaf and hold it as a fan, preach for about 15 minutes, and end the session by 'offering merit' as monks do when they preach a sermon. There is a special chant for offering merits that Ruvan would chant in Pali. The other children accepted his behavior, listened attentively, and gave him due respect. He came to be known as 'Ruvan sadhu' (monk).

The Montessori pre-school was on the compound of the Dombagoda Temple. There Ruvan had his first contact with monks, and became particularly attracted to Ven. Hemarama, who soon learned about Ruvan's memories. Ruvan liked their robes, the pictures of Lord Buddha, and liked to go to their books and handle them. He liked to sketch pictures of the Buddha on the floor and one day he spoke of a monkey. When asked what monkey he was talking about, he replied, "the monkey in Pitumpe." Ruvan stated that he had been a monk in Pitumpe, that there were 3-4 monks in that temple, and that he wanted to become a monk. The Ven. Hemarama knew there was a temple in Pitumpe and suggested to his parents that they make inquiries and take him to Pitumpe. His parents were against this and no inquiries were made. It was not until two years later, after Ruvan entered primary school, that the journalist published his report and the first contact was made with Pitumpe.

At the beginning of our investigation we expected that Ruvan might have learned about Pitumpe from the monks in Dombagoda. However, several witnesses asserted that Ruvan had mentioned Pitumpe before entering pre-school.

Shortly after the visit of the group from Pitumpe, Ruvan's family went to the Pitumpe Monastery with the *Lankadeepa* reporter, the Ven. Hemarama, and several other persons. Ruvan's father said that he instructed the party not to tell his son anything or give him any leads in order better to test whether he could recognize something. According to the *Lankadeepa* report, Ruvan helped in locating the Pitumpe monastery after they arrived in the vicinity.

Table 3.6. List of Ruvan's Behavioral Features as Reported in the *Lankadeepa* Before the Case was Solved

1.	Does not eat at night (monks do not).
2.	Does not want to sleep with his mother (monks do not sleep with women).
3.	Recites in Pali part of Buddha's first sermon.
4.	Does not ask for toys, only pictures of Buddha, which he collects lovingly.
5.	Wants to become a monk.
6.	Sits in the lotus position when he goes with his parents to the temple.
7.	Likes to wear monk's robes when he is at home.
8.	Asks his family not to eat at night and only takes refreshments as monks do.
9.	Does not eat fish or meat.
10.	Likes to read the "pirithpotha" (Buddhist texts for protection).

According to a second *Lankadeepa* article, the group visited the shrine room and there Ruvan pointed to the statue of the monkey made of clay, which is not prominently displayed. He said: "That is the monkey I told you about." In the room of the present chief monk at the Pitumpe Monastery, the Ven. Hematillaka, there were two large framed photographs, each of one monk. Without being asked Ruvan pointed at one of them and said: "This was the chief monk." That photograph was of the Ven. Pannasekhara, the former abbot of the Pitumpe Monastery. This impressed the Ven. Hematillaka. The other photograph was of Pannasekhara's teacher, who previously had also been a chief monk.

In May 1997 we visited Ruvan's former primary school. It was early morning and a group of children were waiting for the school to open. Some of them had been classmates with Ruvan, who had left school the year before to join a monastery. We asked about Ruvan, whom they remembered well. He had been a class leader all his three and a half years in primary school, appointed by the teacher. Would they have liked another pupil as a class leader? No, they said, they liked Ruvan as class leader.

On occasions, Ruvan got his fellow pupils to recite the Five Precepts (compared roughly to the Lord's Prayer in Christianity), and he preached to his fellow pupils. He sat in an elevated position, but they sat on the floor (according to tradition). In his sermons, Ruvan had taught them the importance of behaving well. They said he was always calm. What did they think of his becoming a monk? It was a good thing, they agreed. Evidently they were not surprised by it.

In Sri Lanka a class leader is traditionally the best pupil in the class. The principal allowed us to examine the grade books. The first two years Ruvan ranked first in school performance, and in the third year another pupil shared with him the first rank. In his fourth year he left the school for the 'pirivena' (school for child novices living in monasteries). The principal told us that Ruvan had been popular with the other children, a true class leader, although he did not move much with them. He had a keen memory, was obedient to his teachers and was quiet and peaceful. He did not like to be with girls, not even his sister.

In his early years in primary school Ruvan started to give frequent public pujas at the request of various persons, and his fame started to spread, also through several articles in the newspapers. He conducted these ceremonies, which consist mostly of chanting, with the dignity of a senior monk.

On August 9, 1996, Ruvan was ordained into the ancient Pushparamaya Pathawatta Temple in Rajgama. The monks there had heard about Ruvan, and happened to know some people where he regularly went for meditation. One day Ruvan's family had visited the temple to discuss the possibility of his entering as a monk novice. Then he told his parents: "I wish to stay here; you can go home." Ruvan told us he is happy in the temple, does not miss home, has time to meditate and that there is much to study. The abbot told us that Ruvan is different from the other child novices. He is more calm and composed, and has a better memory and much greater knowledge of Buddhism than they do, and gets on well with them. On the last full moon day he had performed the Bodhi-puja ceremony and did that very well.

Verification of the Case

One of the interesting features of this case is that some of Ruvan's statements were published before an attempt was made to find a person who fitted Ruvan's story. It is of crucial importance to find out whether Ruvan might in normal ways have acquired knowledge about the Pitumpe Monastery and the clay monkey in the temple. We failed to find such a normal way, both for the name of Pitumpe Temple, and for the fact that there was a monkey made of clay in this temple. The monkey was in a scene that depicted Buddha's passing away. Statues of monkeys are almost never found in temples, as far as we have been able to ascertain.

The statement that there were frescoes and wall-paintings in the Pitumpe Temple is also correct. Such wall-paintings and frescoes are not uncommon in temples but those in Pitumpe are of unusual beauty for a temple of such a small size. They were built and painted at the initiative of the Ven. Pannasekhara. The statements about leading the flower offering ceremonies, organizing processions in the temple, and motivating people towards meritorious living, would fit the life of any abbot who is actively engaged in promoting Buddhism among the public, which some (but far from all) abbots do. We traced a younger sister of the Ven. Pannasekhara. She told us that her parents had been very religious and were vegetarians for religious reasons, which is rare in Sri Lanka. Her brother also had been a vegetarian.

Of Ruvan's eight statements, seven are correct and one might be incorrect. There were 3-4 and not 6 monks living in the Pitumpe temple, not counting the child novices. If the child monks were included, Ruvan may have been right. At the time of our investigation there were four child novices in Pitumpe and one monk.

The monk that Ruvan is believed to be referring to is the Ven. Pannasekhara who was born in 1902, became a monk, and lived in the latter part of his life in the small and unimportant Pitumpe Monastery. In 1972 he was appointed chief abbot over the whole Colombo District. This was a great honor and recognition by the authorities of his spiritual and leadership qualities. He came to participate in many important official functions, religious and otherwise, where he was bound to meet other leading clerics of the nation. Ruvan's statements that he led flower pujas and processions and motivated people towards a meritorious life seem a fitting description. The Ven. Pannasekhara died January 9, 1986. Ruvan was born 17 months later, on August 2, 1987.

The Ven. Pannasekhara is not the only candidate for Ruvan's previous personality. Some monks considered the possibility that Ruvan may be referring to the Ven. Nanavasa, who stayed in Pitumpe for two years, disrobed and died two years later in January 1986, then still a young man. However, his personality differed widely from the Ven. Pannasekhara. His relatives described him as shy, an average pupil in school, and not particularly good at chanting. In addition, he had not been as deeply committed to Buddhism as Ruvan, as he abandoned his life as a monk.

Ruvan displayed no recognition of persons, and his statements are few and not specific enough to point clearly to any previous personality. Only by the method of exclusion does Ven. Pannasekhara become a better fit for Ruvan's statements than other monks who lived in Pitumpe in recent times. Ruvan's personality resembles the Ven. Pannasekhara, in that his life is strongly oriented towards Buddhism, he has distinct leadership qualities, enjoys chanting in public, and does it with ease.

Discussion

Duminda, Sandika and Ruvan are the only children speaking of memories of having been monks in over two hundred cases that have been recorded in Sri Lanka. The majority of children claiming previous-life memories speak of untimely violent death. Sandika speaks of dying in a bomb blast; Duminda and Ruvan had long previous lives. Prominent in these cases are deep-seated unusual behavioral traits and interests that fit the ideal behavior of monks. Interestingly, two of these children wanted to become monks again and did so.

We might describe these boys—perhaps a bit too dramatically—as heroically resisting and fighting the constraints they encountered in their families. They developed quite early ideals and goals of a possessive strength, which was not in line with life in their families (particularly in the case of Sandika and Ruvan). In addition, none of them had immediate familiarity with monks with whom they might have identified and modeled their behaviors. Reciting stanzas in Pali by Duminda and Ruvan appear to be cases of recitative xenoglossy (speaking a language that the person has not learned). Xenoglossy is extremely rare. The strength of the past-life memories in our three monk cases falls considerably behind the best of our cases, but the behavioral aspects are outstanding (Haraldsson and Samararatne 1999).

4

CASES IN ICELAND: FROM THE EDDA TO THE PRESENT DAY

The earliest reference to reincarnation and a reincarnation case in Iceland is found in the *Poetic Edda*, a classic recorded in the 13th century. The *Poetic Edda* consists of poems from pre-Christian times, mostly prior to the settlement of Iceland in the 9th and 10th century. One of these poems is *Helga kvida Hundingsbana II*. It consists of 51 verses that describe the life of the heroic warrior Helgi and his beloved Sigrun, his death in battle, and the sorrow of his wife who made her bed on his grave and died of grief and sorrow. At the end of the poem it is stated that they were reborn, his earlier name had been Helgi Haddingaskadi and her name Kara Halfdanardottir.

What about modern times? A question about having memories of a previous life was included in the representative national survey that I conducted in Iceland in 1974. Two percent reported memories of a previous life. When this survey was repeated in 2006, 10% claimed such memories, 8% of the men and 12% of the women. Why this increase? There is no obvious answer to that question. None of the survey respondents were interviewed about their experiences.

In the next two chapters we report on five cases that have come to my attention. Three of them have been published. Two are from modern times and may be considered solved. Both occurred in the same family. The solved cases have intermissions of 7 days and 19 years. Three other cases from distant times and places, permit no investigation, and will be reported in the next chapter.

Einar Jonsson

Dr. Stevenson was informed about this case in a letter in March 1973 from Geir Vilhjalmsson in Reykjavik. Stevenson asked me to investigate it. I interviewed the mother and father of the child and wrote a report for Stevenson about the case. Einar Jonsson was four years old at this time, very shy and did not respond to my questions. Einar's name, as all other names of persons and places, are pseudonyms.

Einar Jonsson was born on July 25, 1969, and lived with his single mother and grandparents in Reykjavik. According to his mother he began at two years of age to say that he had another mother who was living up in the country. He cried often and wanted to go to his "real mother." He spoke often about life in the country, such as "now my grandmother is baking," or "my grandfather is cutting grass." He spoke often about his big brother, and mentioned a big mountain in the countryside. Furthermore he talked about a man who limped, and a tractor that had turned over, and that someone died. You can see his statements in Table 4-1.

Einar's father did not live with Einar and his mother Helga, and there was little communication between his parents at this time, although they later married. The boy rejected his mother, and did not welcome his father's visits when he came to see him. His mother had never heard Einar refer to having two fathers, but she learned that he had been saying this to his playmates at his nursery school.

The farm where Einar's father was brought up was several hundred kilometers away from Reykjavik. His half-brother, Harald, had been driving a tractor to another farm when it turned over at a curve on the road and Einar died instantly. This was on July 18, 1969. Einar was born on July 25 so there were only seven days between Haraldur's death and Einar's birth, which is an extremely short intermission time, especially for a Western case.

Table 4-1 lists all statements that Einar's mother recalled. They were all made before he became four years old.

Table 4-1. Einar Jonsson's Statements about His Previous Life

	Statement	Status
1.	The tractor turned over (and) a man died.	+
2.	He had a big brother.	+
3.	He has another mother who was dead.	-
4.	There was a man who limped (imitates him).	+
5.	The farmhouse was large.	+
6.	There was a mountain behind the farmhouse.	+
7.	The mountain has an unusual shape.	+
8.	There were horses there.	one horse
9.	There was a barn.	+
10.	There was a sheephouse.	+
11.	There was a cowhouse.	+
12.	The house for the cows and the sheep burnt.	small fire 1967
13.	They had skis.	-
14.	He had a bicycle.	?
15.	There was a small boat on the farm.	+
16.	The boat had become broken.	+
+ Statement verified. (13) - Statement did not fit and was wrong. (2) ? Impossible to ascertain; may or may not be right. (1)		

Einar also talked about his uncles, aunt and cousins. He mentioned no names or other specifics about them. Unlike many children with apparent past-life memories Einar never said directly that he had lived before. Thirteen of Einar's statements were correct for the life of Haraldur Olafsson, and 3 incorrect.

In Table 4-1 we have added + if the statement was verified, - if it was found wrong, and ? if it proved impossible to find out if the statement was right or wrong: namely if it fitted the life of Haraldur Olafsson.

Let us comment on individual statements:

1. This statement correctly describes Haraldur Olafsson's traffic accident and death. Einar never said directly that he had driven the tractor. He spoke like an observer watching an event that had happened to someone else. On the other hand he rejected his mother, spoke of having another mother, that he had a big brother and so on.
2. Haraldur had a brother who was a year older than he.
3. Haraldur's mother was still living when Einar was making his statements but absent from Einar who never met her.
4. Marta's father stayed with her on the farm the last six months of his life. He limped. He died when Haraldur was three to four years old.
5. Stevenson and I visited the farm in 1999. The farmhouse was larger than the neighboring farmhouses.
6. There is a mountain behind the farmhouse.
7. The mountain was rather unusual in that it was conical in shape and not with a flat top, as is more common.
8. According to Einar's grandmother they had one horse during Haraldur's lifetime, not horses.
9. Almost all farms in Iceland have barns, sheep and cowhouses.
10. No fire in out-houses but one in the farmhouse that occurred after Haraldur's death.
11. No one in the family had skis. Verified by the grandmother.
12. Einar's grandmother verified that Haraldur had a bicycle.
13. There was a small boat on the farm that was kept on the seashore some distance away.
14. In autumn the boat is hauled higher up the shore, turned over and tied down. One winter the boat was caught by a storm and broken up.

Einar's memories about the previous life vanished at a young age. He had stopped talking about life in the country when Stevenson visited Iceland in 1985 and both of us met Einar.

Can Einar's case be considered solved? Do the statements fit the life of Haraldur Olafsson? Stevenson's and my conclusions were guardedly affirmative, as Stevenson writes in his account of the case (Stevenson, 2003—European Cases of the Reincarnation Type). Tractor accidents are rather common on farms but fatal accidents much less so. Several of the statements would fit most farms but some are very specific, like the one about the broken boat, and that it was kept some distance away from the farm. Only farms near water have boats and it is rare that they are broken. Also rather specific is the statement about the man who limps, and about the unusual shaped mountain behind the farm. Taken as a whole, it seems unlikely that Einar's statements would fit other farms than the one where Haraldur lived.

Ditta Larusdottir

This is a case with meager data that Stevenson and I investigated in 1981. I learned about it from my wife who knew some of the people involved. It concerns Ditta (pseudonym), a girl who was born to Margret Olafsdottir in Reykjavik in 1969. During pregnancy Margret's sister, Gudrun, had a dream about their deceased sister, Kristin, who implied that she was being born as Margret's daughter. Kristin had attended a drama school and acted in some plays on the radio. She had married Einar Grimsson. When she was three years old, Kristin suffered an injury to her head, but she died from an electric shock from a washing machine at the age of 22.

Soon after Ditta's birth the family noticed a prominent birthmark at the back of her head. She was around the age of 2 to 2½ when Margret took her to the bathroom and she noticed a ring on Margret's finger. She asked who had given her this ring? Margret replied that it was her first husband (not Ditta's father). Then Ditta said, "I had a husband too." Her mother told her, "No. You do not have a husband." Ditta insisted, "Yes, I do", and her mother explained, "Little girls do not have husbands." Ditta said, "Well, I have one." Her mother asked about his name—"Einar," Ditta replied. Einar had in fact been Kristin's husband, as was mentioned above. Kristin had been Margret's favourite sister. Ditta never said anything more that might indicate memories of a past life.

Hence we have only her aunt's dream when she stated that she was going to be born as Margret's daughter and the few statements she made to her mother about having had a husband whose name was Einar. When Ditta was two years old she would play at being an actress and wanted to become an actress. Additionally she had a birthmark on her head where Kristin had been injured as a child.

A striking physical similarity between Ditta and Kristin further strengthened the belief of some in Ditta's family that she was indeed Kristin reborn who had died almost 19 years prior to Ditta's birth. By any standard this is a slight case of past-life memories, if indeed it is one, but we spent some time investigating it and Stevenson (2003) included it in his last book, "European Cases of the Reincarnation Type."

In the following chapter we report three unsolved and unverifiable Icelandic cases, apparently from distant centuries. With one exception, pseudonyms are used for the people involved. Two of them are academics.

5

THREE UNSOLVED ICELANDIC CASES: ECHOS FROM A DISTANT PAST?

Kristjan Einarsson from Djupalaek

Kristjan Einarsson from Djupalaek (1916-1994) was a prominent poet and literary figure known for his realism mixed with Oriental idealism, and for taking part in labour and left-wing politics. He wrote a short account of his past-life memories—"I was murdered"—for an edited book on unforgettable events that was published in 1962.

In his six page-long account Kristjan describes events leading up to his death in the previous life. He was part of a religious group that was persecuted and in semi-hiding. He was a tall young man of dark complexion. He describes a long walk over landscape (a flat plain and a beach) that had remained vivid in his mind. He slept one night in the wild and continued the next morning until he arrived at a group of houses partly dug into the slope of a mountain. He was greeted by a man of his age with folded palms who invited him to follow him. He had come there to join a monk-like community. They pray, meditate, sit in silence, and study scriptures.

This community had enemies and sometimes got into fights with them. The enemies looked different, were of darker complexion and shorter. One day they came in greater numbers and a battle followed. Kristjan vividly recalls that he and his compatriots were outnumbered and captured. Their ankles were tied up on a plank placed between two high rocks, and there, all eleven of them, were kept hanging upside down one painful cold night. At sunrise the following morning they heard the footsteps of a few of their enemies. They talked for a while, then one of them stepped forward with a short, sharp spear in his hand. He walked up to the man hanging at the end of the row and stabbed him from behind in the heart. Thus all the men were killed one after the other. Kristjan heard them groan in pain until their murderer came to him. He felt the cold spear pierce his body and screamed in agony until he died.

There is nothing in Kristján Jonson's account that can be firmly placed in space or time. It is evident that the incidents do not take place in Iceland but in a more southern country, perhaps in Asia, Kristjan comments. He states that this is more memorable to him than any event in his present life; also that the landscape is so memorable that he would recognize it if he saw it again. When he wrote his account in 1962, he was still having occasional nightmares about this horrifying incident.

Kristjan does not mention how old he was when these memories first emerged. He died in 1994 so he cannot be asked about it now. I met him a few times but this incident did not come up in our conversation. I had a favourable impression of Kristjan as an outspoken and sincere man. When I asked his son and only child—now a prominent academic—about them, he responded that he knew about his father's past-life memories as far back as he could recall, and that his father often mentioned them.

Gudmund

Gudmund is an acquaintance of mine in Reykjavik whom I have known for several decades. Gudmund has images of a life as a fisherman. These vivid images are of a beach and seeing wooded land where the shore ends a short distance away. He knew that the house he lived in with his wife stood amongst the trees. He was perhaps around forty at the time. One day when he was alone on the shore a group of foreign men attacked him. They were dressed in skin clothes and looked different from the local population. They captured him by casting a net over him. He knew they were catching slaves and domestic animals. He also knew he was going to be taken away to their country, and that he was never going to see his wife and house again.

These images/memories came to Gudmund as an adult around sixty. He felt that the woman in the house among the trees had been reincarnated as his present wife. One gets the impression when talking to Gudmund that his present wife (his second marriage after a long first marriage) was the crucial factor for the emergence of these images as they first emerged when they were sitting at their dinner table. By then they had been married for a few years. These images still come back to him.

The nature of these images cannot be investigated in any way. Gudmund is convinced that they are images of events that occurred in a distant past life.

Arnar

The images of the following case emerged during childhood. They were reported to Stevenson in a letter in the 1970s. The text follows, slightly abridged:

> At the age of 4 till 8 years I spent some summers with relatives who had a farm up in the country a considerable distance from the Reykjavik area where I was brought up. There I sometimes walked with some older children to bring the cows to graze some distance away from the farm. A part of the grazing area was wet with small ponds that were partially grown by high grass. On one such occasion, when I was looking after the cows, I had a memorable experience.

> Here I had a very vivid experience that seemed quite different from usual phantasies and daydreaming. I felt I was reliving something intensely but, at the same time with some sweetness of its own, so that I was not scared or embittered. I felt myself suddenly in a large market square crowded with people.

> Something dramatic had happened that was felt and noticed by all present. Around the square that made up the market place were white

buildings two or three stories high. Somehow I knew this to be the center of the city. On a platform at the wall of one of the houses I stood in a row of a small number of men. In front of us on the platform stood a man asking for offers from the public. We were being sold as slaves. I recognized two men in the crowd, an old friend who wanted to buy me, and another that was my foe and also wanted me. Somehow I knew that catastrophic changes had taken place in the city. There had been a revolt or it had been overrun and captured by a neighboring power or city. Or there had been a mixture of both.

I had been an influential man in the city before the change and knew that most of my former friends had either fled or been killed. The rest of us who were standing there—six to eight perhaps—had been captured. Only this friend of mine in the crowd was left and he was from another province and had come to help me. After several bids I was sold to my enemy for a high price as my friend did not have any more cash with him. The next scene I remember was from an evening in the fields where I had been put to work from sunrise to sunset. It was a large field sloping upwards, and at the end of it was a low forest or rows of trees. It was near sunset and its beauty impressed me and perhaps some mood of my own went into this beautiful but somewhat melancholic impression.

In the third scene I found myself in a hut where I was kept at night, with other slaves I believe. This was a peculiar house as the walls were built of uncut thin trees that would cross at the corners so that the ends of the trees would stand out of the walls at the corners and one could see through the house. I would sleep on the floor chained on one ankle.

Although I remember each of these scenes separately they also were integrated into a whole for I seemed to know the interconnecting events. However, what had happened before these events took place, what my position or work had been, etc., I do not know.

The next scene I remember is standing upright and riding a two wheeled chariot/wagon on a road running through a forest so that I could clearly see a narrow slip of the clear bright sky in the darkness of the night. Somehow I had managed to escape early that night and get hold of a horse and a wagon. In the dark I could dimly see the form of my thick and heavy arms as I held the reins.

I rode till some time next day when I arrived at the farm of my friend who lived in a distant area. I knew that only with him could I hope to find shelter. I also knew him to be a man of some power and influence. I do not remember the scene when I met him but somehow I knew he had welcomed me and told he would do his best to hide me. We knew that my foe and owner would soon come in search of me so he suggested that I hide in high grass that grew in a pond or lake on his land. There it would be difficult to find me. That I did. Later the same day, I somehow knew, my foe came in search of me accompanied by a number of armed men.

The last scene is very clear. I was hiding in the high grass with most of my body covered in water. Spears or arrows were being thrown into the grass around me. One hit me in the chest. There ended my life.

This was my experience. Its vividness and content kept me puzzled for a number of years. It seemed to remain in its vividness and there was something unique about this experience that made it look radically different from usual fantasy or day-dreaming. When I experienced this I felt I was reliving something with an involvement that I had not had with other sorts of experiences. I had the conviction that this had been a real experience in some long since passed time. However, and this puzzles me still, during my childhood I never mentally thought about reincarnation; maybe I just did not know the word or the notion, although I felt that the experience had been real, very keenly perceived and distinctly my own.

From the surroundings and other parts of this experience I suspect that this took place in the Mediterranean area, perhaps in Greek or Roman times. The wagon I drove, the houses and the people give me that impression. Two things puzzled me; when riding the chariot I had looked down on my forearms. They looked thick and muscular; now my arms were slim. Secondly, why did I use a chariot or wagon instead of riding the horse? Much later I read in an old edition of Encyclopedia Britannica that horses in that part of the world were in that time small and only used to drag wagons, not to ride them.

In this case, like that of Gudmund, there is obviously nothing that can be checked. The memories of the chariot caused Arnar to place the images in Greek or Roman times for reliefs/drawings of such chariots are often found from that period. He does not recall having seen such images at the young age when his memories emerged.

6

THREE RANDOMLY SELECTED DRUZE CASES FROM LEBANON

T he more impressive cases get published with greater frequency than 'run of the mill' cases, and hence give readers a skewed impression of the overall quality of the cases that are found in the field. In this chapter I describe three cases that were randomly selected for a thorough investigation. Thirty Druze children were briefly interviewed for a psychological study that I conducted in Lebanon (Haraldsson, 2003). One outstanding case, that of Nazih Al-Danaf, had already been published (Haraldsson and Abu-Izzeddin, 2002) when I decided to select three randomly from the 29 remaining cases.

My Lebanese assistant, Majd Abu-Izzeddin, and I had studied every case that was brought to our attention until we reached the preset number of 30 for the psychological study. We found 19 boys and 11 girls. They lived mostly in the mountainous area to the east and south of Beirut; 23 in rural areas, and 7 in towns. Their ages varied from five to fifteen, with a mean age of 10 years. Their mean age was 2.58 years when they started to speak about a previous life.

Wael Kiwan

We met Wael first in March 1999, at his home in Batir in the mountains 70 km east of Beirut. He was then 11 years old. At the age of four he had started to say that his name was Rabih, that he had been big, not small as now, that he had other parents in Beirut and wanted to know where they were. Later he added other statements: "There was a house with a red brick roof," and he "lived near a house of Allah Wa Akbar" [i.e. mosque] in the "Jal al Bahr," which is a section of Beirut by the sea. He constantly repeated the same story about his death: it was sunset; he saw people coming towards him, and they shot him. You can look up statements in Table 6-1.

Wäel Kiwan, Batir
5 - 3 - 1999

5. Wael Kiwan lived in the village of Batir in the Lebanese mountains. He insisted that he had in his past life lived in the area of Beirut that is close to the sea. His name had been Rabih. He had had two homes, one to which he had to go to by airplane. Rabih had died as a student in California.

Wael's mother and her sister (married to two brothers) are devout Druze and dress in the fashion of a female sheikh in long black garments with a white scarf around the head and over the mouth. Many devout male Druzes are found in the rural areas where they are easily distinguished by their black garments and white headwear. They are particularly co-operative and hospitable, keep their houses spotlessly clean, have healthy lifestyles, and are indeed very nice people.

Wael spoke mostly about the sea and a boat. He would draw a wheel of a boat on paper and say: "I used to stand," and he did circular movement of his hands to show how he moved the steering wheel.

The Search for a Previous Personality

Wael's father would often go on business to Beirut. When he returned Wael would ask him if he had seen his house. It would upset him when his father said no. Wael also told him "If you find it, don't tell them that Rabih has died, because they will cry." He said that they had a balcony, from which he used to jump to the street, that he had two homes, one in Beirut, and another to which he had to travel by airplane. He said to his mother what many of these children do: "My [previous] mother is prettier than you." His parents remembered him making these statements before they started to look seriously for a deceased person who matched what Wael was saying.

Before making any inquiries in Beirut, his father, wife and children sat down with Wael and listed many family names in the hope that he might recognize one of them. He rejected all names until they mentioned the name Assaf. Yes, he said, that was his previous family name. Assaf is a rather common name in Lebanon and is carried by Druze, Christians and Muslims alike.

Wael's father told a Druze friend in Beirut, Sami Zhairi, what Wael was saying about a previous life. Sami promised to ask around. He found a boy called Rabih Assaf whose life seemed to fit Wael's statements. Unfortunately, Sami died three years prior to our investigation of the case, so we were unable to interview him.

About a year after Wael made his first statements, his father took him to Beirut. Accompanied by Sami, they went to a house in the Jal al Bahr section where this boy had lived. Wael ran into the house ahead of the group, and into the apartment on the ground floor. Wael saw a picture on the wall and said, "This is my picture." It was a picture of Rabih Assaf.

They met Raja Assaf, the brother of the deceased Rabih. His mother, Munira, was not at home. Raja brought out a photo album and asked Wael to identify people. According to Wael's father he recognized Rabih's father, sister and a paternal aunt. When they were driving back home, Wael told his father that he was relieved that he had found his previous home. After the meeting with the Assaf family, he spoke little about his previous life and now does not talk spontaneously about it at all. There were further visits between the families. At the time of our interviews Wael occasionally spoke to his previous family over the phone.

Wael came home from school as we were interviewing his parents. By that time he was forgetting his previous memories and he could not tell us anything. By the age of 11 memories of previous life have usually faded away, although some children continue to remember something. At a second meeting in January, 2001, Wael told us that he still remembered how he was shot. It is common that the imagery of the death scene lasts longer than other memories.

Wael's mother told us that Wael gave two versions of his death. The first was that "they" shot him in his head. The second version was that a group of people kicked him and hit him until he did not feel anything; hence his parents assumed that he had been killed.

A week before Wael's birth, his mother dreamt of a grown-up boy who had a moustache, black hair and an open shirt on. The grown-up boy was sweating, and breathing rapidly with difficulty. The boy in the dream looked like the photo of Rabih.

How Close is the Correspondence with Rabih's Life?

A few days later Majd and I visited Rabih's mother, Munira, at her home in the Jal al Bahr section. Munira lives on the ground floor in a four-story house close to the sea. She told us that her son, Rabih, died in South Pasadena, California in January 1988. He had moved to the United States when he was 21 years old, and studied electrical engineering for two years. During the third year he wanted to return to Beirut, but was unable to do so because of the civil war in Lebanon, and did not have enough money either to stay in California, or to return to Beirut.

Rabih was a sensitive boy. He was depressed and attempted suicide by swallowing pills, but was taken to a hospital and survived.

He was staying with relatives in the USA. They did not tell his mother about his first suicide attempt until after he had died. The relatives tried to keep him from attempting another suicide, but on January 9, 1988, he was found dead in the garage. He had hanged himself. This was validated in a telephone interview I had with Abboud Assaf, the relative with whom Rabih had been staying.

Wael never said that he had killed himself. He only said that "they" had shot him but also that a group of people kicked him and hit him until he did not feel anything. Neither Rabih's mother nor his relative in California were aware of any such incident, and we were unable to determine what it concerned.

Table 6-1. Statements Made by Wael Kiwan

	Statement	Status
1.	My name was Rabih. I was big (not small).	+
2.	I have parents. They are not here, they are in Beirut.	+
3.	My house is in Beirut near the sea.	+
4.	My house is near the house of Allah Wa Akbar (mosque).	+
5.	There is a house with a red brick roof.	+
6.	It was sunset and I saw people coming and they shot me.	-
7.	A group of people hit me and kicked me until I did not feel anything.	?
8.	I was often on a boat out at sea.	+
9.	I used to stand and steer the boat with a wheel.	?
10.	I would walk from my house to the sea.	+
11.	My house is in Jal al Bahr.	+
12.	I had two homes, one in Beirut, and one which I went to in an airplane.	+
13.	We had a balcony.	+
14.	I used to jump from the balcony to the street.	+
15.	I used to throw an 'iron' to stop the boat. (Only reported by his aunt).	?
16.	My [previous] mother is prettier than you.	?

+ Statement verified. (11)
- Statement did not fit and was wrong. (1)
? Impossible to ascertain; may or may not be right. (4)

What convinced Munira that Wael was Rabih reborn? When he first visited her home, he asked about the house with a red roof. A house with a red roof had stood behind their four-story building but had been torn down by the time Wael visited there. Rabih had grown up seeing it from their apartment. This, more than anything else, made her believe Wael.

Munira's apartment is on the ground floor and has a balcony. It is easy to jump from the balcony to the street, something Rabih had often done, according to his mother. Wael had mentioned jumping from a balcony to the street before meeting the Assaf family or seeing the house. Rabih's date of birth was August 12, 1964, and he died on January 9, 1988.

Wael repeatedly mentioned a boat. Some relatives and neighbors had boats in a fishermen's harbor at the end of the street some 30 meters down. Most of the boats were rowing boats, but Rabih might sometimes have had a ride on a boat with a steering wheel.

6. Surroundings of the home where Rabih had lived near the sea in Beirut. It fits the description made by Wael Kiwan, such as the close by boat harbour and the old mosque.

Wael had said he lived near a mosque. There is an old mosque approximately 100 meters away from Rabih's house on the same street as the harbor. It is the only mosque in the Jal al Bahr area of Beirut. The statement that Rabih had two homes, one of which you had to go to with an airplane, fits the fact that Rabih also lived with relatives in the United States.

It is interesting that Rabih died in the United States and was reborn in Lebanon. The Druze believe that Druze are always reborn as Druze, and Rabih's reincarnation as Wael fits this expectation. We call cases where rebirth is in a different country than a person's death "international cases." Jim Matlock describes international cases in Chapter 27.

Nadine Maan

Nadine Maan was four years and eleven months old when we first met her in August, 1998. She lives with her parents some 25 km from Beirut, and is the second-youngest of four sisters. Her father is an officer in the security police, and a prize-winning athlete. Her mother works at home.

Nadine remembers her previous name, Randa (or Ranya), and the name of her husband, Ramiz, who strangled her and threw her into the sea. She would show her mother how he did this by placing her hands around her throat.

Nadine wanted to be with her daughter, Reema. She would get a pillow, wrap it in a blanket, and take it with her when they went for a drive in their car. She would put it in the back seat of the car and tell her mother, "This is how I used to put my daughter." Sometimes she takes a pillow, sometimes a doll, and says, "This is my daughter."

Nadine's father has a different memory of when she started to speak about Randa's life. When she was about a year and a half old the family went to Sidon, on the coast, and took a small boat over to an island. When they got into the boat Nadine started shivering with fear. Her sisters could swim but she could not. When her father tried to put her into the water she was extremely scared and grasped his arms in great fear. When they returned home, she told them: "They killed me in the sea." It was after this trip that Nadine started to speak about her daughter, Reema, and her previous life family.

Nadine talked a lot about her memories before she could speak properly. If her family did not understand what she was trying to say, she would get emotional and her neck would become red and swollen. When visitors came she would ask them to take her to her Reema. She would add: "If you do that I will give you a car." She would get involved with babies, wanting to change their diapers and hold them in her arms. If she were asked whether she liked her previous husband, she would say: "Yes, he strangled me, but I loved him." I offered to take her to Reema if she could tell me where she lived. Then she became silent.

Her aunt, Banan Abu Thiab, had observed Nadine's neck getting red and swollen, particularly in her early years when it was difficult to understand what she was talking about. She told Banan that she was at sea and she died. Banan heard from Nadine all but three of the twenty-three statements listed in Table 6-2. She would repeat them over and over again. She was scared of water. Once she tried to strangle Banan's son. When she was asked why, she replied, "He looks like Ramiz."

Nadine would talk on the phone: "Ramiz, I have put the food for you on the table. Send me the car with the driver," and, "Now my daughter Reema should be coming back from school." Nadine still plays at being on the phone with her previous husband. It is not uncommon for previous-life memories of children to be expressed in play. She shows no interest in boys and complains to her father if they speak to her.

Table 6.2. Nadine Maan's Behaviors

1.	She had a fear of sea and water.
2.	Her throat would become red and swollen when speaking about her previous life.
3.	She played at being on the phone with her previous husband.
4.	When playing with other children, she sometimes gave them the names of her previous family.
5.	Once she tried to strangle a young relative. When she was asked why, she replied that he looked like Ramiz.
6.	She liked to put on make-up and lipstick from the time she was two and a half years old.
7.	She likes to wear high heels, dress up, pad her chest to simulate breasts, and look at herself in the mirror.
8.	If someone calls her Nadine, she will sometimes say she is Ranya (Randa).
9.	She used to talk to herself about her previous life.

Nadine's fear of the sea would make sense if Randa had been drowned. Children who remember previous lives often have phobias related to the way the previous person died. The fact that her neck became red and swollen when she talked as a young child about the drowning, is consistent with this too, and it is particularly interesting because it is a physiological reaction. Another example of a physiological reaction in a child too young to explain a trauma in words occurs in a Haida Indian case studied by Ian Stevenson, and described by Jim Matlock in Chapter 22 Nadine's other behaviors are also very similar to what we see in other reincarnation cases.

Searching for the Previous Personality

Nadine's parents knew of no deceased person that fitted her statements when we first visited them. However, when Majd and I returned in January, 2001, they had learned from a distant relative about a young woman who had been on a yacht in Saudi Arabia with her husband and brother-in-law. When they returned to shore they had reported that she had drowned.

At a neighbor's house, Nadine's family were talking about Nadine and how she spoke of having a daughter, a husband, etc. A man, RS, told them that he had been in prison, where he met a man (we will call him SF) who had been accused of choking his sister-in law, Bassima, to death and throwing her body into the sea. SF had been arrested on his return to Lebanon from Saudi Arabia. The father of the drowned woman accused SF and his son-in-law of murdering their daughter. This was evidently a so-called "honor killing" for which there is a tradition among some Muslims if a wife has been—or is assumed to have been—unfaithful.

Majd and I met Bassima's parents in Lebanon. Their daughter and husband had moved to Saudi Arabia, where Bassima died. The Saudi police reported her cause of death as drowning. However, according to the medical report, there were bruises on her back. On hearing this, Bassima's father filed a suit in Lebanon against Bassima's husband and brother-in-law, for they believed that their daughter had been drowned. Two witnesses came forward and testified that Bassima's brother-in-law had told them how he and her husband had drowned her. They had gone out to sea in a rubber motorboat. They held Bassima's hair from the back and pushed her down in the water until she died. They went back to the shore and reported her as being drowned in the sea. One of the witnesses testified. Bassima's husband was sentenced in absentia to hard labor for life. His brother received 10 years' hard labor, later reduced to five years.

Despite the similarities between Bassima's death and Nadine's memories, Bassima's parents rejected the notion that Nadine might be their daughter reborn. Her name had not been Ranya or Randa, her husband's name had not been Ramiz, and they did not own a yacht. To the best of their knowledge, Bassima did not have a store. The only correspondence between Bassima's life and Nadine's statements was that both died at sea, and were drowned. Majd and I had to agree that Nadine was not recalling Bassima's life, and the case remains unsolved.

Nevertheless, this case has remarkable behavioral, emotional and even physiological features; Nadine's throat would become red and swollen when speaking about her murder and drowning, and once she tried to strangle a young relative because he looked like her husband, Ramiz. This illustrates Nadine's intense psychological involvement.

Sasha Chehayeb

Majd and I met Sasha in 1999 at her home in Aley when she was ten years old. By that time her memories had faded away.

It first occurred to her parents that Sasha might be referring to a previous life when she would put a handmade scarf around her head and say: "I am the bride" and "I have a baby." At this time she was one year and four months old and could barely speak. When she was about two and half, they passed a ruined house, and Sasha said to her father, "I am ma wa [baby talk for pain] and then slept." They thought that she might be remembering a previous life, for they understood this to mean, "I was in great pain and that was the end of my life."

One day they were buying petrol, and her father mentioned the name Khalil, the owner of the petrol station. Sasha said: "He is cute." After that she often said that she wanted to go and visit Khalil, but not the Khalil at the petrol station.

At this time her mother was pregnant. Sasha pretended that she was also pregnant and that she was going to call her baby Bashar. She played with a doll she named Bashar. She said that she had been pregnant and she and Khalil were going to call their baby Bashar.

Sasha said that she had heard an airplane and the ceiling collapsed and she fell down. She uttered this after they had driven past an abandoned house in ruins. She had a fear of airplanes. Sasha told her mother: "I am older than you, don't yell at me," indicating that she felt herself to be a grown-up person.

Sasha said that her mother was not her real mother, that their house was not like her previous house, and that she did not have such clothes as she used to have; in short, she was comparing her past and present lives and complaining about the present one.

Potential Previous Personality is Identified

As in the two previous cases, no record was made of statements before a potential previous family was found. This makes the reconstruction of Sasha's original statements and behavior difficult, five years after the families met. Moreover, Majd and I obtained somewhat different views from witnesses of how the first contact was established between Sasha and the family of the deceased woman, Sana, whom Sasha's parents came to believe to be her previous person.

Sana's family was well known in the Druze community. They resided in Abadieh, where some relatives of Sasha's family also lived. In
addition, Sasha's mother was distantly related to Khalil.

On 25 June, 1982, at the time of the Israeli invasion of Beirut, several
rockets bombarded the village of Abadieh. One of them hit the house
of Khalil Zahr, killing seven people, four of them inside the building.
The roof came down over some of them. Khalil lost his wife, Sana, and
his mother, cousin, and daughter.

Khalil and Sana were a young couple who had a particularly loving relationship. Sana was said to have been pregnant with their first
baby. This tragic event became national news and was especially well
known among the Druze community. An obituary of Sana appeared
in a major Lebanese newspaper. We must take these things into account when evaluating this case. Correspondences between Sasha's
statements and facts in the life of Sana have less evidential value than
if the circumstances of Sana's life and death were more obscure. Sasha's statements are listed in Table 6-3.

Table 6.3. Statements by Sasha Chehayeb according to her Parents

	Statement	Status
1.	I want to see Khalil.	+
2.	I am a bride (married woman).	+
3.	Khalil is cute.	+
4.	He has a half-beard.	+
5.	He smokes a pipe.	+
6.	I heard an airplane.	+
7.	The ceiling collapsed and I fell down.	+
8.	I was carried out of the building.	+
9.	I died.	+
10.	I was pregnant.	-
11.	Khalil and I were going to call our baby Bashar.	-
12.	Khalil used to bring me gifts.	?

+ Statement verified. (9)
- Statement did not fit and was wrong. (2)
? Impossible to ascertain; may or may not be right. (1)

Several of Sasha's statements seem to fit Sana: Khalil was a handsome man, had a half-beard and smoked a pipe; the ceiling fell down on Sana and others in the house; she was carried out of the building and died a few minutes later. The relationship between Sana and Khalil was described as particularly loving, so it is likely that Khalil often brought Sana gifts.

Particularly interesting is the statement about what Khalil and Sana were going to name the child they were expecting, as this would only have been known by the closest family members. It has been difficult to ascertain this name: Khalil's sisters, Hayat and Hanan, were not sure about it. They agreed that it had a 'sh' sound in it, and was a Muslim name. Hayat said: "Maybe Rashad was the name," Hanan said, "Maybe Bashar." Both are Muslim names. The sisters agreed that Bashar was probably the name Khalil and Sana had planned for their baby if it was a boy. When we finally reached Khalil, however, he told us that Sana had not been pregnant at the time of her death, but if she had had a son she would have named it Omar, not Bashar.

Meetings between Sasha and Members of Sana's Family

We interviewed several members of Khalil's and Sana's family. We wanted to check some claims of recognitions.

Hayat is the head teacher of a school in Abadieh. She first met Sasha's mother, Thurayah, when Sasha was about five or six years old. Thurayah told her that her daughter was talking about Khalil (not the Khalil at the gas station,) adding that Sasha said that Khalil had a half beard, smoked a pipe, always brought her gifts, and that her previous mother was "different from her." Hayat told Thurayah that she and Khalil would soon come and visit Sasha to see what might happen. Hayat and Hanan were Khalil's sisters and that is why Sasha's mother wanted to talk to them.

Two or three months after Thurayah visited Hayat, Hayat and Khalil had still not paid a visit to Sasha. Thurayah therefore took Sasha to Hayat who showed her some photographs. She opened a big album and asked Sasha to look at them. On the first page was a photo of a young couple. The moment Hayat opened the album, Sasha pointed to the couple and said: "This is Khalil, not Khalil the owner of the petrol station, and this is Sana." The picture was an engagement photo of the couple. Hayat said to Sasha, "Sana was big and you are small," and Sasha replied, "I was the big Sana." Hayat showed her other family photographs, but she did not mention any more names. Hayat was rather impressed with Sasha's recognition of this one photograph, however.

Zahr Adnan and her brother, Hassan, are cousins of Khalil and were the first close relatives of Khalil and Sana that Sasha met. One day Thurayah came with Sasha to visit her grandfather's family, who lived in a house close by. Sasha started playing with children outside. By chance she came with these children into Zahr and Hassan's house. She happened to see a family photo on a table with some 10-15 people, relatives of the Adnan family. Sasha pointed to a man in the photo and said: "This is Khalil." She added that Khalil had shaved off his beard (which was true). She also said that she did not like the tie he was wearing. This photo had been taken after Sana's death. Sana and Khalil had visited Hassan and Zahr in this house not long before Sana died but there was no recognition of them or their house.

Emma Najjar, the wife of Sana's uncle Sleiman, told us that Zahr brought Sasha to her house one day. When she walked into the flat Sasha said, "Auntie Emma." Mrs. Adnan brought her some photos to look at. Sasha pointed to one and said: "This is uncle, not Thurayah's grandfather, Said." What Sasha said was correct. The man was Sasha's paternal uncle Sleiman. The uncle she pointed at was Emma's husband, Sheiman, but she did not mention his name. Then Emma saw, or picked out, another picture. "This is me," Sasha said, and she mentioned another name that Emma no longer remembers, but someone who had been a friend of Sana's. Sasha wanted the photo and Emma gave it to her. Sana was indeed in the photograph and her friend was on a hospital bed. Sasha had shown us this photo when we visited her. Sasha did not make any statements about her previous life. Was Emma impressed with Sasha? Yes, slightly impressed, she replied.

Aniseh Najjar, Sana's mother, first heard about Sasha from her sister-in-law, Emma. Two or three months later, Sasha and her mother visited her when Aniseh was staying overnight in Wadi and Wadia Najjar's house. Sasha was shy and did not approach her. When asked, Sasha could tell Aniseh her name and the name of her husband (Sana's father), but did not recognize the name of Sana's brother whom Sana had loved very much. Aniseh believes that Sasha had been told her name and that of her husband, Fuad. Aniseh took Sasha to another room to be with her alone and showed her several photographs. She first showed her a photograph of her husband (Sana's father) and asked who was in the photograph. "My uncle," Sasha replied. To a photo of Khalil, Sasha also replied, "Uncle." For all the men she replied, "Uncle."

Aniseh thought that Sana had been pregnant, but Sana never told Aniseh about any particular name she would give to the child. Aniseh was unimpressed by Sasha. Aniseh said that Sasha had not recognized anyone in the photos, and said nothing to convince her that she was her deceased daughter reborn.

Maarouf Zahr owns a grocery store in Abadieh. Sasha's parents told us that when Sasha was two-and-a-half to three years old and they were visiting Aley, she saw a man, became scared and said: "This is the last man I saw in my previous life." Sasha's father was slightly acquainted with Maarouf, and later learned from him that after the rocket attack he had carried Sana, who was seriously injured, from her house to a neighbor's house, where she died. We interviewed Maarouf. He had been 60-70 meters from the house when the rocket hit. He ran towards the house to help the injured people. He and Khalil's father, Mohammed, who had been in the house but escaped unharmed, carried Sana to a neighbor's house. Sana told Maarouf to go back and get Khalil. When he returned a few minutes later she had expired. Hayat was in Khalil's house when it was shelled and was also injured. She saw Sana seriously injured on the floor and saw how her father, Mohammed, and Maarouf Zahr carried Sana out of the building shortly before she died.

Khalil Zahr met Sasha accidentally for the first time at a social gathering some time after her meeting with Aniseh. When Sasha saw Khalil she told her mother that Khalil had changed, for he used to have a "half-beard;" now Khalil had no beard. They met only briefly. Sasha asked him, "Do you still smoke a pipe?" He did not answer. Khalil knew that this was Sasha and asked about her story from his sister Hayat. Khalil now lives in Saudi Arabia and we were not able to meet him.

Sana's father died in a car accident in 1993. Sasha cried a lot when she heard about the news. She had never met him.

Sasha's case contains few statements, some recognitions, and some behavioral features. Its principal weaknesses are that the child and alleged previous family are distantly related, Sana's death was well known in the area, and the investigation took place several years after the statements and recognitions were made and observed. It might, however, be pointed out that Sana's death occurred seven years before Sasha was born and hence it is unlikely to have been an active topic of conversation at that time.

It is interesting to note the differences between how various members of Sana's family perceived the evidential value of the case. Sana's mother, Aniseh, found nothing to make her think that Sasha might be her daughter reborn. Hayat, Maarouf Zahr, Hassan and Emma, on the other hand, were impressed with Sasha's recognitions of photos. Different members of the alleged previous family sometimes hold different views regarding the possibility of the case being viewed as 'solved' or not, depending on what they themselves have witnessed. Sometimes differences in the socio-economic status of families can play a role, but that seems unlikely in this case.

Discussion

What do these three randomly selected Lebanese cases reveal? Parents of all three children are convinced that their children have genuine previous-life memories.

In the case of Wael Kiwan we find a high correspondence between his statements, many of them quite specific, and the life of Rabih. Only the mode of death differs. The present and previous families were complete strangers and lived far apart.

In the case of Nadine, we could not confirm any correspondence except the mode of death with the life of the person that Nadine's parents suspect to be her previous personality. A convincing match with a previous person has not been found. The leading statements are the mode of death; the murder and drowning of a young mother by her husband at sea. The search for such an event is difficult as Lebanon has a long coast with thousands of boats and yachts, and there is no centralized recording of persons drowned or missing at sea. Besides, civil war was raging in Lebanon for many years with the consequent breakdown of law enforcement. During this period, the authorities might not have investigated such a murder. This case has proved unverifiable. On the other hand, it has interesting features, apart from the memories—deep emotional involvement, acting out her memories in play, and her throat getting red and swollen at a very early age when she could not speak properly. Unsolved cases can have quite interesting features and are often as developed as solved ones (Cook, Pasricha, Samararatne, Maung, and Stevenson, 1983a, 1983b)

In the case of Sasha, her statements are few and there is correspondence with the previous person. The case is weakened by the fact that

Sasha's family were related to Sana and the circumstances of her death were well known in their community. Sana's mother rejected Sasha as Sana reborn, whereas some other relatives did not. From the point of view of Sasha's parents, who know the case best and observed it develop, there is sufficient evidence to accept the case as evidential, but for outsiders, the evidence is meager.

These three cases lay bare some of the difficulties that face the researcher when researching them and, even more so, when attempting to interpret them. There are no cases without some weakness and few have no merits at all. Two out of our three randomly selected cases were possibly/probably solved, one albeit weakly. Two are stranger cases, and one a same-family case. The random selection of the cases is not strongly biased and representative in a limited way. Interesting features appear in all of them. Apart from the alleged memories, reincarnation cases often have puzzling features such as deep emotional involvement, expression of memories in play, and physiological effects, as in the case of Nadine.

7

SRI LANKAN CASES WITH WRITTEN RECORDS BEFORE VERIFICATIONS

In the majority of reincarnation cases, the family of the child had identified the previous person before investigators learned of the case. Then all the investigators can do is to try to reconstruct the development of the case and its verification as well as they can. Cases with written records made before verifications are very important, but we have relatively few of them. In this chapter, we report four such cases from Sri Lanka. All are remarkable in some way, and yet, in their basic features, are representative of the 64 cases I have investigated in that country. One has birthmarks at the location of injuries that led to the death of the person whose life the child seemed to be remembering. Stevenson has published a paper with three other Sri Lankan cases with written records.

Dilukshi G. Nissanka

We learned about this case through an article in the *Weekend* edition of *Sun*, a leading Sri Lanka newspaper. Dilukshi is the only child of her parents who live in Veyangoda in the Gamphaha District. Dilukshi's mother told us that her daughter began to speak about a previous life when she was less than two years old. She spoke about a life in Peravatte, Dambulla, where she had drowned in a stream. To her parents' dismay, she refused to call them mother and father and requested to be taken to her earlier home. She was born on October 4, 1984, and we interviewed her mother in November, 1989. You can read Dilukshi's statements in Table 7-1 (Haraldsson, 1991).

7. Dilukshi Nissanka insisted that she had lived in the far away Dambulla area and drowned when she fell into a river. Nearby had been a grocery shop that was run by a young man called "thin boy". Dilukshi made many verifiable statements about her previous life.

Dilukshi's parents tried hard to get their girl to stop this talk about a previous life, even by threatening her, but in vain. In the end, when Dilukshi was almost five years old, they gave up. They contacted a relative, Sunil, who made a phone call to the abbot of the famous Dambulla rock temple, which is a frequent place of pilgrimage in Sri Lanka. The abbot, the Ven. Sumangala, also an archaeologist, asked Sunil to write a letter listing the statements that the girl had been making. With that in hand, the Ven. Sumangala made enquiries around Dambulla and did not find a deceased child that fitted Dilukshi's statements. He therefore contacted a journalist friend, who quickly made his own investigation, interviewed the girl's parents and published an account in the Sinhalese and English editions of *Weekend*.

Dharmadasa Ranatunga in Dambulla read the account in *Weekend*, wrote a letter to Dilukshi's father, and mailed a photocopy to the Ven. Sumangala. A few days later the two fathers met and, soon thereafter, Dilukshi was taken by the journalist and her parents to Dambulla, where the Ven. Sumangala joined them. According to them, the girl led the way to Ranatunga's house some four miles from Dambulla town. After recognition of objects and persons at the Ranatunga's home, and verifications of her statements, the Ranatunga family accepted her as their daughter Shiromi reborn.

Table 7-1. Statements made by Dilukshi G. Nissanka according to the report in *Weekend* on September 10, 1989

	Statement	Status
1.	My mother lives in Peravatte in Dambulla.	+
2.	My brother and I fell into the stream and I came here (died).	+
3.	A stream with a footbridge over it skirts the paddyfield near the house.	+
4.	Our house is near Heenkolla's boutique.	+
5.	We used to buy provisions in Heenkolla's shop.	+
6.	The roof of their house could be seen from the small Dambulla rock (punchi Dambulla gala).	+
7.	We played on the smaller rock. I played shopkeeper (mudalali) in the boutique. There was a little doll in our boutique.	+
8.	One day I climbed the Dambulla rock and my brother and I fell down.	?
9.	There is a public drinking cistern (pinthaliya) at Dambulla temple.	+
10.	I went to school by van.	+
11.	Father took me in the van to school.	?
12.	I have friends and we have been in Colombo.	+
13.	My father is the owner of a metal quarry.	+
14.	Father is fair in complexion.	+
15.	Mother is very fair.	-
16.	Younger brother is very dark.	-

17.	She (Dilukshi) was known as Suwanna.	-
18.	Mother was Swarna. Cannot remember father's name.	-
19.	My mother wears a housecoat with beautiful buttons.	+
20.	My brothers, Mahesh (elder) and Thushara (younger) are waiting for me in our play boutique.	-
21.	Two children fell into the stream while playing near the footbridge.	?
22.	My mother is not like you, aunt. She loves me very much.	?

+ Statement verified. (13)
- Statement did not fit and was wrong. (5)
? Impossible to ascertain; may or may not be right. (4)

The distance from Veyangoda to Dambulla is about 80 miles. Dilukshi's parents had no friends, relatives, or other connections with Dambulla, which is a small town in a rural area. They had visited Dambulla once in early 1984 on their way back from a pilgrimage to Anuradhapura.

We are in the unique position of having copies of three documents with Dilukshi's statements about her previous life before any person was found which fitted her statements—Sunil's letter to the abbot of the Dambulla Temple; notes by the journalist from his interview with Dilukshi's mother; and his report in *Weekend*. Furthermore, we have a letter dated September 15, 1989 from Mr. Ranatunga to Dilukshi's father with a copy mailed to the Ven. Sumangala where he writes that he has read the report in *Weekend* and he describes some facts about his daughter who drowned on September 27, 1983, at the age of nine. Let us examine individual statements that Dilukshi made. There are 22 in the *Weekend* record, and 13 in Sunil's letter with slight discrepancies between a few items. The difference in the number of items is most likely due to unequal thoroughness on the part of the recorders.

Table 7-2. Statements made by Dilukshi G. Nissanka
according to B. A. Sunil's Letter

	Statement	*Status*
1.	She lived near Dambulla in her previous life.	+
2.	Near the road where you turn there is a small vegetable boutique.	+

3.	There is a very thin boy there.	+
4.	She and her younger brother slipped on the big Dambulla rock.	+
5.	When you climb the stone steps of the Dambulla (temple) you can see the roof of her house.	+
6.	Her father has a large stone quarry in Dodamwatte (orange garden).	+
7.	On the road near the house the bus runs that goes to Sigiriya.	+
8.	Father had plenty of money.	+
9.	Her mother wears a housecoat with big buttons.	+
10.	She was in the 5th grade.	-
11.	In the house there are two dogs.	+
12.	On the two sides of the house are grown two big flowering trees.	?
13.	She and her two younger brothers go to school in the morning by van.	?
14.	Her house is near the paddyfield.	+

+ Statement verified. (11)
- Statement did not fit and was wrong. (1)
? Impossible to ascertain; may or may not be right. (2)

Let us look at a few items. "My mother lives in Perawatte in Dambulla" (*Weekend*). "She lived near Dambulla" (Sunil's letter). Both statements mention that Shiromi lived near Dambulla but not in Dambulla town. When the Ven. Sumangala discovered that no village existed by the name of Perawatte, he turned the case over to the journalist. Perawatte literally means a gova fruit (pera) garden (watte). Dilukshi's mother told us that her daughter had sometimes called her home in her previous life perawatte because of the number of fruit trees growing there. Her father explained that there were a number of gova fruit (pera) trees at a house close by and also many other fruit trees around. The location has an abundance of trees that bear fruits. Dilukshi was describing a characteristic of her previous location.

Wimala is the sister of Shiromi's mother and lived with the family for two years. Although Wimala was nine years older than Shiromi, they went to the same school, were close to one another, and spent most of their day together. Wimala told us that when the gova trees were bearing fruit, Shiromi always insisted that they go through Perawatte on the way home from school, a place near her home, which she called by that name because of many gova trees. We visited this

77

place, which is close by, and has many gova trees. Another example of child-like name giving is the second item on Sunil's list, where Dilukshi states that her father had a large stone quarry in Dodamwatte (garden of oranges). Shiromi's father works in a tile factory in Anuradhapura where oranges are also grown.

"My brother and I fell into the stream and I came here (died)." Shiromi died by drowning in a nearby stream or canal that is about three yards wide and a yard and a half or more deep. On that day Wimala and five or six other children were with her at the canal bathing and washing linen. Wimala noticed that Shiromi had disappeared, and a few hours later she was found drowned at the bottom of the canal. Shiromi knew how to swim and it was assumed that she had fallen on a rock that protrudes into the stream and lost consciousness because an injury was found on her head.

8. Dilukshi and Erlendur standing on the bank of the river that she recalled having fallen into and drowned.

"A stream with a footbridge over it skirts the paddyfield near the house." Slightly upstream and opposite Ranatunga's paddyfields there had been a footbridge across the canal. It was torn down a few years ago, and a concrete footbridge was built some 15-20 yards further down the stream. This item corresponds well with Shiromi's statement of the location.

"Our house is near Heenkolla's boutique. We used to buy provisions in Heenkolla's boutique. Near the road where you turn is a small vegetable boutique. There is a very thin boy there." Near Ranatunga's house, as one leaves a footpath, and enters the road towards to the school, there is a house with a small shop. It had been closed down because of insufficient business five months before we first visited the area. The shopkeeper's brother told us that his younger brother had been called Heen (thin) Malle (younger brother) since he was a boy and suggested that Shiromi might have called the shop Heenkolla's (kolla = boy) boutique, or the shop of the thin boy. We were shown the licence for the shop that sold groceries and vegetables. It was the only shop that Shiromi would have passed on her way to school. This item is quite specific and an excellent fit with Dilukshi's statement. In 1990 we met Heen Malle, who at the age of 27 was a slender man, and he remembered Shiromi buying in his shop.

"The roof of their house could be seen from the small Dambulla rock (punchi Dambulla gala)." Some 30-40 yards from the Ranatunga's house is a large flat rock, less than a yard high from the ground. Shiromi's mother, and independently her sister Wimala, told us that Shiromi had called this rock the small Dambulla rock and often played there with her younger brother. We verified from that rock that the roof of their house could be seen between some trees and bushes. This rock is the only one of its kind near the house.

"We played on the smaller rock. I played shopkeeper in our boutique. There was a little doll in our boutique." According to Shiromi's mother her children had often played on the low rock near the house, and also played boutique.

"One day I climbed the Dambulla rock and my brother and I fell down" (*Weekend*). She and her younger brother slipped on the big Dambulla rock (Sunil). According to Shiromi's parents, this may well have happened because they often visited the Dambulla rock temple and walked up the long footpath and the many steps up to the ancient temple, which is hewn into the slope of the boulder-like rock. It can be seen from far away and there is a beautiful view of the surrounding countryside.

"There is a public drinking cistern (pinthaliya) at Dambulla temple" (*Weekend*). There was a drinking cistern near the beginning of the way up to the temple, which had been placed there by a family that lived close by, according to Shiromi's parents and Ven. The family moved away a few years ago and since then no drinking cistern is placed at the roadside for thirsty visitors. We will let these comments of individual statements suffice.

How do Dilukshi's Statements Fit the Facts of Shiromi's Life?

Shiromi died one year and a week before Dilukshi was born. Dilukshi's statements differ widely in potential verifiability. Some concern objective facts and are clearly either right or wrong. Others, such as whether Shiromi played boutique, had a doll, or slipped on the way up to the Dambulla temple, are either so general that they might fit almost any child, or are such minor events that they are unlikely to have been remembered by witnesses. Of the 17 statements that seem potentially verifiable, 12 correspond at least partially with Shiromi's life, whereas four (15, 16, 18, and 20) are definitely wrong. Statements about location and places fare well, whereas four names of persons are wrong, unless we accept that the two names for Shiromi's brothers were really meant for playmates, which children in SriLanka frequently refer to as brothers and sisters. The names Suwanna for Shiromi and Swarna for Zeila start with the correct sound. This is a very interesting case with many direct hits.

A documentary on Dilukshi's case, *Past Lives: Stories of Reincarnation* was made by Storyhouse Productions in Washington D. C. and aired in the United States in 2003 on the Discovery Channel and in Asia and Germany.

When I met Dilukshi again in 2006 she still had some of her old memories while others had faded away. She occasionally visited her previous family and exchanged gifts with them, had completed secondary school and was looking for a job, which is difficult in Sri Lanka. She seemed rather unhappy about her prospects.

Pretiba Gunawardana

Pretiba Gunawardana was four years and two months old when we first met him and his mother in November, 1989, at their home in Pannipitiya, some 20 miles southeast of Colombo. Tissa Jayawardane, my interpreter, had learned about the case from a friend. It was only after we convinced Pretiba's mother that we would not publicize the case in Sri Lanka that she was willing to talk to us. Pretiba had made his first statements about his previous life after suffering high fever for a week when he was a little over two years old. Since then, he frequently spoke about his previous-life memories (Haraldsson, 1991).

Pretiba was strongly built and healthy looking and spoke to us without shyness about the memories that he insists he has about his previous life. He had lived in Kandy (using the Sinhalese name Maha Nuwara), that is the main city of central Sri Lanka. His former name was Santha Megahathenne, and he had lived at number 28 Pilagoda Road. His car had caught fire, he was burnt on his right leg, hand and mouth, was taken to the hospital and "came here" (died). His mother told us that he often mentioned two names: an older brother Samantha and an older sister Seetha. His father later told us that Pretiba often said he wanted to see them. According to his mother, he talked more often about names than events. He had no unusual behavioral traits that seem to relate to his statements. His 42 statements are listed in Table 7-3.

Table 7-3. Statements made by Pretiba Gunawardana about his Previous Life

	Statement	Status
1.	Often mentions Samantha aya (elder brother).	?
2.	Often mentions Seetha akka (elder sister).	?
3.	Elder sister was married.	?
4.	Mentions Loku aya and Loku akka (big/elder).	?
5.	Mentioned Dhamman Sadhu, a relative of father's brother.	?
6.	They had a car and a bus.	?
7.	His car had been burned (with much smoke) with him in it.	?
8.	Right hand, leg and mouth had been burned.	?
9.	Admitted to Nuwara hospital, plaster placed on his body.	?
10.	After that he came to this place (died and was born here).	?
11.	He had been to India and to a Hindu temple (kovil).	?
12.	He had a passport.	?

13.	Mentioned name of Natapati (Nathapathi), visited Natapati Devalaya (kovil) while in India.	?
14.	Brought from India some items for his mother (saris and buttons).	?
15.	He lived at number 28 Pilagoda Road in Nuwara (Kandy).	?
16.	He lived upstairs in a house.	?
17.	His father was old.	?
18.	His father had a car.	?
19.	His father wore eyeglasses.	?
20.	Father had gone abroad and returned.	?
21.	Mentions a fight between snake and katussa.	?
22.	He had a girlfriend but did not like to marry that girl.	?
23.	They had a house with land around it.	?
24.	He had an uncle.	?
25.	They had paddyfields.	?
26.	Balansena worked in the paddyfields.	?
27.	There was a temple near the house.	?
28.	There was artwork of elephants at the temple.	?
29.	He went to Sunday temple school.	?
30.	They had a refrigerator.	?
31.	They had a pettagama (large wooden box).	?
32.	He had a good wristwatch.	?
33.	Mentions mother's younger sister.	?
34.	Husband of mother's young sister had a lorry and was a businessman.	?
35.	His name was Santha Megahathenne.	?
36.	He had a friend called Asanga.	?
37.	Bandara also lived there.	?
38.	He wore trousers.	?
39.	He was attending school.	?
40.	They had a bank account.	?

| 41. | His (former) brother looked like the brother of his (present) mother. | ? |
| 42. | Attanayake lived close to our house and had a lorry. | ? |

? Impossible to ascertain; may or may not be right. (42)

We asked Pretiba if he would like to go to Kandy. He was quick to say yes. He said he could find his house, but when we asked him if he knew its whereabouts he replied with no. His father had not been willing to search for the previous person, and his mother shared the common fear of mothers that she might lose her child if the previous family were found. Previously Pretiba had told his parents that he wanted to go to Kandy to collect his things.

In Kandy we made inquiries about Pilagoda Road and names resembling it. Post office authorities told us that there was no such road in Kandy city nor any village or area by that name in the Kandy District. We also made inquiries about the name Megahathenne, which Pretiba had given as his former family name. Some Sri Lankans use the name of the village they come from as a family name. A village by the name of Megahathenne is near Galagedara some 15 miles from Kandy. Inquiries there yielded no information about any person having the characteristics described by Pretiba, and Pilagoda Road was not found in the village. The name Megahathenne was not found in the Kandy telephone directory.

We expressed the wish to take the boy with his family to Kandy, and his parents accepted. With Godwin Samararatne as my interpreter, we made the three-hour drive up the scenic road to Kandy, which leads through many villages and towns. As we were approaching the bridge over the Mahaveli River at the other side of which is Kandy city, and were driving through a busy street, the boy became quite animated. He spontaneously said, "There is Maha Nuwara," which is the Sinhalese name for Kandy city. As we crossed the bridge over the Mahaveli river—one of a few bridges on the way to Kandy—he correctly remarked, "This is Mahaveli Ganga" (ganga = river). Neither we nor the parents had mentioned this name nor given any indication that we were about to enter Kandy.

We drove down Peradeniya Road, the main street into Kandy, to the Temple of the Tooth— the chief landmark of Kandy—and around the Lake. Apart from these two statements, Maha Nuwara and Mahaveli Ganga, there was no comment from Pretiba that indicated recognition or knowledge of the area, nor did he express any wish to see a particular spot, though he definitely enjoyed the journey.

We failed to find any person that fitted Pretiba's statements. One possibility would have been to go through the admission records at Kandy hospital in the hope of finding the name of Santha Megahathenne. This was beyond our means as there were thousands of admissions every year.

Without revealing the boy's name or address the main features of the case were publicized with the parent's permission in an interview with me on December 11, 1990, in the widely circulated *Dinamina* and its English edition *Daily News*. We obtained no response from readers. We have no evidence that Pretiba's alleged past-life memories correspond to any objective facts. It remained unsolved like so many Sri Lankan cases, in fact about two thirds of them.

Thusita Silva

Thusita (pseudonym) was born on June 16, 1982, in the small town of Elpitiya in southwestern Sri Lanka. In 1988 she moved to Panadura, which is 18 miles south of Colombo. Tissa Jayawardane heard about the case from neighbors and interviewed the girl and her mother in June 1990. In November the same year I interviewed Thusita and her family with Godwin Samararatne as interpreter. Thusita's father had died a few years earlier (Mills, Haraldsson and Keil, 1994).

Thusita had started speaking about a life in Akuressa at the age of two and a half years. She said she had fallen from a narrow suspension footbridge into the river and drowned; the hanging bridge was not far from her house. She had a husband and had been pregnant at the time. Her father's name had been Jeedin Nanayakkara and she had lived in a house larger than the mud hut where her present poor family was living. Her mother had a sewing machine, she had a yellow bicycle, and she had worked in a hospital. In the interview with Tissa Jayawardane, Thusita had further stated that her husband had thrown himself into the river in an attempt to save her and had almost drowned. She said that he had been a postman, that they had had a car, that there was a big gate in front of their house, and that she had a brassiere. Her statements are listed in Table 7-4.

Thusita's mother stated that her daughter had a phobia of bridges and water. Earlier she had mentioned more names, but neither she nor her family remembered them when we interviewed them. By then Thusita seemed to have forgotten some of her earlier memories.

9. Thusita Silva recalled having lived in far away Akuressa as a member of a Nanayakkara family. She insisted that she had drowned when she fell into a river from a walking bridge near her home.

Table 7-4. Statements made by Thusita Silva

Statement	Status
A. Statements made 11/26/90 to Erlendur	
1. I am from Akuressa.	+
2. My father's name was Jeddin (Nanayakkara).	-
3. My father's name was (Jeddin) Nanayakkara.	+
4. I had a bicycle.	+
5. The bicycle was yellow.	-
6. I went to work by bicycle.	-
7. I rode my bicycle alone (by herself).	+
8. I worked in a hospital.	-
9. I wore a white hospital uniform with a cap and shoes.	-
10. The hospital was some distance from my house.	+
11. Mother wore frocks (skirts).	?
12. Mother had a sewing machine.	+
13. I had two striped frocks (skirts).	?
14. There was a river or stream some distance away (from my house).	+
15. The hanging bridge (wel palama) broke.	+
16. I fell into the river.	+
17. I drowned.	+

18.	I was pregnant when I drowned.	+
19.	I had a husband.	+
20.	My former house was larger than my present house.	+
21.	Its walls were colored.	+
22.	I had a niece (sister's daughter).	-
23.	My former father was called appa (my present is dada).	?
B. Items reported to Tissa Jayawardane, but not to Erlendur		
24.	There was a big gate at her former home.	+
25.	Her husband jumped into the river to save her.	+
26.	Her husband was a postman.	-
27.	They had a car.	+
28.	She wore a brassiere.	?
+ Statement verified. (17) - Statement did not fit and was wrong. (7) ? Impossible to ascertain; may or may not be right. (4)		

Thusita's family claimed to have no connections of any kind with Akuressa, and none of them had ever been there when Thusita was talking about her previous life. Akuressa is some 30 miles from Elpitiya where Thusita was born and 78 miles from Panadura. Some considerable time after she started to talk about these things, her brother traveled to Akuressa, but did not learn of or find anyone corresponding to her statements. Upon returning home, he scolded Thusita for telling lies. Later he beat her for talking to Tissa Jayawardane.

In the summer of 1990, Tissa visited Akuressa that has a population of about 20,000. He learned that a young woman with the married family name of Nanayakkara had drowned after falling into a river from a narrow suspension bridge, but was unable to meet any members of the family. In November 1990, I visited Akuressa with Godwin Samararatne and found the relatives of a Chandra Nanayakkara who had drowned by falling off the suspension bridge. The house of her in-laws was some 100 yards from the bridge. We interviewed two of Chandra's sisters-in-law, a close friend of the family, her husband Somasiri Nanayakkara, and her brother. All these persons were cooperative and answered all inquiries.

Chandra had drowned in 1973 at the age of 27, after falling off the suspension bridge that she and her husband were crossing. A plank that Chandra stepped on apparently gave way, and she fell into the swollen river. Her husband jumped into the river to rescue her but almost drowned himself. Chandra's body was found three days later some distance down river. She had been seven months' pregnant at the time. A document in the coroner's office confirmed that Chandra had died in December 1973 "by choking after swallowing water when the deceased fell into the River Nilwala from the suspension bridge." This is the only suspension bridge in the area. After Chandra Nanayakkara's drowning, the bridge was repaired, but in 1990 it was back to its earlier state of disrepair. Several people have fallen into the river since, but no one has drowned.

10. Thusita claimed to have fallen from a hanging bridge near her home in the town of Akuressa and drowned. In that town we found a hanging bridge close to the home of a Nanayakkara family. Their daughter-in-law had drowned falling off the bridge.

Briefly stated, the inquiries confirmed that there was a suspension bridge in Akuressa, and that a married, pregnant woman, had fallen from it and drowned. The name of her father-in-law (not her father) was Edwin (not Jeedin) Nanayakkara. In Sri Lanka married women commonly refer to their father-in-law as father. Her family (the in-laws) had owned a car (uncommon in Sri Lanka) and a bicycle. Their house was larger than Thusita's home and had a big gate made of bamboo.

Some of Thusita's statements were found to be incorrect: The bicycle had been black, not yellow; Chandra had never been a nurse but a cousin and close friend of hers had been; Chandra's husband had been a bus driver, not a postman (his elder brother was a postman); and she had not had a sister who had a daughter but had a sister-in-law who had daughters. The other statements are too general to be of much value.

We planned to take Thusita to Akuressa for tests of recognition, but her brother forbade that.

Chatura Buddika Karunaratne

Chatura was born on 20 April, 1989, in the rural area of the Kurunagala District. At the age of three he started to speak about a previous life. He had been going through the forest in a truck when a group of people fired at him; he was in the army. He was hit in the neck, his face was covered with blood, and a helicopter took him to the doctor. He described his earlier home and surroundings: He lived in a village near Narammala and lived in a house with a tiled roof. Close by there was a thatched hut and in the hut was a small store run by his father. The house where they lived was pink. Near the house was a lake and tortoises lived in the lake. They had a parrot who could talk, etc. (Haraldsson, 2000).

Martin, a retired farmer and mason, overheard in a shop that there had been an article in the newspaper *Divaina* about Chatura's statements. He read the article and thought it was describing the life of his son, Dayananda, who had joined the army and died in April 1986 as a result of injuries suffered in a bomb blast and had been brought to hospital by helicopter. Dayananda's family lived eight miles by road from Narammala in a house with a tiled roof. Close by there had been a hut with a shop which he owned and where his son used to sell groceries until he joined the army. Near their house was a small lake with tortoises living in it. All this corresponded to what Chatura had been saying.

Martin decided to visit Chatura's family. He asked his local village headman (government official) to join him. They first visited the village headman of Chatura's locality, and all three went to Chatura's family. During this visit, and another with his wife the following day, Martin and his wife became convinced that Chatura was describing events in the life of their son Dayananda.

The *Divaina* journalist, Nandasena, learned about this new development and brought three and half year old Chatura to the home of

Dayananda's parents. In *Divaina* he reported that the boy had been given a warm reception by Dayananda's parents, who accepted him as their son. Dayananda's mother brought some old clothes that had belonged to her son; the boy complained somewhat angrily that only his long trousers were there and that they had been worn and torn by someone else.

Dayananda's mother asked the boy if he could remember the house where they used to live. Chatura said he had not lived in this house but in another one somewhere else, which was true of Dayananda. They had only recently moved to the present house, which is located on the same premises about 100 yards away. They went to the house where they used to live. There an old woman walked up to the boy and asked him if he could remember her. He looked at her for a while and said she was his grandmother. Dayananda had lived longer with his grandmother than with his parents. Inside the house the boy made the comment: "Now you have electricity," something they had not had when Dayananda lived there. Hanging on the wall he saw the scales that had been used in the shop. He made the comment: "These are the scales we used to weigh things with. Don't you have the store now?" He then asked the late Dayananda's mother to take him to the store but it had been torn down. Chatura also identified one of his old friends who was in the crowd.

The journalists asked Dayananda's father what he thought about the helicopter and Landmaster tractor that Chatura had mentioned. Dayananda's father stated that he had said to his son that if he had a tractor he could plough the fields easily. Dayananda had told him that the army auctions tractors which they confiscate from the Tigers (Tamil rebels fighting for a separate Tamil homeland) and they could be bought cheaply. At the next auction he wanted to buy a tractor for his father. But Dayananda never came back. He was caught in a bomb blast, was flown by helicopter to a hospital in Polonnaruwa and later transported to Colombo, where he died.

This, in short, is the history of the case as it stood when we first met Chatura's family and other witnesses in late November 1992. Chatura's mother told us that he had first mentioned a previous life by talking about shooting. He told that he had been shot in two places and that he was taken to hospital by helicopter. He only mentioned one name related to his previous life, Narammala, near where his former parents live. If taken to Narammala he could find his house and his younger brother and sister. He also said, "My mother in Narammala is not like you [slim], she is fat."

Chatura was afraid whenever he heard a helicopter. He was also fearful of balls that children play with, thinking that they might be bombs. He often talked about army trucks, camps and soldiers, and liked songs about the army that he heard on the radio.

We met Martin, Dayananda's father, in November 1992. He became quickly convinced that the report in Divaina was referring to his son. At first, he said, he was full of doubts for he could not believe that a thing like this could happen.

Dayananda had been born and lived with his family at their home near Narammala until he joined the army in 1985. After leaving school he had worked as a mason for two years but did not like it; so his father built for him a small shop with a thatched roof. He had lived in a house with a tiled roof, only a few yards away from the small shop where he sold groceries and sweets for about a year. He wanted to go abroad but, failing to do so, he decided to join the army.

Dayananda had only served eight months in the army when his parents were notified that he had been seriously wounded. They rushed to the Polonnaruwa hospital to be with their son, and accompanied him when he was transported to Colombo, where he died. Dayananda remained unconscious after the blast and was not able to speak to them. Dayananda was given a military funeral at his home.

We confirmed some of Chatura's statements when we visited Dayananda's family, including those regarding the tiled roof and the lake where Martin used to go swimming with his son. This lake is some 15 minutes' walk away. Tortoises still live there according to Dayananda's father. Dayananda's family now live in a house with a thatched roof, but earlier they had lived in a house with a tiled roof that is only a short walk away and is also on their property. This was confirmed by close relatives now living in the house.

With the kind help of Major-General Pagoda, we obtained a document from a military court of inquiry regarding the circumstances of Dayananda's death. On the morning of April 15, 1986, Dayananda was in a group of 14 soldiers in two army trucks who had been ordered to proceed on a route-clearing patrol from Wakaneri (close to the east coast of Sri Lanka) to the Poonani Post Office, and from there to the Namal Adi junction. On the way, the trucks were caught in a massive landmine blast. Dayananda was found unconscious near the vehicle, which had overturned and was completely wrecked. A few soldiers were killed and others severely wounded. Dayananda was taken by helicopter to a hospital in Polonnaruwa, and later by ambulance to Colombo. He never regained consciousness and died on 18 April 1986.

As soon as Chatura started to talk about a previous life, he told that he had been shot in two places and pointed towards the birthmarks near his neck and left ear. When Dayananda's parents had visited him in the hospital he had a bandage around his head and neck. Bandages covered his left ear. A photograph of Dayananda's body at his funeral shows his face bare, but his head and neck are covered with bandages, and also his left ear, which suggests that he suffered injuries to this area of his body. Chatura's birthmarks match Dayananda's wounds. They have darker pigmentation than the surrounding skin. One is on the lower part of the jawbone and the other is on the neck/throat below the jaw.

There are two aspects of this case; the memory aspect and the birthmark aspect. Regarding the memory aspect we have the great advantage that Chatura's statements were recorded by three independent interviewers before a potential previous person was found. Chatura seems to have added on statements as people repeatedly asked him about his previous life. Perhaps he was being unduly pressured to respond. Table 7-5 shows his statements. The number of verified statements drops from 71% in the first interview to 52% and 47% respectively in the interviews that followed. Many of the correct statement are highly specific, such as regarding the circumstances that led to his violent death.

Table 7-5. Statements Made by Chatura That Were Recorded in 1992 Before Search Was Made for a Previous Personality

Statement		Interview Date			Status
		June 7	June 14	June 12	
1.	He lived in a village near Narammala.	D[a]	N[b], D	T[c]	+
2.	He lived in a house with a tiled roof.	D	N, D		+
3.	Close by there was a thatched hut.	D	N, D	T	+
4.	In the hut there was a small store.	D	N, D	T	+
5.	The store was run by his father.	D			+
6.	Near the house was a lake.	D	N, D	T	+
7.	Tortoises lived in the lake.	D	N, D	T	+
8.	He had been going through the forest in a truck.	D	N, D	T	+

9.	A group of people had fired at him. (People surrounded the truck and started to shoot).	D	N, D	T	-
10.	He was hit in the neck.	D	N, D	T	+
11.	The crowd trampled on him and walked away.	D	N, D		-
12.	The wounds were treated at his home.	D			-
13.	He was in the army.		N, D		+
14.	His face was bathed in blood.		N, D		+
15.	He fell down and pretended he was dead.		N, D		?
16.	A helicopter arrived and took them to the doctor.		N, D	T	+
17.	The house where he lived was pink.	D	N, D		+
18.	His family had a Landmaster tractor.	D	N, D	T	+
19.	He ploughed paddy fields (with the Landmaster).		N, D	T	+
20.	They had parrot at home in a cage who talked.		N, D		+
21.	His mother loved it, gave it food mornings and evenings.		N, D		+
22.	His father's name was Perera.		N, D	T	-
23.	His mother's name was Mangalika.		N, D	T	-
24.	His mother was fair and round like a ball, not like his present mother.		N, D	T	?
25.	Their house had three rooms.		N, D		+
26.	Kumari was his sister.		N, D	T	-
27.	Kumari occupied the corner room.		N, D		-
28.	He had an elder brother.		N, D		-
29.	His brother's name was Mahesh.			T	+
30.	He switched on a cassette recorder and danced at home.		N, D		+
31.	His mother didn't make oil cakes for the New Year, she made (Western-style) cakes.		N, D		-
32.	His name was Suduputha.			T	-
33.	There was a red flash lamp where he stayed.		N, D		-

Total number of statements	14	29	17

Interviewers: [a]Divaina; [b]Nandasena, Divaina; [c]Tissa Jayawardane

+ Statement verified. (20) ; - Statement did not fit and was wrong. (11)
? Impossible to ascertain; may or may not be right. (2)

8

WORLDWIDE BELIEF IN REINCARNATION AND LIFE AFTER DEATH

This book focuses primarily on past-life memories and on the spiral or circular model of human life's progression. Survey data about belief in life after death and reincarnation reveal different basic assumptions in the population regarding man's nature and the ontological status of consciousness and the psyche. We can distinguish four basic views:

1. Death is the end of our existence: This is the dominant scientific, secular view that assumes that consciousness is produced by the brain's activity and comes to a final end by the death of the body. All memories are stored in the brain and are gone forever when the brain disintegrates. This view is not new, for the Roman, Lucretius Carus (99-55 BC), argued for it two thousand years ago:
    *   Mind matures and ages with growth and decay of the body.
    *   Wine and disease of the body can affect the mind.
    *   The body is stunned by a blow.

- If the soul is immortal why does it not have memories of its previous existence?

2. The agnostic view: It is impossible to know if we live on after death or not.

3. The Christian, Muslim and Judaeic view: We come into existence by birth and have an eternal life ahead of us when we die.

4. The concept of reincarnation: It is found in pre-Christian Europe, with Pythagoras and Plato in Greece, in pre-Christian Ireland, Germany and Scandinavia, as well as in Buddhism and Hinduism in Asia. According to this view we lived on earth before we were born into the present life, and we will be born again in a new body some time after we die. Verified past-life memories that some children insist they have seem to contradict the dominant scientific view.

How widely are these different views held by the modern-day populations of Europe and America? Let us first look at the findings of the European Values Survey conducted in 2008-2010 (*See http://www.europeanvaluesstudy.eu/page/survey-2008.html*). The survey contains two relevant questions:

Question 1.   "Do you believe in life after death?"

Response alternatives: Yes, No, Don't know.
The mean results for 44 European countries was that 44% answered yes (believe in life after death), 41% do not believe in life after death and 15% do not know what to believe. The total sample was huge, 62,816 respondents. Thus, slightly more Europeans believe than disbelieve in life after death, with large national differences. The percentage of believers in the large nations of Europe was; Italy (58%), Great Britain (46%), Spain (42%), France (40%), Russia (36%), and Germany (27%) with large differences between East- and West-Germany.
The greatest believers are Malta (84%), Poland (67%), Kosovo 72%), Northern Ireland (65%), Iceland (63%) and Ireland (62%). The lowest are Albania (21%), Germany and Montenegro (27%), Denmark and Hungary (33%).

Question 2.   "Do you believe in reincarnation i.e., are we born into this world again?"

Response alternatives: Yes, No, Don't know.

The mean result for the 44 European countries was that 21% believe in reincarnation, 65% do not, and 14% do not know what to believe. The percentage of believers among the large nations of Europe; Russia (26%), Great Britain (24%), France (22%), Spain (20%), Italy (17%), and Germany (16%).

A cross-tabulation for the two questions (see Table 8-1) shows that 36% reject any form of survival after death, 15% are agnostics, 28% believe in life forever after death, and 21% believe in reincarnation. It is interesting to note that among those who believe in life after death, 38% believe in reincarnation. Reincarnation is a major form of belief in survival. This is more prominent if we ignore the doubting Thomases—the agnostics who are sitting on the fence and cannot make up their mind (sometimes deleted in surveys). Then we find that 46% of believers in life after death also believe in reincarnation.

Table 8.1. Cross-Tabulation of Beliefs in Life after Death and Reincarnation

		Do you believe in reincarnation? (Q31)			
		Don't know	Yes	No	Total
	Don't know	3,701 5.9%	936 1.5%	4,376 7.0%	9,013 14.5%
Do you believe in life after death? (Q30B)	Yes	3,178 5.1%	10,473 16.8%	13,911 22.4%	27,562 44.3%
	No	1,540 2.5%	1,770 2.8%	22,338 35.9%	25,648 41.2%
	Total	8,419 13.5%	13,179 21.2%	40,625 63.3%	62,223 100%

The German speaking countries, East and West Germany, Austria and Switzerland show remarkable differences, as can be seen in Table 8-2. Notice the large difference between West Germany and the former communistic East Germany.

Table 8-2. Percentage of Believers in Life after Death and
Reincarnation in German-Speaking Countries

	Life after Death	Reincarnation	Both
Austria	61	29	47
Western Germany	45	28	59
Eastern Germany	9	17	56
Switzerland	53	28	49

The World Values survey (Inglehart et al, 2004) was conducted in 1999-2002 and included data from six major American countries and three Asian countries. See Table 8-3.

Table 8-3. Percentage of Believers in Life after Death and
Reincarnation in the Americas

	Life after Death	Reincarnation	Both
United States	81	25	31
Canada	75	32	43
Argentina	63	39	62
Brazil	71	57	80
Chile	82	49	60
Mexico	76	43	57

Brazilians score particularly high on belief in reincarnation, higher than any nation of Europe and America. A fair number of cases have been found in Brazil and we devote a chapter to them. Only India reveals greater belief with ninety-one percent believing in reincarnation. Fifty percent of the Japanese share this belief, about as many as believe in life after death (51%), whereas 28% do in Turkey—presumably mostly Alevis among whom a number of cases have been investigated by Stevenson and Keil. That covers all the data we have so far from the Americas and Asia.

Summing up; we can safely conclude that belief in reincarnation is widely held around the globe. That is not only in Asia but also in the Americas and Europe, more so than most people would probably have guessed.

9

RESEARCH AROUND THE GLOBE

The first part of this book deals exclusively with my research of children who insist they remember a past life. It gives the story of my involvement. It began in 1969 as I came to know Professor Ian Stevenson when I was doing an internship in clinical psychology in the Department of Psychiatry at the University of Virginia.

Stevenson was a former head of the department with an outstanding academic career. He had at this time become heavily involved in studying children who claimed to remember a past life. He travelled widely to pursue his investigations, to Asia, Europe, Africa and the Americas, truly around the globe.

In the 1950s he had begun to collect and compare published reports of cases that he could find. In 1960 he published his award-winning essay: "The evidence of survival from claimed memories of former incarnations." In 1961 he started field work with a trip to India and was surprised by the abundance of cases he could find there. There followed investigations in Sri Lanka and among the Tlingit in Alaska. Studies in other countries soon followed. In 1966 he published his now-famous *Twenty Cases Suggestive of Reincarnation* with cases from India, Sri Lanka, Brazil, Alaska and Lebanon.

Stevenson is the father of reincarnation research. He was born in Canada in 1918 of British parents. When he passed away in 2007 he had studied far more cases than all other researchers combined, and published numerous books and papers about them. His work is monumental. In 1990 he was joined by the child psychiatrist, Jim Tucker, who is now Stevenson's successor at the Division of Perceptual Studies at the University of Virginia that Stevenson founded in the 1960s. Tucker (2013) has emphasized the study of Western cases, particularly American. See his *Return to Life: Extraordinary Cases of Children who Remember Past Lives.*

Apart from Stevenson there were some other early investigators, notably the Brazilian engineer Hernani Guimarães Andrade, who investigated many cases in his country. Guy L. Playfair, who knew Andrade and worked with him, gives a good review of his investigations in *The Flying Cow: Exploring the Psychic World of Brazil* (1975, 2nd ed. 2011) and in *New Clothes for Old Souls* (2006), in which I also had a hand.

In the late 1980s Stevenson became interested in getting other researchers involved to see if the cases they investigated bore similar features. He invited three of us to undertake independent studies in different countries. One of them was me, then at the University of Iceland; the Harvard-educated Anthropologist, Antonia Mills, later Professor of First Nation Studies at the University of Northern British Columbia in Canada; and the German-born Psychologist, Jürgen Keil, professor emeritus at the University of Tasmania in Australia.

Antonia Mills met Stevenson in 1984 when he was looking for someone to continue his careful studies of reincarnation cases with the indigenous people of British Columbia. She used Stevenson's systematic methods to study cases among the Beaver and Gitxsan First Nations (Mills 1988a) and then received a grant to continue the study with the Gitxsan and Witsuwit'en First Nations (Mills 1988b). Stevenson hired Mills to join him at the Division of Personality Studies 1988-1994, whence she studied more cases in India and in British Columbia Canada, and did a comparison of children who remember previous lives and those with imaginary playmates.

Jürgen Keil, Antonia Mills and I all accepted Stevenson's invitation to do a replication study. I did my investigations in Sri Lanka and later in Lebanon, Keil in Turkey, Burma and Thailand; Mills did her investigations in India as well as among the indigenous people in Canada. We all published papers on our investigations, and found that the cases had the same general characteristics as Stevenson had discovered and that they required a paranormal interpretation. "Normal" explanations were not adequate. One of us, Jürgen Keil, favoured a different interpretation than Stevenson and thought that the children were somehow reaching out and absorbing psychic "thought bundles" left by deceased persons.

In India, Satwant Pasricha investigated many cases with Stevenson and later on her own. Other notable researchers in India are Gaj R. S. Gaur and Kirti S. Rawat who investigated a large number of cases, some of them with Stevenson and Pasricha.

Towards the end of the 20th century researchers turned up in Europe, notably Dieter Hassler in Germany and Titus Rivas in Holland. Hassler (2011) has published the book *...frueher, da war ich mal gross. Und... Indizienbeweise fuer ein Leben nach dem Tod und die Wiedergeburt* and also a book on past-life regressions.

Hassler (2013) has published an interesting case in English that contains several features commonly found; a premonition by the subject's mother; announcing dreams; the subject's behavior relating to the opposite sex of the previous personality; a special ailment affecting the subject and his special skills. The case is rendered particularly unusual because it involves a chance encounter between the subject's mother and the previous personality at the moment of the latter's death in a traffic accident, suggesting that the case could have evolved because this encounter offered an incentive for the previous personality to reincarnate with this particular mother.

Titus Rivas (2007) has written a book with Kirti S. Rawat, *Reincarnation: The Scientific Evidence is Building*. In 2004 Rivas published a Dutch case that he was able to solve. A three-year-old girl (pseudonym Christina) had a detailed nightmare in which she died in a fire. This dream included intermission memories of picking her present mother. The nightmare triggered her to repeatedly talk about her past life. Rivas tracked a fire that matched most of her statements. The fire was a major tragedy that was reported in regional newspapers. Recently he also found a brother of the victim that best resembled the girl's description, who confirmed that his sister's personality matched that of the girl who was remembering her past life (personal communication). The girl's mother had heard about the fire when she was a teenager. Her physical appearance and activities at that time matched her daughter's intermission memories.

Stevenson's research has not been without criticism; most notably from the American philosopher, Paul Edwards, who wrote the highly critical (1996) review *Reincarnation: A Critical Examination,* that, as Roy Stemman puts it "is marred by sarcasm and needless jibes." Edwards' book has been criticised by several knowledgeable scholars, such as John Beloff of the University of Edinburgh, and Robert Almeder of Georgia State University, who critique Edwards' view that "any argument for any form of personal post-mortem survival is indefensible."

I once asked Stevenson what he thought of his critics. He did not seem much concerned and replied that their criticism "was stimulating," stimulating him, I understood, to do more research of high methodological quality.

My co-author, Jim Matlock, has recently investigated some cases, which he reports on in the second part of this book. He founded an active online discussion group "Signs of Reincarnation" that has brought to light interesting personal experiences from the numerous participants of the group.

In Britain, Roy Stemman (2012) wrote *The Big Book of Reincarnation: Examining the Evidence that We have All Lived Before.* He also edited and wrote a lot about reincarnation cases in his magazine *Reincarnation International,* later renamed *Life and Soul,* to reflect a broader interest in phenomena related to evidence for survival. He has done more than anyone in Britain to make the subject known to the public. He explored cases in Lebanon when he was invited to take part in the documentary, *Back From the Dead,* that was made by Granite TV for Channel 4.

A British experiencer, Jenny Cockell (1993), self-investigated her own case, which was later re-investigated by Mary Rose Barrington (2002).

Documentaries in which I was involved include:

Past Lives: Stories of Reincarnation. Storyhouse Productions, Washington D.C. Producer, Andreas Gutzeit. Broadcasted in the United States on April 1, 2003 on The Learning Channel (Discovery Communications). Aired on Discovery International December 29, 2003.

Reinkarnation — nur ein Mythos? Storyhouse Productions for Learning Channel and Spiegel TV. Spiegel TV in VOX and XXP, October 2002. (German version of Past Lives: Stories of Reincarnation). A Tamil version was broadcast in Asia.

Children's Past Lives. A Zenith North Production for Channel 4, UK. Producer, Laura Granditer. October 2000.

In Search of the Dead. BBC Wales in cooperation with PBS, WXXI-T Rochester, New York. Producer, Jeffrey Ieverson. 1992.

Other documentaries:

"Back From The Dead" in a series called To "The Ends of The Earth" that dealt with various topics. It was made by UK company, Granite TV, for Channel 4 and was first broadcast on May 18, 1998. The producer was Chris Ledger. It has subsequently been shown around the world.

10

BRIGHTER AND MORE MATURE?

S tudies of cases of the reincarnation type (CORT) have been almost exclusively concerned with the verifiability of statements
that the children have made about their alleged previous life; that
is, do these statements correspond to events in the life of a particular
deceased person? There are, however, many other questions that can be
asked. The psychological make-up of children with past-life memories
is of great interest. Do they differ psychologically from other children?
Could their psychology contribute to an explanation of their claims?

For example, could normal psychological or socio-psychological
factors lead a child to make claims of remembering a previous life?
Psychiatrist Eugene Brody (1979) proposed that psychological features
like a rich fantasy life, the need to compensate for social isolation, high
suggestibility, dissociative tendencies, attention seeking, and disturbed
relations with parents may cause a child to claim past-life memories.
Stevenson has pointed out that subjects who claimed a life in a socio-
economic class different from that of their families seemed to remember a life in a higher class more often than one in a lower class. Some
of Stevenson's critics have used this to suggest that the children are
fantasizing, but Stevenson's statistics do not support this except in India and Sri Lanka. Could this point to "escapist fantasies?"

Those who live with the young children know them best. They sometimes report to investigators that they are more mature than other children, and speak more like grown-ups than children.

Stevenson asked me in 1973 to undertake a psychological study of cases that he had investigated in India. This project came to an early and abrupt end when I met with a serious traffic accident in Northern India that made me unconscious for almost two hours and took me half a year to recover from. Travelling by car in India is a risk to your life! In my case, the driver fell asleep and drove into a tree at the roadside when we came at last down to a wide straight flat road after driving down winding mountain roads from Kalimpong to Siliguri in Northern India.

In the late 1980s Stevenson was looking for researchers to replicate his studies of children's reincarnation claims and he asked me if I would like to participate in the project. Sri Lanka, we thought, might be the ideal place for such a replication study. Sri Lanka is a country in which a few cases can be found every year. In the early 1980s I had visited Sri Lanka briefly with my wife during my study of Sathya Sai Baba. I liked the country and found it interesting. It would not be difficult to find a new interpreter there, which was important for both Stevenson and me, as that would guarantee that my investigation was truly independent of his. Besides, Stevenson had a group of people there who would inform us if they learned of a new case.

First Sri Lanka Study

I accepted on the condition that I would be given the opportunity to study enough cases to conduct a psychological study, and that meant a minimum of thirty cases. In the 1990s, after several field trips to Sri Lanka, I had investigated enough cases for such a study. A few years later I followed it up with another psychological study in Sri Lanka and then one in Lebanon several years later (Haraldsson,1997, 2003; Haraldsson, Fowler, and Periyannanpillai, 2000).

The main concern of these studies was the cognitive development of children who claim to remember previous lives, and the question of whether they differ from other children on some of the above-mentioned psychological factors. Do the abilities and personalities of children reporting past-life memories differ significantly from children in general? Do they show a greater tendency to confabulate than other children? Are they more suggestible? Do they tend to live in social isolation? Are there indications of a greater tendency for dissociative processes than in other children?

The subjects of my first study in Sri Lanka had all been reporting past-life memories at the typical age range of two and a half to five years. They were compared with an equal number of children with no such memories. At the time of testing, all the children were between seven and thirteen years old. Both groups were administered a battery of psychological tests as culture-free as we could find them. In addition, we interviewed the parents and teachers of the children and administered questionnaires about their behavior. We also obtained the school examination records for every child. We wanted this to be a thorough study.

Of the total of 64 children whose cases I investigated in Sri Lanka, 20 had made statements that, upon examination, were found to fit facts—at least some facts—in the life of some person who had lived before they were born. They were solved cases. In 44 cases no person was found whose life corresponded to the child's statements. These cases were unsolved.

Children with active past-life memories are usually aged two to five years. Few objective psychological tests exist to assess the factors of interest to us in children so young. Furthermore, these children are rare and difficult to find, and a meaningful comparison of them with other children requires a sample of adequate size. In order to get a sufficiently large sample, all available subjects up to age thirteen were included. Since tests that can be used with children younger than seven are rare, the children in our sample ranged in age from seven to thirteen years. At this age most of the children had stopped talking about their past-life memories but all of them had, at an earlier age, talked about them for some period of time.

The cases of twenty-two of these children had been investigated by me and detailed reports were published on five of them (Haraldsson, 1991; Mills et al., 1994). Eleven of them were solved and an equal number unsolved. Eight cases had been investigated by Stevenson but no report published on them. Three were solved, two unsolved, and information was not available for three of them. At the time of testing, the average age of these 30 pairs of children was nine years and four months.

I found an experienced Sri Lankan Psychologist to work with, Mrs. Vimala Periyannapillai. We visited each child unannounced at her or his home. The family or teachers in the school that the child attended helped us to find another child in the neighborhood, without past-life memories, to act as a control, i.e., for comparison. The control child was always of same age and sex as the child who had spoken about the previous life.

This study involved a lot of driving, for the children were scattered through a large part of Sri Lanka. We had a safe driver and the good company of Rohana Kumara, who drove me on practically every trip, from Colombo up to Kandy, as far north as to Anuradhapura and Vanuniya and as far south as Kataragama. In short, we covered all Sri Lanka, with the exception of the northern and eastern parts of the country, where civil war was raging. On one of our trips there was a suicide bomb blast in Colombo, but we were out of town that day. An attack on the Sri Lanka Reserve Bank made a whole street look like a war zone. I was not in the country but arrived afterwards to witness the devastation. Every window had been shattered in the hotel where I used to stay, for it was next to the bank.

After the testing had been completed, we expressed our appreciation with a gift of sweets and ball-point pens to the tested child and to other children that might be in the family. Without exception, the families were helpful and cooperative.

The difference between the children with past-life memories (whom we thought of as "our" children) and the comparison group (control group) proved greater than we had anticipated. Our children scored much higher on a vocabulary test (Peabody Picture Vocabulary Test) and thereby showed greater knowledge of words and better understanding of their language. This finding was substantiated by higher school grades for their mother tongue, Sinhala. Our children had a mean score of 69.68 for Sinhala, compared to 52.83 for the control group. The results of a general test of intelligence (Ravens's Progressive Matrices) also gave significantly higher scores for our children, indicating greater capacity to reason by analogy. There were indications that our children's memory might be better too.

A suggestibility test (Gudjonson Suggestibility Scale) showed that our children were definitely not more suggestible than other children and had significantly fewer confabulations than other children did. The role of suggestibility has been favored by critics who correctly point out that the cultures in which cases are most readily found have a strong belief in reincarnation. Those who put forward this hypothesis as a sufficient explanation of the cases overlook the fact that parents often try to suppress the children talking about their past-life memories. Usually the children vehemently oppose such attempts to suppress them, as discussed in a journal paper by Stevenson and Chadha (1990). A good example of such persistence against parental opposition occurred in the case of Dilupa Nanayakkara (Haraldsson, 1991). Her Roman Catholic parents tried in vain to get her to stop speaking of her previous life.

Another memorable case is that of the Muslim boy, Mohammed Izzan, who claimed to have been a Buddhist and requested to be sent to a Buddhist school. His father vehemently opposed but in the end the child's mother yielded to Mohammed's wish and applied. The principal of the Buddhist school rejected him because he was Muslim. A journalist heard about the case and it was published in a newspaper. The President of Sri Lanka happened to read the account and ordered the principal to accept the boy into his school. This caused a violent reaction by the father and his friends. Mohammed's house had to be placed under police protection day and night and the father divorced his wife. Regarding this case, it must be stated that in spite of considerable efforts it has not proved possible to verify the boy's statements. The case remains unsolved.

In cases of the reincarnation type, the children often say to their mothers that they are not their real mothers, that the real mother is somewhere else and that they want to get back to their real family. This is fairly common and something the mothers do not want to hear. When the children demand that their parents take them to their previous home or try to find their previous home, the mothers often fear that they may lose their child. My colleague in India, Satwant Pasricha (2011), found that many of the mothers she interviewed were initially tolerant of their children's past-life memories but, after the cases were solved, they started to worry that their children would be taken away by the previous families and started to try to suppress their talk.

Suggestibility may play a role in reincarnation cases but evidence shows that it may be a factor in only some of the cases. Stevenson and Chadha (1990) and Mills (1989) report how they have observed children withstand considerable pressure from their parents to stop talking about their memories, sometimes resulting in the children being scolded and even beaten. This brings to mind our remarkable case of Thusita Silva in the chapter "Four Remarkable Sri Lankan Cases" that we were able to solve after her brother had failed to do so; he then scolded the girl for what he thought were her lies.

We asked the parents of subjects and controls to assess the school performance of their children and also checked their school grades. The mean grades for children with past-life memories were much higher than for the control group. The superiority of "our" children is obvious when we look at their rank in class. They obtained better grades than 74% of their class. Their teachers also rated "our" children as better students, said they worked harder, behaved better, and learned more. Cognitively, in Sri Lanka anyway, children with past-life memories are superior to their peers.

Second Sri Lanka Study

Three years later I conducted another psychological study in Sri Lanka, with a different group of children. This time the children were about two years younger—the mean age was seven years and ten months. There were 14 pairs of boys and 13 pairs of girls. Again our children obtained higher scores on the cognitive tests than the controls but not large enough to reach significance. Again their grades were significantly higher, as they did better than 86 percent of their class. The control group did better than 61% of their class, which indicates that they were more gifted than a randomly selected control group should have been. This might explain why our children did not get significantly higher results on the cognitive tests than the control children although they scored in the predicted direction. These two Sri Lankan studies combined show that children with past-life memories are cognitively more gifted than their peers. They are brighter.

Lebanon Study

Lebanese children claiming past-life memories did not differ from their peers regarding the extent of their vocabulary and other cognitive abilities. Nor did their school performance differ from other children in their class. According to their teachers, they did not differ from other children in how hard they worked, how appropriately they behaved, or how happy they were. The findings in Sri Lanka were not confirmed. Why we can only guess. One factor may be that the Druze often make a case on very meager grounds whereas Sri Lankans demand more evidence. Thirty pairs of children participated in the study, 19 boys and 11 girls, belonging to the Druze community with a mean age of 10.62 years (Haraldsson, 2003).

We have one psychological study from Western countries where be-lief in reincarnation is not widely held. Tucker and Nidiffer (2014) of the University of Virginia tested 15 US children with past-life memories. Their conclusion, "The participants in the study overall demonstrated above average intelligence, with a number of children demonstrating superior intelligence." In short, the intelligence of the 15 American children is well above the average child in the United States. This con-firms our finding that children with past-life memories are, as a group, brighter than their peers. What about their behavioral and personality development? We will examine that in the next chapter.

11

SCARS FROM A
DISTANT PAST?

Wè examined in our last chapter how the cognitive performance of children with past-life memories compares with other children. The results of our tests and investigations showed that children with past-life memories were more intelligent and made better grades in school than their peers without past-life memories. Now let us look at the behavioral traits of these children. Do children with past-life memories differ from other children in this respect also?

To answer this question, we needed the assessment of the mothers of our subjects and controls. They filled out The Child Behavior Checklist which is essentially a list of statements about problems that children may have, or characteristics that can sometimes lead to problems. The sum of these characteristics yields a "Problem Score."

First Sri Lanka Study

We found a large difference in our first study in Sri Lanka (Haraldsson, 1995). The Problem Score was 41 for our group and 27 for their peers, a highly significant difference. Let us look at the prominent characteristics that made them differ. Children with past-life memories score higher on a large number of them: argues a lot; is nervous, high-strung or tense; feels she/he has to be perfect; likes to be alone; is withdrawn, does not get involved with others; is confused, seems to be in a fog; is too concerned with neatness and cleanliness; talks too much; is too fearful and anxious; gets teased a lot; threatens people; is self-conscious and easily embarrassed; is stubborn, sullen or irritable; talks and walks in sleep. We also found that our group was as socially active and competent as their peers. There was no sign that they were withdrawn or had problems interacting socially.

Two features are particularly noticeable in these findings. Our children tend to be obsessive-compulsive, and they show "oppositional" characteristics: They are argumentative, stubborn, excessively talkative, sometimes threatening to other people, and at times they have or show more than one personality.

Second Sri Lanka Study

Let us compare these findings with our second Sri Lankan study (Haraldsson, Fowler, and Periyannapillai, 2000). Fowler is a psychologist in the Department of Child Psychiatry at the University of Virginia whom I had known for some time. He was interested in this study so I invited him to join me and Vimala in evaluating the test material. Our participants were 27 pairs of children and their parents, 14 pairs of boys, and 13 pairs of girls. They ranged in age from five years and five months to ten years and two months, with a mean age of seven years and ten months. The pairs were equated for sex, age, and general background; social and family demographics. The first study was overwhelmingly confirmed. We found much the same thing. Children with past-life memories were said to: argue a lot; have certain thoughts or obsessions; brag and boast; feel that she or he has to be perfect; fear animals, situations and places; are highly strung or tense, exhibit nervousness; show sudden changes in mood or feeling; experience nightmares; don't eat well; are too concerned about neatness and cleanliness; daydream or get lost in thought; talk too much; are secretive; have temper tantrums; display hot tempers, are self- conscious and easily embarrassed. There were a few less prominent characteristics as well.

We added the Child Dissociation Checklist to our second study. Our children were much more likely to show rapid changes in personality;

daydream frequently; have intense outbursts of anger; and refer to themselves in the third person, probably that of the previous person. Our children exhibited a high degree of dissociation, obtaining a score of 6.59 compared to 1.67 for the control group. Their dissociation score is similar to the score obtained by sexually abused girls in the USA. Dissociation is considered a defense mechanism to ward off unpleasant experiences.

These findings bring to mind that children who report past-life memories are often characterized by unusual behavioral features that are in line with the person they claim to have been in the previous life. For example, children who tell us that they have been monks may take up behavior that is characteristic of monks, and want to dress like monks, etc. As I have discussed in the chapter "I was a monk," the rapid changes in personality may be related to these behavioral features. They may swing back from one personality to another, be confused, and have difficulties integrating the two.

Could dissociation explain why children come up with past-life memories? Possibly, but what speaks against this view is the fact that, in over a third of the cases in Sri Lanka, we find a substantial degree of correspondence between their account of the previous life and the facts in the life of a person who died before they were born, and some of these facts can be highly specific in nature.

Furthermore, these children frequently have phobias associated with the previous life; they may have birthmarks that correspond to wounds that led to their death, like in the case of Purnima; and they may even possess knowledge and skills that they are not known to have acquired in their present lifetime. Purnima described in detail how incense was made, although her parents did not know it.

The Teachers form of the Child Behavioral Checklist was filled out by the teachers of our children and the controls. Let us keep in mind that teachers only observe children while they are in school, and classes are large in Sri Lanka with up to 40 children. However, the teachers noticed that our group scored higher on the following items than their peers did: Feels she/he has to be perfect; likes to be alone; not unhappy, sad or depressed; not disobedient at school; gets along with other children. Furthermore, while in school our children learn more, behave better and work harder, and are more adaptive than their peers.

The Family Questionnaire measures discord within families that might cause children to seek "escapist" phantasies. This questionnaire did not reveal any difference in the number of conflicts within the families of our two groups. Children with previous-life memories live in normal families.

Lebanon Study

The Sri Lankan children with past-life memories differ in many respects from their peers. I wondered if we would find the same characteristics among children in other countries. Lebanon, with a different culture and religion, seemed ideal for comparison. I investigated 30 cases among Druze in Lebanon (Haraldsson, 2003), where cases are more easily found than in Sri Lanka. When a child may possibly be talking about a previous life, the Druze are generally quicker to accept it as a genuine case than are the Sri Lankans.

The cognitive tests revealed no difference between the two groups. "Our" Druze children were *not* more gifted than their peers, which had been the case in Sri Lanka. However the behavioral characteristics turned out to be the same in both countries. Our children had a higher "Problem Score" on the Child Behavior Checklist, 45.10, as compared to 27.70 for their peers. Our children were more unhappy, sad or depressed than their peers; preferred being with older kids; had more worries; were too fearful or anxious; had temper tantrums or a hot temper, and so on.

Our children also scored higher on the Child Dissociation Checklist, 1.47 compared to 0.23. Significant items were: daydreams frequently, and refers to him/herself in the third person. Close to significance were having intense outbursts of anger and showing rapid changes in personality.

To conclude, elevated dissociation scores in Sri Lanka and the high Problem Score in both countries opens up the question that our children may be traumatized by abuse or neglect. We looked for signs of abuse, such as bruises or fear of parents, or evidence for physical or emotional neglect, but found nothing of that sort.

When I presented our findings at conferences, two colleagues, an expert on post traumatic stress disorder (PTSD), and an experienced clinical psychologist, brought to my attention that the findings of the Child Behavior Checklist and the Child Dissociation Checklist revealed symptoms that are characteristic of persons with an identifiable trauma, namely phobias, fears, outbursts of anger, and nightmares.

The World Health Organization has determined that three things are required to diagnose post traumatic stress disorder (PTSD):

a) The patient must have been exposed to a stressful event or situation of exceptionally threatening or catastrophic nature.
b) There must be persistent remembering and 'reliving' of the stressor in intrusive 'flashbacks', vivid memories.
c) The patient experiences difficulty in falling or staying asleep; irritability or outbursts of anger; difficulty in concentrating; hypervigilance; and exaggerated startle response.

Seventy-six percent of children in the combined Sri Lanka samples speak of memories of a violent death and so do 77% of our Lebanese sample. In the absence of any exceptional life-threatening situation in their present life, could the persistent images of violent death serve as a stressor and cause the symptoms of PTSD? The majority of our children frequently relive and speak about their past-life memories of how they died. The World Health Organization criterion for PTSD, the symptom of outbursts of anger, is clearly present. Other items are not specifically surveyed in the Child Behavior Checklist or the Child Dissociation Checklist but fearfulness, phobias (related to memories of a violent death), sudden changes in mood and feelings, and aggressiveness are likely to be related to hypervigilance and an exaggerated startle response. It should be emphasized that the presence of PTSD was not systematically assessed so these findings require further investigation. We must also mention that signs of PTSD were not found in all our children, in fact in relatively few, but enough to find a significant difference between them and their peers.

If the post-traumatic hypothesis is true, we would expect those who speak of violent death to have higher Child Behavior Checklist and Child Dissociation Checklist scores than those who do not report memories of a violent death. This is confirmed for CBCL and not for the CDC. There are strong signs of fear, anxiety and aggressiveness in our children. It seems that our *post hoc* finding of PTSD can be seen as a signal of distress and explain why many of our children are demanding a lot of attention. Are the symptoms of PTSD scars from a distant past? This seems quite plausible.

Do we see any confirmation of this in Tucker's and Nidiffer's U.S. study? Two of their 15 participants scored high enough to indicate significant dissociative behavior. So there is some confirmation. Tucker mentions that some American cases have included nightmares and possible post-traumatic play, but that was not found in this particular sample. Inferring from the Sri Lanka and Lebanon samples, one would expect a confirmation of PTSD if the majority of the children recalled a violent death. Regretfully, it is not stated or known how many of the 15 subjects of the U.S. sample recalled a violent death.

Tucker's final comments: "In general, though, I wouldn't say that most of the children have PTSD, many talk repeatedly about traumatic memory. Also, in the cases in which the previous person died an unnatural death, over 35% of the children show an intense fear of the mode of death, the kind of avoidant behavior that is a part of the official criteria of the DSM (Diagnostic and Statistical Manual) criteria for PTSD" (2013, p. 141).

This must be seen as a confirmation of our finding that some children with previous-life memories are traumatized. It seems highly likely that this stems from memories of a violent death, namely that these are scars from a distant past.

12

HOW LONG DO PAST-LIFE MEMORIES LAST?

How common is it that children retain past-life memories into adult life? How persistent are these memories? Are certain kinds of memories likely to last longer than others? To find answers to these questions, I conducted interviews with groups of adults in Sri Lanka and Lebanon who spoke of previous-life memories when they were children.

It has been assumed that the memories fade away in most instances. Stevenson writes "Children who remember verified previous lives (solved cases) continue speaking about them to an average age of just under seven and a half years, whereas children having unverified memories stop speaking about the previous lives at an average age of under six" (2001, p. 109). This is based on his observations of a great number of cases that he followed until the children became older and, in a few cases, into adult life.

Tucker expresses a similar view: "Most of the children stop by the age of six or seven, and not only do they stop talking about the previous life, they often deny any memories of it when asked... Children vary, and some subjects report that they still have past-life memories even into adulthood just as some individuals report having a fair number of early childhood memories when they are adults. Nonetheless, the vast number of subjects seem to have forgotten all about the past life after a few years" (2005, pp. 90—91).

Sri Lanka Study

My first persistence study was conducted in Sri Lanka where Stevenson had investigated over a hundred cases between 1960 and 1980 and published several reports on them. I studied over 60 cases in Sri Lanka in 1988 to 1998 and some of the earliest investigated cases were 19 years or older by the time the persistence study was made in 2005-2006. The age limit was set at 19 years to be considered an adult.

A 49-item questionnaire was developed for the study. We traced and interviewed 42 subjects in Sri Lanka: 30 were from Stevenson and 12 from me. The mean age for Stevenson's subjects was 36 years and 22 for mine. There were 17 males and 25 females.

38% percent felt sure that they had memories which were a continuation of their childhood's past-life memories. 17% had no memories, and 45% had memories only because their family had been speaking about them or they remembered only what they had *said* as children.

It is often advisable to ask more than one question to get at the same fact. We therefore phrased another question: Do you still have clear memories of your past-life? 12% did. Do you still have some memories? 33% did. Or do you have no memories at all? 55% had no memories.

Lebanon Study

We asked the same questions to 28 adults in Lebanon who had past-life memories as children who were extensively interviewed by Stevenson and associates approximately 34 years earlier. Their mean age was 40 years; the youngest was 28, and the oldest 56 years. There were 19 men and 9 women.

The results were partly similar to Sri Lanka. 43 percent had memories they considered a true continuation of their childhood memories, whereas 38% did so in Sri Lanka. Regarding the clarity of the memories, 43% had clear memories (12% in Sri Lanka), 43% some memories (33% in Sri Lanka), and in 14% the memories had faded away compared with 55% in Sri Lanka. Here there is a large difference. The Lebanese retain their memories much better than the Sri Lankans. It should be added that it is much easier to find cases among Druze in Lebanon than among Sri Lankans.

Table 12-1. Number of Adults Reporting Past-Life Memories
That They Had When They Were Children

	Do You Still Have Memories of a Past Life?			
	Many / Clear Memories	*Some / Vague Memories*	*All Have Faded Away*	*Total*
Yes, a continuation of childhood memories.	17	20	0	37
Yes, but I'm not sure of their source.	0	2	0	2
No, I only remember what I said as a child.	0	3	7	10
No, I only remember what my family says.	0	1	10	11
No, I no longer have any memories.	0	0	10	10
Total	17	26	27	70

Would it be possible to check how truthfully these individuals were telling us about the extent of their past-life memories? We asked the relative who knew each subject best. In most instances this was the mother. Sometimes we had to travel far to find her. In some instances no close relative could be found, was out of reach, or had passed away. No unexpected discrepancies were found between the testimony of the subject and the closest relative.

What do adults with memories of their distant past remember most clearly? Firstly, people they had known, and secondly, events that had led to their death and how they died. This was true for both countries. It is interesting what a prominent role memories of dying play in past-life memories. These deaths are, as we have already mentioned, predominantly violent due to accidents, murder and, in rare instances, suicides.

Our questions do not only concern how many adults have retained some memories. No less interesting is to know how much of their childhood memories are still remembered by those who have retained some memories. The adults were therefore asked about what they remembered. Most of them were interviewed by Stevenson when they were children and very few by me. I made it a principle not to look up

Stevenson's old files before the study to exclude the possibility that I might influence their recall of what they remembered as children.

Those in Sri Lanka who considered their memories a continuation of childhood memories had made on average 29 different statements as children. At the time of the study they recalled only seven. In Lebanon the same figures were 30 statements as children and nine as adults. This is similar in both countries. The adults recalled about a quarter of their old memories, and had forgotten three quarters of them.

This opens up the question of the rate of forgetting normal childhood memories. We found no studies that throw substantial light on this. We asked our participants what events they remembered from their preschool years. We were surprised how little they remembered. Some could not recall anything at all. Our general impression is that past-life memories may be better remembered into adult life than normal memories from preschool years.

The Effect of Having Past-Life Memories

How have the past-life memories affected the lives of the individuals who have them? Have they proved to be a hindrance or did they enrich their lives? About half of the adults in both countries stated that their past-life memories had been helpful and had a positive impact on them. Some reported positive as well as negative experiences when their past-life memories became known in the community. A few complained that the impact had been negative, such as excessive attention being given to them, and too many people wanting to hear about the previous life. A few children had been teased by other children, even nicknamed or considered odd. For about a third the memories had made no difference one way or the other.

We asked many questions. Did they in retrospect prefer the previous or present life? In Sri Lanka 55% preferred the present life, 13% preferred the past life, and 33% had no preference. The results from Lebanon were not greatly different, 68% preferred the present life, 21% the past life, and 12% had no preference. The main finding is that the majority in both countries preferred their present life.

How had these children fared in life as they matured and became adults? The great majority in both countries expressed general happiness with how their life had developed. In Sri Lanka 7% were unhappy with their situation and even fewer in Lebanon, which is a considerably more developed country. We have no figures for the general population to compare with our data.

It seemed that our subjects received a higher degree of education than their peers. In Lebanon 39% had received some college or university education and one-fourth in Sri Lanka. As was to be expected, the number of those who received only compulsory education was higher in poorer Sri Lanka than Lebanon.

As far as we could ascertain the participants were generally leading normal productive lives. They were found in various professions; we had a mathematican, an engineer, a computer expert, housewives, teachers, sales representatives, truck drivers, a sculptor, an entertainer, a stage magician, and so on. The magician—an interesting man to talk to—was a bit apart from the rest. He was the only Christian in the group; all the others were Druze. He was also unique in another way. He had reinterpreted his experiences since he was a child. He still thought they were genuine memories of events that had actually taken place, but for him they had become memories of someone else that he had somehow picked up. He was the only person who came up with this interpretation.

In Sri Lanka 87% of our adult group were reasonably satisfied with their occupation, and in Lebanon they were practically the same, namely 89%. On the whole the data indicates that our subjects had fared well in life, probably somewhat better than the average population in their respective countries.

Phobias are a common characteristic in children claiming past-life memories and are often associated with memories of how they died in the previous life. Do the phobias tend to disappear as the child grows up? In Sri Lanka 45% had some fears as children and two-thirds believed that these were related to their previous life. More than half of them still had these fears. In Lebanon almost a third had fears as children and a quarter of them believed they were related to their past life. These fears or phobias seemed to have been rather resistant. A portion of our Lebanese participants still had their fears as was the case in Sri Lanka.

In many solved cases there were visits between the present and previous families and an exchange of gifts. In 24 of the 51 solved cases these visits continued into adulthood. In three cases in Lebanon the presumed previous family did not accept a child as having been a member of their family, but I do not recall such a case in Sri Lanka. Sometimes some member of the previous family accepted the child and others did not. Same-family cases are common in the USA but there was only one in Sri Lanka and two in Lebanon.

What are the main conclusions that we can draw from these two studies? First, they indicate that past-life memories are more frequently retained into adult life than previously assumed. Second, there are indications that past-life memories may be relatively better remembered into adult life than normal memories taking place at the same early age. Third, it seems that children with past-life memories reach a higher educational level than their peers. This comes as no surprise as psychological studies have shown that they tend to be more mature than their peers at an early age. Fourth, it was most common to remember important people they had known, how they had died, and events that led to their frequently violent and premature death. Fifth, some fears and phobias that were related to how the person had died in the previous life tended to last into adulthood. Sixth, there were no indications of any detrimental effects of having had past-life memories.

13

BETWEEN DEATH AND REBIRTH

In a few cases, our children speak of memories from the period after they died and before they were reborn. I found three such cases, two in Sri Lanka and one in Lebanon. These cases generally fall into two categories: memories of observing what happens in the physical surroundings after they pass away and, secondly, memories of the non-physical realm in which they live after they die. Some children may have both kinds of memories.

Let me first describe the case of Purnima, as presented in chapter 1. She told her parents and me how she had died in a traffic accident when a bus ran over her as she was taking incense to the market on a bicycle (Haraldsson, 2000). Then she added:

> After the accident I floated in the air in semi-darkness for a few days. I saw people mourning for me and crying, and saw my body until and including at the funeral. There were many people like me floating around. Then I saw some light, went there and came "here" to the town of Bakamuna (where she was born).

This is how Purnima described how she saw her lifeless body and followed how people were mourning her. Interestingly Purnima not only describes her physical surroundings but also observations of what was happening in the realm in which she found herself, namely that many people who had died were floating around.

This leads me to the second Sri Lanka case, that of Duminda Ratnayake, as presented in chapter 3, who remembered a life as a senior monk. After his death he recalls being among the "devas" (angels, minor deities, beings of light) in heaven (Haraldsson, 1999). Sometimes, his mother told us: "He would point up to the sky and say that is where I stayed." Regrettably I failed to ask Duminda and his mother if he spoke of any further details about his life among the devas.

In the unpublished Lebanese case, Rabah Zar Elldin recalled what happened in his physical surrounding immediately after he died. He was shot in the civil war that raged in Lebanon in the 1960s and 1970s. After he died he recalls seeing his comrades and feeling helpless for not being able to warn them about the actions of their enemies that he was able to observe.

Stevenson describes several cases of memories between the death and rebirth of a person, usually referred to as intermission cases. One of them was a Finnish case that he investigated (Stevenson, 2003). The child, Samuel Helander, recalls that after his death he had been in a place that had a lot of coffins and some of them were open. Evidence suggests that Samuel had recalled events in the life of his mother's younger brother, Pertti. He had indeed been taken to a mortuary where his body was kept after he unexpectedly and suddenly died at the early age of eighteen.

Another interesting Stevenson case concerns Michael Wright who recalled events in the life of Walter Miller who had been his mother's boyfriend. She later married another man with whom she had Michael. Coming from a dance Walter had driven off the road when drunk and died in the accident only 18 years old. Michael correctly recalled having been carried over a bridge after the accident.

Stevenson describes the case of Ratana Wongsombat from Thailand. She had many memories and recognitions of being a Chinese religious woman in Bangkok who died after an operation at the age of 43. She recalled her ashes being scattered at a bodhi tree (sacred to Buddhists) instead of being buried there as she had requested in her will. She also described being with a deva visiting heaven, which brings to mind Duminda's statement of being among the devas.

Three further cases that Stevenson describes:

Bongkuch Promsin from Thailand remembered how Chamrat was murdered by two men at a fair. "The murderers had stabbed him in several places, taken his wristwatch, and neck chain, and afterwards dragged his body into a field." Furthermore Bongkuch stated that he (the then discarnate Chamrat) had stayed at a bamboo tree near the murder site until he saw his father, in rainy weather, whom he then followed home.

Disna Samarasinghe (a subject in Sri Lanka) remembered that the body of Babanona (of life she recalled) had been buried near an anthill; the burial site had been chosen only after Banaona's death. Veer Singh, the subject of another case in India, claimed that after death in the previous life he had remained near the house of the previous family.

The Thai monk, Chaokhun Rajsuthajrn, to whose case I referred earlier (in describing the futile efforts of his parents to suppress his memories), remembered that after dying in the previous life he had attended the funeral of the person whose life he recalled. At this time, he said, he had a sense of lightness and seemed to move easily from place to place. He thought he was in charge of the ceremony and was receiving his guests. In fact, however, he was invisible to the participants, who went on with the ceremony with no suspicion of his presence (Stevenson, 2001, p. 112).

Some subjects claimed to have engaged in poltergeist activity after they died. One of them, Stevenson reports, said that he had thrown a stone at a man who later became his father; another that he had broken a plank on a swing on which some people were playing. Stevenson continues:

The second, more common type of memory of the period between death and presumed rebirth is that of another realm where the subject claims that he sojourned—usually not knowing for how long—after death in the previous life and before his birth in the present one. Disna Samarasinghe gave a rather circumstantial account of her stay in such a place after the death of Babanona, the old lady whose life and death Disna remembered. The clothes one wore were rich and elegant, she said, and they needed no washing. One could have food, which appeared when one wished for it, but there was no need to eat. She met a kindly "ruler" who eventually advised her to get herself reborn, but did not tell her where (Stevenson, 2001, p 112).

Jim B. Tucker has made a consistent effort to find American and Western cases. In his books, *Life Before Life* and *Return to Life,* he describes a few he has found where children describe memories from the realm where they were after their death. Many of them are same-family cases. The cases briefly stated:

William, who claimed to have been his mother's father, "said that he floated up after dying, and talked about being in heaven" (Tucker, 2005, p 172).

Sam, who recalled being his grandfather in the previous life, talked about seeing God and said "that his body shot up to heaven when he died and that someone else died at the same time he had." In addition, Sam talked about seeing Uncle Phil in heaven (his grandfather's best friend) (ibid. p 172).

Patrick, his deceased half-brother reborn, spoke of "speaking to a relative in heaven named 'Billy the Pirate' who told him about being shot at close range and dying while up in the mountains. Patrick's mother reported that she had never heard about such a relative but, when she called her mother to ask about Patrick's statements, she learned that a cousin with the nickname of Billy the Pirate had in fact died that way" (ibid., p 172).

In the archives of the Division of Perceptual Studies at the University of Virginia, detailed reports are kept and coded of 2,242 cases of children claiming past-life memories; among them my 64 cases from Sri Lanka and 32 from Lebanon. Jim Tucker has calculated that 199 of these 2,242 children report memories of their funeral or the handling of bodily remains in the previous life, and 247 describe other events happening in their terrestrial surroundings after they died.

In 253 cases we find memories of being in another realm, as Duminda experienced when being among the devas. And 116 children report memories of conception or being born. We will report more on such cases in a later chapter, particularly in the research conducted by Prof. Masayuki Ohkado at Chubu University in Japan.

To sum up; among the 2,500 cases there are 217 children who report at least one of the above experiences and some of them had more than one kind of experience, like our Purnima. Most of the intermission memories cannot be verified in any way. However, they are highly interesting and more so when we consider how some of them resemble experiences that people report close to or on the threshold of death, such as in deathbed visions and near-death experiences. Furthermore, it is interesting that statements about intermission memories are more commonly made by children who have detailed memories of their past life, many of which have been verified, such as in the case of Purnima.

Are the experiences that children report remembering between their death in the past life and birth in the present life, related to any other phenomena we know? Two immediately come to mind, death-bed visions and near-death experiences. In the next chapter we explore some similarities.

14

BETWEEN THE TWO REALMS: DEATHBED VISIONS

T wo phenomena are highly relevant and are related to memories of the after death realm that children with past-life memories tell us about. Sometimes just before people die they experience deathbed visions and sometimes,when people are close to death, they find themselves in the other realm but turn back to life, namely, they have a near-death experience. We will deal with these separately.

Deathbed visions do sometimes occur when a person is on the threshold between life and death, in other words, about to die. I was deeply involved in one such study: the Osis and Haraldsson cross-cultural study of deathbed visions. We conducted over 800 interviews with US and Indian doctors and nurses about their observations of hallucinatory/visionary experiences among terminal patients. In deathbed visions deceased people are seen by the dying, mostly friends and relatives; they usually appear with the purpose to take or guide the patient to the non-physical realm. This brings to mind Purnima's experience of many people like her floating around after she died, with the exception that they seemed inactive whereas, those appearing to the dying, seem to be there to receive the dying and take them to the realm of those who have already passed on.

Below are some cases taken from our book about this major project *At the Hour of Death* (Osis and Haraldsson, 1977, 2012*)*. Many alert patients reported visions, which appeared in some way to be suggestive of another world.

A dying sixteen-year-old girl had just come out of a coma. Her consciousness was clear when she said to the respondent: "I can't get up," and she opened her eyes. I raised her up a little bit and she said, "I see him, I see him. I am coming." She died immediately afterwards with a radiant face, exultant, elated. It is clear that the girl saw someone and wanted and did go with him.

A sixty-five-year old cancer patient seemed to be clear and rational when he would look into the distance; these things would appear to him and seemed real to him. He would look up to a wall, and his eyes and face would brighten up as if he saw a person. He would speak of the light, brightness and saw people who seemed real to him. He would say, "Hello," and "There is my mother." After that he closed his eyes and seemed very peaceful.

All of a sudden (the doctor reports) she opened her eyes. She called her (deceased) husband by name and said she was coming to him. She had the most peaceful, nicest smile just as if she were going to the arms of someone she thought a great deal of. She said, "Guy, I am coming." She did not seem to realize I was there. It was almost as if she were in another world. It was as if something beautiful had opened up to her; she was experiencing something so beautiful and wonderful.

Well, it was an experience of meeting someone whom he deeply loved. He smiled, reached up, and held out his hands. The expression on his face was one of joy. I asked him what he saw. He said his wife was standing right there and waiting for him. It looked as though there was a river and she was on the other side, waiting for him to come across. He became very quiet and peaceful—serenity of a religious kind. He was no longer afraid. He died a very peaceful death.

These were American cases. Did we have deathbed visions in India? Yes, indeed. Here is one taken from *At the Hour of Death* that was first published in 1977, and last in 2012, and has appeared in many translations and editions:

An Indian female diabetes patient kept uttering words. I listened because the relatives thought she wanted to tell me something. She told me her mother, who had died many years ago, had come, calling her to accompany her to the land of God. When I told this to her relatives, they asked me to tell her not to go. They took this as a bad omen; that she was dying and nothing could be done. The patient said she was going and seemed happy about it. "I am going; mother is calling me. I am going to the land of God." These were her last words. Before this experience, the patient had expected to recover.

A Hindu patient in his sixties was hospitalized because of a bronchial asthmatic condition. His doctor's prognosis predicted a definite recovery. The patient himself expected to live and wished to live. Suddenly he exclaimed. "Somebody is calling me." Afterward he reassured his relatives, saying, "Don't worry. I will be all right," but the "call" seemed to have been more potent than he himself thought. The patient died within ten minutes.

In deathbed vision some patients who were in pain, miserable and scared, seemed to take a peek at the "other-world" reality and become "exultant" and "radiant"—eager to go into it.

Sometimes the apparition might be a total surprise. A man, 50, with coronary disease, saw an old friend who had been dead for some time. "Why (he named the person), what are you doing here?" These were the last words he spoke before he died.

In deathbed visions we found not only experiences of deceased persons, but also less frequently experiences of angels, other deities (we called them religious figures), or beings of light that may resemble Duminda's experiences of being among the devas.

Below is a short American case reported about a 10-year-old girl. In this case the appearance of the angel apparently has a purpose. This is often expressed in deathbed visions: namely, the angel comes to take the patient away into another realm of existence.

The mother saw that her child seemed to be sinking and called us (nurses). She said that the child had just told her she had seen an angel who had taken her by the hand—and she was gone. That just astounded us because there was no sign of imminent death.

The next case is about an American housewife:

> She suffered a heart attack but seemed to have every hope of recovering. She was really calm and quiet—cooperative, not apprehensive. Then she looked at the ceiling and said, "I see an angel. He is coming for me." Afterwards she was even calmer, more serene. Very soon she became unconscious and died the next day.

> One of the Indian cases involved a young Hindu woman in her twenties, who had been brought to a large hospital in Delhi because of tetanus. She was clearly conscious when she told her nurse that she saw a deity called Murti, who said to her, "I have come to take you." She told her relatives that she was going with him and refused medicine which might hold her back. The girl was convinced that she would die in a few minutes, and within fifteen minutes she expired.

In some cases the patients identified the entity appearing to them as a deity, like in the case above. In this category we would consider appearances of Jesus or the Virgin Mary by Christians. These appearances are likely to have been molded by cultural expectations for who knows what Jesus looked like. Perhaps some of these "beings of light", or Duminda's devas, would have been identified by these patients as their favorite religious figure.

Were all of these mere hallucinations? To test this we created the "hallucinogenetic index" which consisted of a diagnosis of stroke, brain injury, uremic diseases, high fever, certain medications and sedation, all of which can in some instances cause hallucination. Some possible hallucinogenic factors were present in 33% of US patients and 18% in India. This shows that the majority of patients were not affected by hallucinogenic factors, and patients with brain disturbances saw fewer apparitions with take-away purpose than patients without hallucinogenic factors. Patients who had a clear state of consciousness saw more peaceful take-away apparitions than patients with impaired clarity of consciousness.

Peter and Elizabeth Fenwick (2008) interviewed over 40 carers, nurses, doctors, chaplains, etc., in hospices and nursing homes, about their observations of what the Fenwicks call End of Life Experiences (ELE). The carers not only experienced the archetypal "take-away visions" but also many other wider and more subtle phenomena associated with the death of people they had cared for. One of the interviewees said: "It is about letting go of this physical world to prepare for what is going to happen next." Once the patients started to have experiences of someone visiting them, they took this as a sign that the end was near, "I know then that they are almost certainly going to be peaceful as they let go of this world, and they have got this peace to look forward to what's next."

Another stated; "Suddenly my gran sat up in bed and smiled; she said 'I am going now and here is Dad and George come to meet me.' She then died, still with this big smile on her face."

There were cases in which otherworldly beings—angels or whoever—are asked to wait a few moments before taking them away.

Sometimes end of life experiences involve hearing:

"My father was at his bedside, deeply distressed, but my grandfather quietly said to my father, 'Don't worry, Leslie, I am all right. I can see and hear the most beautiful things and you must not worry.' And he quietly died, lucid to the end."

Note that Leslie's father could "hear the most beautiful things." This brings to mind the case of a retired acquaintance of mine who had held a high position at the University of Iceland. He had been an amateur singer all his life, singing in various choirs. This is how the incident was reported by his wife:

> One morning when I woke up he told me that he had heard such extraordinarily beautiful singing. I woke up around seven in the morning and he asked me, "Did you hear the beautiful singing?" Because of this strange question I wondered if he was confused, although there was no other sign of it and he had not been earlier. I understood this happened just as he was waking up, perhaps in a dream. "Such beautiful magnificent singing," he said. He had never heard such beautiful singing in his life. There was singing and there were many people around listening. "I thought there might have been a choir," he added. I went to the kitchen to make coffee. Then we sat up in bed reading. He appeared in good health but a few hours later he unexpectedly collapsed and died instantly.

The carers that the Fenwicks interviewed felt confident that End of Life Experiences are not drug-induced and insisted that "drug-induced hallucinations are of a quite different quality from true end-of-life visions, and had a quite different effect on their patients." A good confirmation indeed of the Osis-Haraldsson's finding over thirty years earlier.

In *The Art of Dying* the Fenwicks report many cases of deathbed visions that have the same features as Osis and Haraldsson found.

I was nursing my friend who had definite views that there was no afterlife. In her last couple of hours she became very peaceful and arose from her unconsciousness. Periodically, she said clearly and happily such phrases as "I will know soon," "Come on, get on with it then, I am ready to go now," and "It is so beautiful." She would immediately lapse back into unconsciousness after uttering these phrases. She was very obviously content, happy, and at peace. It was a wonderful experience for her partner and me.

A wife gave this account of her husband's final moments:

"He was losing consciousness. I looked at him; he was looking fixedly at something in front of him. A smile of recognition spread slowly over his face, as if he was greeting someone. Then he relaxed peacefully and died."

Sometimes the dying have an experience of something amazing that greatly astounds them, great beauty or whatever. Famous are the final words of Steve Jobs as recorded by his sister, Mona:

"Before embarking, he'd looked at his sister Patty, then for a long time at his children, then at his life's partner, Laurene, and then over their shoulders past them. Steve's final words were: OH WOW. OH WOW. OH WOW."[1]

---

[1] http://www.nytimes.com/2011/10/30/opinion/mona-simpsons-eulogy-for-steve-jobs.html?pagewanted=all&_r=0

15

THOSE WHO RETURNED: NEAR-DEATH EXPERIENCES

I n the last chapter I described experiences, visionary and auditory, that some people have during their last hours. We also have those who return, are unconscious and unresponsive for a while, but come back to life and consciousness and report remarkable experiences while they were apparently in an unconscious state. These are called near-death-experiences (NDEs). Accounts of such experiences are well known from long-distant times. In *The Republic*, Plato describes the case of Er, a soldier who was thought to have been killed in battle but who just before his cremation came back to life and told the story of what he had seen in the other world.

It was not until the last third of the 20th century that serious attention was paid to these experiences. This was particularly the case in hospitals when patients close to death, such as after cardiac arrest, accidents, etc., regained consciousness and related what had taken place around them while they were unconscious. Physicians such as Michael Sabom (1982), Bruce Greyson (2000), and Pim van Lommel (2010) became interested and started to collect accounts and interview patients..

Research shows that 12% to 18% of patients who had cardiac arrests and were resuscitated had near-death experiences. Furthermore, about two thirds of those who have near-death experiences, also report mystical experiences during their brush with death, such as a feeling of unity with the ultimate reality; divinity, nature, or cosmos; in short, generally accepted criteria of religious experiences found within religion itself, such as the experience of union with God, communication with God, and being in the presence of God (Greyson, 2014). They had a strong sense of William James' four criteria of a religious experience: ineffability, noetic quality, transiency, and passivity.

Some patients not only observed what took place in the physical space around them, but claimed also to observe otherworldly realms, and they were deeply touched by their experience. This interests us because of the similarity to what children with past-life memories tell of their intermission experiences; that is after they die and before they are reborn.

Bruce Greyson of the University of Virginia is one of the chief investigators of near-death experiences. He has defined NDEs as profound psychological events with transcendental and mystical elements, typically occurring in individuals close to death, or in situations of intense physical or emotional danger.

Here is a case reported by another NDE investigator, the cardiologist Pim van Lommel:

> ...What happened was that I had suddenly become aware of hovering above the foot of the operating table and watching the activity down below around the body of a human being. Soon it dawned upon me that this was my own body. So I was hovering over it, above the lamp, which I could see through. I also heard everything that was said: "Hurry up bloody bastard" was one of the things I remember them shouting. And even weirder: I did not just hear them talk, but I could also read the mind of everybody in the room, or so it seemed to me. It was all quite close, I later learned, because it took four and a half minutes to get my heart, which had stopped, going again. As a rule, oxygen deprivation causes brain damage after three or three and a half minutes. I also heard the doctor say that he thought I was dead. Later he confirmed saying this, and he was astonished to learn that I'd heard it. I also told them they should mind their language during surgery.

The case above is essentially an out of body experience without any encounter with non-physical beings, people or deva-like. Still these experiences are important, for elements in them can often be verified. They are, hence, an indication that NDEs with encounters with non-physical beings and realms can be veridical, namely, describe actual facts. Let us quote two cases from Van Lommel that include such encounters:

> Suddenly I recognized all these relatives. They all looked around thirty-five years old, including the little brother I'd never known, because he had died during the war when he was two years old, before I was born. He had grown a lot. My parents were there, too, and they smiled at me, just like the others.

> At the age of sixteen I had a serious motorcycle accident. I was in a coma for nearly three weeks. During that coma I had an extremely powerful experience . . . and then I came to a kind of iron fence. Behind it stood Mr. Van der G., the father of my parents' best friend. He told me that I couldn't go any further. I had to go back because my time hadn't come yet. When I told my parents after waking up, they said to me that Mr. Van der G. had died and been buried during my coma. I couldn't have known that he was dead.

The cases above describe experiences of deceased people and there are others that describe experiences of angels, devas, or otherworldly beings, rather like Purnima and Duminda observed in their intermission period. Intermission memories of children with past-life memories, deathbed visions, and near-death-experiences share common elements and are essentially the same.

Sent-Back Cases

In some of the NDEs the sick patient about to die is explicitly sent back by some otherworldly being, either a person, angels, or deva-like entities. Such was the case above when Mr. Van der G. told the experiencer that he could not go any further: his time had not come yet. A number of such cases were reported to Osis and me. We called them *sent back cases.* Two examples:

> She said her father and mother [both deceased] were coming to meet her and take her far away. The three of them were going along a hill when her parents suddenly told her to go back. She turned back and left them. The next morning, approximately six to eight hours after

the experience, her condition improved. I [her doctor] had expected her to expire that night. I realized how seriously ill she was, how close to leaving.

"I see God." He started to cry and moan that he was going to die. He just stared out into space as if he were really seeing God. When I returned half an hour later, he was a changed man, a very happy countenance. He said that God told him it was not yet time for him to go.

Examples of the sent-back cases indicate that such visions are not to be taken literally. It is interesting that the sent-back or come-back cases, as Osis and I called them, saw more religious figures and fewer apparitions of the dead than those who had deathbed visions.

Many patients spoke of seeing beautiful landscapes, gardens, and scenery that was a source of joy to them and made them happy to die when the time came.

An American housewife felt that she had visited heaven. She said that she had been in that beautiful place. "If heaven is like that, I am ready."

16

SPONTANEOUS CONTACT
WITH THE DEPARTED

I have written about two kinds of intermission memories. First, memories of observations of the after-death world, like Duminda who recalled being with the devas. Secondly, intermission memories of events taking place in the physical world, like Purnima who—after she died— observed people mourning her and saw her funeral.

There are also experiences and observations that are the other way around, namely the living perceiving those who have died—like in deathbed visions, but without being on the threshold of death. A major large-sample survey, the European Human Values Survey, was conducted in most countries of Western Europe in the early 1980s. One if its many questions was: "Have you ever felt as though you were really in touch with someone who had died?" Twenty-five percent of the Western Europeans had, every fourth person, and 31% in the USA. The figures varied widely between nations from 9% to 41%. In Table 16-1 you will find the results for the participating nations (Haraldsson and Houtkooper, 1991).

Table 16-1. Percentages of Respondents from Western Europe and the United States Who Answered Yes to the Human Values Survey Question, "Have you ever felt that you were really in touch with someone who had died?"

"Have you ever felt that you were really in touch with someone who had died?"					
Belgium	18	Denmark	10	Finland	14
France	24	Great Britain	26	Holland	12
Iceland	41	Ireland	16	Italy	34
Norway	9	Spain	16	Sweden	14
West Germany	28	WESTERN EUROPE	25	UNITED STATES	41
Total number of respondents = 18,607					

What did people experience when they felt "really in touch with someone who has died"? The European Values Survey tells nothing about that. How were the deceased perceived? Who were they? Under what circumstances did people feel really in touch with those who had died? We sought answers by interviewing 450 persons who reported such experiences (Haraldsson, 2012). Highly interesting patterns and characteristics emerged.

Particularly interesting was the fact that every seventh case took place at the time the person died. Two examples:

I was a member of Parliament for 18 years and during that time I was in contact with many men who later became good acquaintances. One of them was Karl Kristjánsson, MP. We were friends, and kept in touch on and off after we retired. One winter's day I went out to the stable as I usually did after lunch. When I had been shovelling for a while, I suddenly felt Karl Kristjánsson standing in front of me in one of the stalls in the stable. He says something rather peculiar: "You were lucky, you did fine." That was all, and then he disappeared. That evening his death was announced on the radio. While pondering about the incident and trying to figure it out, I learned that he had suffered a heart attack and been brought to Reykjavik City Hospital where he died. I had been admitted to that hospital a year earlier after suffering a similar attack. I luckily recuperated and could go home, whereas he died. In that context, I understood his words, "You were lucky, you had good luck."

Another case:

I lived in Sandgerdi where we had just bought a house two months ago. I was alone in the house. My husband was out working. Suddenly I see that a man enters through the front door and goes to the kitchen. This happened suddenly and was over. I then felt a strong smell of liquor. I never use alcohol. Well, then my husband comes home, and he says: "Who has been here?" Nobody I tell him. "Oh, there is such a strong smell of liquor." Yes, I say, but nobody has been here. The next day my husband comes home for supper and says: "No wonder there was a liquor smell here yesterday.... Erlingur from whom we bought the house was missing in Siglufjord yesterday." He had been drunk and it was feared that he had fallen into the harbour and drowned. Two weeks later his body was found floating in the harbour. When this incident occurred we had no idea about what had happened.

A study conducted in the United Kingdom over a century ago revealed the same; every seventh case of apparitions of the dead occurs on the day of death.

The cases varied greatly; two-thirds were visual, over a quarter auditory and the rest were tactual, olfactory, or consisted of a vivid sense of presence. Some were a mixture of these, as in the case of Erlingur above that was both visual and olfactory.

Some of the cases were quite innocent:

I sat in a chair in my room and was reading. Then I looked up and saw my deceased grandmother standing in front of me, as fully alive. I told my mother about this the following day. She said "That is nice, it was her birthday." I had not remembered it.

Here is an auditory case:

This happened when I was a teenager. I was alone, fishing, on a small boat. Suddenly I heard a voice that says I should leave the fishing line and row ashore. I heard this quite clearly. It was said to me in an ordering tone. I did as ordered. I do not know why, but I found it so odd. Just as I am about to arrive at the harbour suddenly there sweeps over a violent storm. I barely managed to dock. I did not recognize the voice, but later I connected it with my brother who had recently drowned. The fisherman believed that this warning of impending danger had saved his life.

The tactual cases were particularly common with widows and widowers:

The night after my husband died I could not sleep. I was at home in my bed and very lonely. Suddenly I sensed him standing by my bed. He seemed to be covered in something like mist. I saw him and felt his hand as he stroked my head and he recited part of a well-known poem that was about how good it was to rest and then wake up one day surrounded with eternal joy. I felt quite differently after this.

Some experiences were only a vivid sense of an invisible presence, as if telepathic:

I was out in the country and going to visit my grandfather. I was having a pleasant trip and stayed at Blanda town for two nights, or rather was going to. I was not in any hurry. All of a sudden I sensed my grandfather right there with me. I instantly knew that he had passed away. I went to the post office and made a call. It was confirmed that he had died the day before.

Some cases revealed a message or purpose:

This happened shortly after my father died. I was in bed, sleeping, but woke up and felt there was something at my side. I saw my father there. I looked at him, reached out, and felt him. He was just as he had been, wearing a blue shirt over his underwear. He got out of the bed and walked to the room he had lived in which was across from mine. As he walked, he pointed to the wall without saying a word. On that wall there was a large clock that he had earlier asked me to deliver to his grandson in Reykjavík.

In this case his father was reminding him to fulfil his promise. In the great majority of cases no particular purpose is evident according to our respondents except perhaps to let the person know that the deceased person "is there."

There were also cases of warning and rescue at sea, like the young fisherman who heard a voice that ordered him to row ashore. Also cases of guidance, healing, relief, and giving comfort. Some felt they were being watched over from "the other side." Lots of interesting stories. Can we trust them? We only have people's words for them.

Some cases have the advantage of more than one witness. The following case was reported by a well-known attorney in Iceland:

It was just after graduation in 1939. I was coming home from a dance. I hadn't tasted a drop of alcohol. It was about four o'clock in the morning and full light as we were in the middle of summer. I was walking over a bare hill on my way home from town. There comes a woman towards me, kind of stooping, with a shawl over her head. I don't pay any particular attention to her, but as she passes me I say: "Good morning," or something like that. She didn't say anything. Then I notice that she has changed her course and follows me a bit behind. I got slightly uneasy about this, and found it odd. When I stopped she stopped also. I started saying prayers in my mind to calm myself. When I came close to home she disappeared. I lived in a house on the compound of a psychiatric hospital where my father worked. I went up to my room. My brother, Agnar, wakes up and says half asleep: "What is this old woman doing here? Why is this old woman with you?" And I tell him not to speak such nonsense but to continue sleeping although I knew what he meant. I did not see the woman at that time but my brother appeared to see her when he woke up. I went out to get some coffee. When I returned Agnar gets up again and says: "Why has this woman come back?" And I tell him not to act like that, that there is no woman in here, that he is confused and should go to sleep.

At lunch the following day I say to my brother: "What nonsense was this last night? You thought you saw a woman in our bedroom." "Yes," he said. "I felt as though an old woman came with you into the room." Then our father— a psychiatrist working in the hospital— became attentive and asked me "Did you see something last night?" I told him that I had seen this woman. "That is strange," he said. "Around three o'clock this morning old Vigga died." What I had seen fitted her description perfectly.

We approached our respondent's brother. He remembered this incident and that his brother had told him what he had seen. When asked whether he had himself seen the woman, he replied: "I saw the vague image of a hag.... but not clearly. When I woke up I saw a woman come in with him. It was a patient that always kept inside. I think, it was her."

Another case with two witnesses:

Shortly after our father died I came to his house with my brother. We knew that there was nobody in the house and then we heard the old man at his desk. He was walking around, opened the door and closed it again. Both of us stopped and listened when we entered the house and then I remarked: "I guess there is no doubt who is up there."

"No there is no doubt about it," my brother replied. Both of us went upstairs, no one was there. We had heard this so clearly. He was 85 years when he died, walked slowly, you know; had the typical old man's way of walking.

We contacted our respondent's brother who said he remembered clearly that this event had taken place but no details. When we read the account to him, he said it all came back to him, and confirmed his brother's account. One of the brothers was a medical doctor, the other a bank director. Their father had been a nationally known scholar and writer.

We also have cases that were indirectly verified, like the following:

Jakob was a patient in a sanatorium where I worked. He was sometimes depressed, and I tried to brighten his stay with a bit of humor. One day I said to Jakob that he should visit us because he came from the same county as my husband and they would enjoy talking about the people from there. Jakob said yes to that, and I said to him: "Do you promise to come tomorrow." "Yes, yes, I promise," he said. During the night, I woke up, and all strength is taken away from me. I am unable to move. Suddenly I see the bedroom door open, and on the threshold stands Jakob, with his face all covered with blood. I look at this for a good while, unable to speak or move. Then he disappears and it felt as if he closed the door behind him. I became my normal self, called my husband and told him about the incident: "I swear that something has happened at the sanatorium." I telephoned in the morning and asked if everything was all right with Jakob. "No", said the nurse, "he committed suicide this very night."

We interviewed the husband. His wife had awakened him in the middle of the night and told him about what she had seen. They did not know the fate of Jakob until in the morning. He was found drowned some hundred yards downstream from a walking bridge over a river close to the sanatorium. The post-mortem report declared cause of death as "suicidum submergio," i.e., suicide by drowning. It further states that there were "two large wounds on his head and the cranium much broken." This fits the woman's description that she saw Jakob "with his face all covered with blood." The river is shallow and flowing over sharp rocks of lava that must have caused the severe head injuries.

This case has two common characteristics, the appearing person suffered a violent death and he appeared on the night he drowned himself. Thirty percent of our large case collection concern violent deaths—mostly accidents—four times as many as actually suffer a violent death in the population. On the day people die, and also when they die violently—which is mostly sudden and unexpected—many of them seem to have an urgent motivation to communicate with the living. This was also found over a century ago in a British survey. The Icelandic experiences proved very similar to those reported in Britain over a century ago in the first large-scale surveys of apparitions/afterlife encounters (Gurney, Myers and Podmore, 1886).

Violent death also plays a prominent role in past-life memories. 78% of my Sri Lankan and Lebanese children recall how they suffered a violent death, 4% recall a natural death, and 18% do not remember their mode of death.

Next we will turn our attention to after-death contacts through mediums. The percentage of the violently dead who communicate through mediums is also considerably higher than the percentage of violent deaths in the population.

17

CONTACT THROUGH MEDIUMS

In the last chapter we discussed spontaneous experiences of the deceased that some people have on rare occasions and over which they have no control. In the mid-19th century a new form of contact with the departed emerged through the spiritualistic movement. It started in the United States and quickly spread to Europe. Psychically gifted persons—mediums—appeared on the scene. They had, or were assumed to have, the gift of direct contact with deceased persons at special sittings—séances—that usually took place in the dark. There the deceased—the spirits –more or less took control of the medium's body, spoke through them, or communicated in other ways to those who were present around them. The medium served as a middle man between the living and the dead.

With some mediums, called physical mediums, this contact was accompanied by gross physical movements, such as the levitation of objects, and the medium's playing musical instruments without any visible hand touching them and, with a few mediums, voices of the deceased could be heard around them. The spirits often identified themselves and described events that had occurred to them in their earthly lifetime. The invisible spirits not only communicated through the medium but also interacted physically with the physical environment.

Allow me to describe some aspects of two Icelandic mediums, Haf-steinn Bjornsson (1914-1977) and Indridi Indridason (1883-1912). Let us start with Hafsteinn. I already mentioned that over two-thirds of children who claim to have past-life memories speak of having suffered a violent death. Perhaps we may also call them "those who returned quickly" as they usually remember episodes from a life that came to a sudden end only a year or two before they were born.

In mediumship, we also find more communicators who had suffered a violent death than the percentage of violent deaths in the population. Most of these communicators are quite peaceful, but sometimes they are aggressive and disturbing when they first appear. Let us first take the case of Runolfur Runolfsson—nicknamed Runki—in the medium-ship of Hafsteinn Bjornsson.

Runki first appeared at Hafsteinn's séances in the first winter of his me-diumship. He created a major disturbance, swearing and verbally abusing the sitters, and he was not willing to reveal his identity. This went on for a while. One evening, a man attended the sitting who, the spirit commu-nicator claimed, was living in the area where he had lived before he died. He said his leg was missing. It was in a wall of the house that the sitter had recently bought. The spirit wanted the leg to be duly buried. The sitter was ready to look for the leg if the spirit would reveal his name.

Reluctantly he agreed in the end. After some search and inquiries a leg was found in a wall in the sitter's house. It had washed up on the shore many years ago, and nobody knew to whom it had belonged. It was lying around in this wooden house until a carpenter doing some repair work decided to place it within one of the walls.

Runki had suffered a tragic death, had been drunk and fallen asleep on the beach on his way home; the tide washed him out and he drowned. In the record of his burial it was stated that a part of his body was missing. Runki had drowned over half a century before he appeared at Hafsteinn's sittings.

At Runki's request, the leg was duly buried by the clergyman of his parish. Runki turned peaceful and became Hafsteinn Bjornson's prin-cipal control, an outspoken and distinct personality who was much liked by the sitters (Haraldsson and Stevenson, 1975).

Indridi Indridason (1883-1912) is the greatest medium who lived in Ice-land, and his mediumship is amply described in contemporary source and protocols (Haraldsson and Gissurarson, 2015). In September 1907, Indri-di visited a clergyman living on the Westman Islands off the southern coast of Iceland. One day, while he was out walking with the clergyman's daughters, he told them he saw a dead man about whom he made some mocking remarks. The man he saw was in his shirt-sleeves, with a belt around his waist. First Indridi saw him in connection with a lady they had met, and then again when they passed a certain house in the village. The man who lived in that house had committed suicide the previous autumn by drowning himself in the sea. Before doing so, he had taken off his hat, coat, and waistcoat, because these garments were found on the shore.

After Indridi's return to Reykjavik, strange disturbances started in the medium's apartment that he shared with a student, and during séances. For instance, in the night following the October 3 meeting, the light was turned off in their rooms in the middle of the night, and Indridi claimed to see the man in the shirt-sleeves whom he had seen on the Westman Islands.

Two days later Indridi's main control requested that a prayer should be offered for a certain person who had slipped into the séance.

At a later séance, the controls said that, Jon, the person who had committed suicide, was now at the séance, in control of "the power" and in the worst of tempers. The wicker chair in which Indridi sat was thrown about on the floor and finally turned upside down with Indridi thrown out of it onto the floor. Other disturbing movements followed.

On the evening of December 7, 1907, Indridi and the student had gone to bed as usual. A lamp was burning on a table between the beds. Suddenly a plate, which had been standing on a bookshelf in the front room, was thrown onto the floor and came down in the bedroom. Indridi's bed was pulled about one foot away from the wall. Indridi was terror-stricken. After that members had to stay with him at night for some time, and all regular sittings stopped.

Einar Kvaran stayed with Indridi and the student during the night of December 8. He lay in Indridi's bed by the north wall while Indridi and student occupied the other bed—he with his head nearest to the window and the medium with his head at the other end of the bed. A lamp was burning on a table between the beds (no electricity in Reykjavik at this time). A while later the student's slippers, which had been under his bed, were thrown into a hand-basin which stood in the room.

Next, the end of the bed in which the medium and the student were lying was raised and lowered alternately and the bed shaken. The medium shouted that he was being dragged out of bed, and was terror-stricken. The student took his hand, pulling with all his might, but could not hold him. The medium was lifted above the end of the bed against which his head had been lying, and was pulled down onto the floor, sustaining some injuries to his back from the bedstead. At the same moment a pair of boots, which had been under the bed, were thrown at the lamp, breaking both the glass and the shade.

Indridi was dragged head first along the floor into the front room. He tried strenuously to hold onto anything he could, and both Einar Kvaran and the student pulled at his legs, while he was pulled along. Finally they managed to get under his shoulders, which they had great difficulty in lifting, and brought him back to the bed. Indridi's legs were then lifted so forcefully that the student could not weigh the leg down. Einar grasped the other leg but could not force it down either.

At this point all three left the experimental house and went to Einar's home, where some activity continued during the night in spite of all the lights being on.

The next evening Indridi went back to his apartment accompanied by three people to protect him. During that night, a small table standing between the beds at the head of Indridi's bed was lifted up and fell on his bed, making a loud noise. Later it was smashed against the wall and broke into pieces. No other major phenomena took place that night.

The next night, Indridi stayed in the experimental house with two people to protect him. Candlesticks and a brush were thrown around, and the table between the beds was lifted up onto Indridi's bed. One of the protectors then lay on top of Indridi on the bed, and so it went on. The bed in which the two of them were lying suddenly moved about a foot from the wall, although one of them pushed with his foot with all of his might against the other bed. At the same time, he had to use all his strength to hold Indridi down on the bed. The table between the beds levitated high up and came down on his shoulders and he received continuous knocks on his head from the table top.

Then they lit an oil lamp, which stood on the chest of drawers between the washing tables in Indridi's bedroom, and also three candles in the front room. At this point they decided to leave the house. One of them, Brynjolfur, described what followed:

> Indridi was starting to dress again and was putting on his trousers, but I walked into the outer room and stood there. Then Indridi screamed for help once more. I ran to him into the bedroom. But then I saw a sight that I shall never forget. Indridi was floating horizontal in the air, at about the height of my chest, and swaying there to and fro, with his feet pointing towards the window, and it seemed to me that the invisible power that was holding him in the air was trying to swing

him out of the window. I didn't hesitate a moment, but grabbed around the medium where he was swinging in the air, and pushed him down onto the bed and held him there." (Thordarson, 1942, p. 31)

Then all three of them stood side by side and walked backwards out of the room in order to be able to defend themselves against more assaults. Then they all rushed out and went to Kvaran's home.

The violent phenomena that started on December 7, 1907 lasted until January 6, 1908. On January 4, 1908 the destructive disturbances reached their climax when around fifty occurrences were observed and recorded in the Minutes book.

We will let that suffice. In the end Indridi's controls seem to have found means of controlling Jon. He became peaceful and helpful in producing phenomena, and became Indridi's "great friend."

Members of the Experimental Society succeeded in getting a photograph of Jon from the Westman Islands. They showed Indridi some photo albums. In one of them was Jon's photo among many similar photographs. Jon's photo was immediately recognized by Indridi, although those who tested him gave him no hint whatsoever, on the contrary, they tried to mislead him.

Indridi was truly a middleman between the two worlds.

Michael Tymn writes online in a customer review at Amazon.com: "D. D. Home is often referred to as the greatest physical medium on record, but Home may have to relinquish his top spot to Indridi Indridason of Iceland now that we have a record of his phenomena set forth in English by Drs. Erlendur Haraldsson and Loftur R. Gissurarson in their book, *Indridi Indridason: The Icelandic Physical Medium*, released recently by White Crow Books."

It would go far beyond the purpose of this chapter to give even a short account of his phenomena. Let a brief résumé suffice of the different kinds of phenomena that were reported about him in various contemporary sources and protocols:

Raps, cracking sounds in the air, knocks responding to the sitters' demands, some of them loud and heavy, and knocks heard on the body of the medium.

Direct voice phenomena were a prominent feature of Indridi's phenomena. Protocols of 47 sittings show that direct voice phenomena occurred at 77% of Indridi's sittings compared with 8% at 48 sittings with D. D. Home.

Movements and levitations were frequent, of objects, small and large, light and heavy, and over short or long distances within a room or hall and sometimes quite high. Some of these objects moved as if thrown forcefully; at other times their trajectories were irregular. Sometimes objects were found to tremble. Curtains were pulled back and forth on request by the sitters.

Levitations of the medium. Many instances of levitation are reported, often with the medium holding onto another person. During violent poltergeist phenomena, the medium was dragged along the floor and thrown up into the air so that his protectors had difficulty pushing him down.

Light phenomena. Fire-flashes or fire-balls, small and large fire-flashes on the walls. Luminous clouds as large as several feet across, sometimes described as a "pillar of light" within which a human form appeared.

Playing of musical instruments as if by invisible hands, and sometimes while they were levitating and moving around in mid-air. Winding of a music box by itself.

Materializations. The shadow or shape of materialized fingers were seen, or a hand or a foot, or a full human figure. Sitters touched materialized fingers, limbs or trunks that were felt as solid. Once a monster-like animal (mixture of a horse and a calf) was seen by Indridi, and another person observed outside a séance.

Gusts of wind, cold or hot, were common, strong enough to blow paper, sometimes far away from the medium, and sometimes as if someone was blowing air from their mouth.

Olfactory (odor) phenomena sometimes occurred; a sudden fragrant smell in the presence of the medium, sometimes other smells, such as seaweed. The odor would sometimes cling to a sitter after being touched by the medium.

Fixation of objects or the medium. Sitters could not move objects or stop them from moving or push them down when they were above the ground. The sitters could not move the medium or his limbs.

Dematerialization of the medium's arm. The medium's shoulder and trunk was inspected through touch by several sitters, yet the arm was not detected.

Sense of *being touched*, pulled and punched by invisible hands; also of being kissed.

Sounds heard around the medium, laughter, footsteps, buzzing sounds, clatter of hoof-beats, and the rustling noise of clothes as if someone was moving.

Direct writing. Writing appeared on paper without human touch.

Two or more phenomena occurred simultaneously, which was deemed impossible for one person to do, such as a musical instrument moving quickly in mid-air while being played, or two widely different voices singing at the same time.

Automatic writing in which Indridi's handwriting would change significantly.

Mental phenomena; information was communicated that was not available to any of the sitters by normal means. A fire burning in Copenhagen was described at a time when there was no telephone or radio contact with Iceland.

Controls and individual communicators revealed knowledge that the medium could not have known about them.

In the summer of 1909 Indridi fell sick and never fully recovered. Later it was found that he had contracted tuberculosis, the great killer in those times. He was admitted to a tuberculosis hospital where he died on August 31, 1912, only 28 years old.

Prof. Nielsson, one of his leading investigators, wrote:

> I had a talk with him some 24 hours before he died. He was fully conscious, but extremely weak. His voice had become so weak that I had to pay great attention to hear what he was saying as I sat by his bedside. I felt it unthinkable that he would not be aware of his deteriorating condition. I asked him if he was ever aware of his friends from the beyond. "Yes, often," he replied. "Every time I get drowsy I become aware of them." "Are you never aware of them, when you are fully awake?" I asked. "Yes, I see them also when wide awake, particularly when it is getting dark." His certainty of them was as profound as his certainty of me.

Brynjolfur Thorlaksson played the organ at Indridi's séances and became his personal friend. He writes in his memoirs (Thordarson, 1942): Indridi Indridason, the medium, was the most amazing of all men I have come to know in my life, and has become more memorable than all other men.

18

MEMORIES OF BIRTH AND LIFE IN THE WOMB

We have discussed past-life memories, intermission memories—and memories/contacts from the time when or after we die. The last group of memories includes experiences of deathbed-visions and near-death experiences, and contacts of the departed with the living, primarily through spontaneous experiences and through mediumship. If our spiral model of life's progression is true, then after staying in the realm of the departed for a while, we descend into new physical life. There follows a life in a mother's womb that ends with birth into the light of day and being and becoming a new breathing body.

Inspired by findings by earlier researchers like Chamberlain (1988) who reported cases of children claiming to have "in the womb" or birth memories, the Japanese obstetrician and gynaecologist, Ikegawa (2005), conducted a survey among parents that showed a surprisingly high percentage of children with "in the womb" or birth memories.

Ohkado (2015) used an online marketing research company to survey 10,000 randomly selected women in their 20s to 50s. They were asked:

Q1 a. Do you know that there are children having birth memories (talking about memories of being born)?
    b. Do you know that there are children having womb memories (talking about being in the womb)?
    c. Do you know that there are children having prelife or "life between-life" memories (talking about memories from before being in the womb)?
    d. Do you know that there are children having past-life memories (talking about a past life)?

Q2 a. Do you have a child aged 3 to 12 and, if you do, has he/she ever talked about memories of being born?
    b. Do you have a child aged 3 to 12 and, if you do, has he/she ever talked about being in the womb?
    c. Do you have a child aged 3 to 12 and, if you do, has he/she ever talked about memories from before being born?
    d. Do you have a child aged 3 to 12 and, if you do, has he/she ever talked about a past life?

The women who answered positively to at least one of the four questions listed in Q1 and Q2 were given a second round of the survey and asked further questions. Among them: At what age did the child first talk about the memories? Did the child do it spontaneously or after being asked? Were there special circumstances in which he/she talked about the memories? Did the memories contain any element that seemed verifiable? Table 18-1 shows the results for women who had a young child.

Table 18-1. Number of Mothers with a Child Aged 3 to 12
With and Without Four Types of Memory

	Type of Memory			
	Birth	*Womb*	*Pre-Life*	*Past-Life*
Child has memories	974 (16.2%)	1905 (28.1%)	369 (13.3%)	96 (4%)
Child has no memories	5051 (83.8%)	4481 (71.9%)	2415 (86.7%)	2286 (96%)
Total no. of mothers	6025 (100%)	6786 (100%)	2874 (100%)	2286 (100%)

Note: The total number of responses for the four types of memory is not the same because not all the mothers answered all the questions, probably because they were not familiar with one or more of the types of memory in the questionnaire.

This shows a remarkably high percentage of women who claim that their children had memories of being in their womb (28.1%) and of their birth (16.2%). These figures are not far from those obtained by Ikegawa in 2005 and confirm his findings that some children have memories of life in the womb and of how they were born. It is also interesting that 13.3% of the mothers report that their child had spoken about intermission (pro-life) memories, and 4% had spoken about past-life memories. Cases of past-life memories have been found and investigated in Japan, e.g., by Ohkado (2013).

84 mothers answered the stage two questions sufficiently for further analyses. Most of the children with womb and birth memories talk about them at a very young age, in fact 93% and 95% respectively are aged two to five. This is about the same age as children do with past-life memories. Very few children are older when they start to talk about womb or birth memories. We see the same well-known pattern from children with past-life memories that Stevenson discovered decades ago and others have since verified.

Not all children spoke spontaneously about their womb and birth memories. In fact, well over half of them, 60.5% and 68.0%, spoke only about womb and birth memories after their mothers asked them, while well over half of them spoke first spontaneously about their intermission or prelife memories, and over two-thirds spoke spontaneously about their past-life memories. See Table 18-2.

Table 18.2. Spontaneous Talking vs.
Prompting with Four Types of Memory

	Type of Memory			
	Birth	*Womb*	*Pre-Life*	*Past-Life*
Child talked spontaneously	158 (39.5%)	272 (32.0%)	87 (57.6%)	26 (70.3%)
Child talked after being asked	242 (60.5%)	578 (68%)	64 (42.4%)	11 (29.7%)
Total no. of children	400 (100%)	850 (100%)	151 (42.4%)	37 (100%)

Ohkado mentions that the higher percentages of spontaneous cases in prelife and past-life memories will probably reflect the fact that these two memories are not as widely known to parents as the other two types of memories.

Many parents noticed that their children talked about these memories under certain circumstances, especially at bedtime, but often also at no specific time, or when having a meal or a bath. See Table 18-3 for details.

Table 18-3. Circumstances under which
Children Talked about Their Memories

	Type of Memory			
	Birth	Womb	Pre-Life	Past-Life
During or after bath	32 (8%)	67 (7.9%)	11 (7.3%)	0 (0%)
At bedtime	179 (44.8%)	356 (41.9%)	63 (41.7%)	20 (54%)
At mealtime	40 (10%)	79 (9.3%)	15 (9.9%)	5 (13.5%)
At no specific time	149 (37.3%)	348 (40.9%)	62 (41.1%)	12(13.4%)
Total no. of children	400 (100%)	850 (100%)	151 (100%)	37 (100%)

The mothers were asked if they considered that their children's memories contained any verified elements? For birth and womb memories they believed overwhelmingly, as can be seen in Table 18-4, namely 87% and 71%. Regretfully many mothers left this question unanswered which gives this finding added uncertainty.

Table 18-4. Presence vs. Absence of
Verified Elements in Children's Memories

	Type of Memory			
	Birth	Womb	Pre-Life	Past-Life
Verified elements present	156 (86.7%)	219 (70.6%)	21 (42.0%)	4*
Verified elements absent	24 (13.3%)	91 (29.4%)	29 (58.0%)	28
Total no. children	180 (100%)	310 (100%)	50 (100%)	32 (100%)

* For past-life memories, the questionnaire asked whether the person spoken about had been identified or not. In one of the affirmative cases, the "remembered" past-life was that of a non-human.

Did the mothers consider their children's memories real or fantasy? They overwhelmingly considered them real for birth, womb, and prelife memories, 87%, 83% and 69% respectively.

Some of the mothers provided the reason for why they believed that their children's memories were verified. Some of them correctly pointed out the people who were present when they were born. Children who were delivered by Caesarean section said they had been surprised by the sudden exposure to bright light. Other children started to sing the songs their mother often listened to while they were in the womb.

Some children claimed to have chosen their mother before conception, and—according to their mothers—they correctly described the wedding ceremony or other specific situations. One of the mothers having a child with past-life memories believed that the child was her mother reborn because the child talked about something only her mother knew. Another believed that the child had been a baker she knew because the child explicitly said so. The Japanese researchers did not attempt to verify any of this but thought it worth pointing out that sometimes the children's memories were quite specific and convincing enough for the parents to believe in their reality.

The researchers point out in their report that the participants (parents) were all women and believe that the figures would become dramatically lower if this survey had been conducted with men, that is, the fathers. Interviews with a few children revealed that children would not talk about their memories to their fathers since they would not take them seriously. Many children feel frustrated by their fathers' refusal to take them seriously. It might well be that the fathers' disbelief would change if Ohkado's and Ikegawa's studies became more widely known.

19

WHAT CAN WE CONCLUDE?

Not very long ago there were only religious arguments—better termed dogmas—for continued life after death. Spiritualism appeared on the scene in the second half of the 19th century. Alleged communications with the dead through mediums sometimes revealed intimate knowledge of a deceased person's life and were considered a proof for the existence of that person in another world. There followed systematic studies of apparitions of the dead, which offered further indication that those who had died continued to live. There followed studies of deathbed visions, and more recently, of near-death experiences (NDEs). Studies of NDEs in medical settings by physicians gave them added credibility, resulted in more publications in scientific journals, and led to increased discussion of their relevance for the question of survival. Some of these researchers argued that NDEs offered real evidence for continued life after the dissolution of the physical body. Not that these conclusions did not meet with criticism and rejections, but this research led to serious discussions. Gradually there had emerged a radical change: religious dogmas were no longer the sole argument for life after death.

Around the middle of the last century Stevenson started his monumental work on cases of children of the reincarnation type (CORT) who claimed memories of a past life. I got involved at the invitation of Stevenson, and investigated around one hundred such cases. These investigations are the core of this book and the reason for publication. I also got Jim involved because of his wide knowledge of this field.

Cases of the reincarnation type differ a lot in evidential quality and content. We have outstanding cases, many weak cases, and a large number of unsolved cases. Some children only make statements that contain no leads that can be followed up and hence verified or falsified. However, the outstanding solved cases—perhaps ten percent or more of the total number of cases-have some challenging characteristics:

- The child pupports to have memories of a past lifetime and these memories are found to fit events in the life of a person who died before the child was born.
- Does not accept their home and family. Says their family is somewhere else.
- Wants to find their previous home.
- Two thirds or more speak about a life that ended in a violent death.
- Many have phobias and fears related to these memories.
- Some have symptoms of post traumatic stress disorder that is most likely caused by preoccupation with memories of a violent death.
- Often have specific psychological characteristics, such as being gifted and doing well in school.
- Birthmarks—formed before the child is born—are found in some cases, and are often related to the wounds that led to the child's death in the previous life—think of the cases of Purnima and Chatura.
- In rare cases we find physiological features related to the claimed mode of death in the previous life—think of the case of Nadine.
- Evidence of skills/knowledge how to do something, is found in rare cases.

This list consists not only of memories, but also of motivational, bodily, and physiological factors and complicated skills and knowledge of how to do something. The theory that all these features can be explained by the child's sensing some "thought bundles" (Keil, 2010) seems unsatisfactory to me. Unbelievable as it may appear at first sight, the reincarnation theory best fits the data and the various features of the cases.

That is in short what we can conclude—at least as I see it. From the reincarnation theory follows the circular/spiral model of human life's progression. Circular because life, death, life, death, life, follows in succession, and spiral—that is my theory—as it may involve gradual development of various kinds, just as the life of humanity has been progressing through more refined religions, slow and gradually enwidening development of democracy and—last but not least—through the development of science in the last few centuries. Our past-life investigations are a part of science, that is finding answers by putting questions to nature by gathering and analysing data. All of this—development of science, democracy, and religion is pointing towards a very different future for humanity than we had a few thousand—nay a few hundred years go. This is a spiral development, not only a circular one, and I assume the same to be the case with development of individuals as with the development of humanity as a whole.

Let us go back to the circular/spiral model. We have data to support it—weak though this may look. We have cases of past-life memories that peak with lives,which ended a year or two before the person was born, and are from a life that ended abruptly. These are predominantly cases of quick return after violent death at an early age. I have sometimes wondered if these cases could be exceptions to the law of how reincarnation works—one might even ask if they might be abnormal in some way. Should that be correct, it could mean that there is generally a much longer time between lives. Memories of verifiable past lives with long intervals are rather rare exceptions. Could they primarily be found in a person of high spiritual development, like in the case of Duminda, which might still count as a relatively early reincarnation?

We have a few intermission memories, and then there is apparently in most cases a long time lapse until the person is fast approaching physical life again. Then we find—that has been gradually emerging—memories of being in the womb and of being borne.

What happens in the long time lapse I just mentioned? The physical body is very much a part of the image of ourselves. When that is shed we still have our feelings and memories—our ego. Could it be that during the normal reincarnation process there is also a shedding of most of this ego/individuality, with its memories, feelings, attitudes, etc? We would then live in pure consciousness, perhaps emerge with the great Oneness and experience unity with the core of existence. We can only speculate. After that a new descent begins.

Any hints to support this long time lap? In my chapter "Spontaneous Contact with the Departed" we find that most contacts are around the time of death; about half take place within a year, over eighty percent within ten years and, after that, exceedingly rarely. The same is true with contacts through mediums when they seem to be genuine contacts. If this is right, there follows the long time lapse—which should support my speculation about the reincarnation process—and then a new descent into physical existence.

INTRODUCTION
TO PART 2

E rlendur invited me to contribute to this book to broaden out and contextualize his important contributions to reincarnation studies. While he has been busy investigating reincarnation experiences, mediumship, apparitions, and other "paranormal" phenomena in Iceland, India, Sri Lanka, and Lebanon, I have been for the most part comfortably ensconced in my armchair. I have had time to read widely and think generally, to spot patterns in data from places around the world and reach the theoretical insights about past-life memory and reincarnation, which I will be sharing with you.

I am an anthropologist by training but am well acquainted with the data of psychical research. I teach an inter-disciplinary course called *Signs of Reincarnation* and my lectures will become part of a book of the same title. I mention the course and book because Chapter 20 is based on them and I cite my book (Matlock, in prep.) as a source of information in other chapters. As I write these words, the book is not yet ready to send to the publisher, but I expect it will be by the time you read this.

Along with Iris Giesler-Petersen, I manage a Facebook group also called *Signs of Reincarnation*. This group supports the interactions of researchers with the public and provides a forum for discussions about reincarnation. It also allows the public to bring their experiences to the attention of researchers. I have learned about several interesting cases through the group and will describe them later on, together with cases investigated by others and reported in the scholarly literature. My investigative methodology is different from the usual one though, and I would like to comment on it at this point.

The reincarnation case studies, which Erlendur and others have conducted are based on extensive fieldwork, but I have rarely had the time or resources to engage in that. I have followed the same principles of interviewing multiple first-hand witnesses and gathering photographs, medical records, and other documents, but I have carried this out for the most part through email, instant messaging, and Skype. I know that Erlendur has not always felt comfortable with this approach, but I have found no reason to question any of the things I report and I believe that my cases make significant contributions to the discussion of reincarnation and past-life memory.

I have come to believe that reincarnation is the only intellectually honest interpretation of the evidence that has been accumulated. In my view, the crucial questions now are what reincarnation means and how it works. I will be getting on to those issues, but I will first take us back to the beginning, with a history of the belief in reincarnation.

20

IN THE BEGINNING

There are many ideas about how the belief in reincarnation got started. Some authorities suppose that it was suggested by the changing seasons, the alternation of day and night, or other recurring cycles of nature. Others see it as a denial of death, a human reluctance to face up to mortality. Many have assumed that it began in India and spread from there to the rest of the world.

British anthropologist, Sir Edward Burnett Tylor (1832-1917), advanced a very different theory in his book *Primitive Culture* (Tylor, 1920), first published in 1871. Drawing on the reports of travelers, missionaries, and colonial administrators, he pointed out many commonalities in the beliefs and conduct of tribal peoples throughout the world. He attributed these commonalities to a concern with spirits and their interaction with the living, a perspective he termed "Animism."

Animism is all about spirits, many of them spirits of the dead. Tylor traced the animistic spirit concept to dreams and trances in which human figures appeared, as well as to what we now call out-of-body and near-death experiences and apparitions. He remarked on how commonly reincarnation beliefs appeared in tribal societies and identified an empirical source for them too, in announcing dreams, physical resemblances, and tell-tale behaviors. Tylor considered animism to be humanity's most primitive religion. Whether animism really qualifies as a religion is debatable and Tylor certainly was wrong to place it first in an evolutionary sequence that culminated in the Christianity of Victorian England. On the other hand, there is no question that he was right that people in small-scale, indigenous societies subscribe to an animistic way of thinking and that the animistic world view is grounded in observation and experience.

To give some examples: When Jesuit missionaries first went to live with the Huron Indians by Lake Ontario in the 1600s, they discovered that they believed that if a person bore a close resemblance to someone deceased, he was that person reborn, and they buried children along footpaths to facilitate the return of their spirits in the community. When Russian Orthodox priest, Ivan Veniaminov, was with the Tlingit Indians of Alaska in the early 1800s he found that they looked to announcing dreams and birthmarks to identify who a new-born had been before so that they could give it the same name. Many African peoples, also, use signs to identify children as returning ancestors and to bestow names. Similar beliefs and practices appear throughout Asia and the Pacific, including Australia. In Europe, one finds beliefs and signs of reincarnation in Scandinavia and among Celtic peoples of France and the British Isles.[2]

Memories of previous lives are rarely mentioned in the early accounts and it has taken until recent decades and the efforts of workers like Ian Stevenson and Antonia Mills to get well developed cases of reincarnation from tribal societies. There is no doubt about the widespread appearance of the beliefs and supporting signs, however, because they turn up in formal cross-cultural studies. These are studies conducted with large groups of societies with no known historical connections to one another. The more widespread a cultural feature is, the older it is presumed to be. Cross-cultural studies have found reincarnation beliefs in between a third and a half of tribal societies in their samples, from every inhabited continent and from different regions within each continent.-

Given the widespread distribution of the belief in reincarnation in tribal societies, it seems unlikely that the belief originated in India and diffused from there. It is more likely that the Indians picked it up from

---

[2] For references to the Huron see Thwaites (1897, pp. 273, 283) and for the Tlingit, Veniaminov (1840, p. 58). For other tribal beliefs and practices, see Matlock (1993), available online at http://jamesgmatlock.net/wp-content/uploads/2013/12/Reincarnation-Ideologies-and-Social-Correlates.pdf. Erlendur described Icelandic beliefs and cases in Chapters 4 and 5.

tribal peoples in their area. In fact, the earliest Indian religious texts, the Vedas, do not contain clear references to reincarnation, but it is prominent in the commentaries called the Upanishads, written after 600 BCE. This was about the time that the Hindus made contact with the Dravidian tribes of northern India and anthropologists have documented Dravidian reincarnation beliefs.

The Hindus did not simply adopt the belief in reincarnation from the Dravidians, though; they incorporated it into their religious system, adding the doctrine of karma. In the Vedas, karma has the meaning simply of "action," or more specifically ritual action, but in the Upanishads it takes on a moral coloring. Karma becomes linked to ethical behavior. Good and bad deeds in one life help shape the circumstances of later lives. This notion of karma is found also in Buddhism, Jainism, and Sikhism—other religions that began to develop in India around the same date.

Hinduism, Jainism, and Sikhism remained largely confined to India for a long time, but within two centuries Buddhist monks and adepts were moving out of that country, proselytizing and converting people to the north, south, and east. Buddhism reached what are now Sri Lanka, Myanmar (Burma), and Thailand in the 3rd century BCE. It is thought to have reached China in the 3rd century CE, but didn't reach Tibet and Japan until the 7th and 8th centuries. Buddhism also moved west, in the direction of Greece, but it didn't get that far. Already in antiquity there was a variety of religions around the eastern Mediterranean, each with its own idea of what happened after death and its own system of ethical justice.

The Greeks heard about reincarnation from Turkish tribal peoples and from the Egyptians around the same time that the Hindus were becoming acquainted with it, but in ancient Greece it is most closely associated with Pythagoras (ca. 570-495 BCE) and Plato (ca. 428-348 BCE). Pythagoras claimed to remember having lived before as the Trojan fighter Euphorbus and to have recognized his shield when he saw it lying in a temple. He founded a community where he encouraged the recall of previous lives through contemplation, but because he believed in oral teaching and left no writings, we have no details on his techniques. Plato did not remember previous lives but he had a theory that our present-life knowledge derives in part from things we learned in past lives and remember subconsciously.

Plato held that a thousand years passed between lives, during which time spirits did penance for their sins in Hades. In the so-called Myth of Er in *The Republic*, Er describes how spirits returning from Hades and others coming down from higher realms were allowed to choose their next lives from a set of possibilities presented to them, then were made to drink from the River of Forgetfulness (the Lethe) to wipe clean their memories before moving on to their new bodies. The idea that penances were paid before reincarnation appears in odes written by the poet Pindar as well, and is probably one reason the Greeks never adopted the karma doctrine. If one paid the price for one's wrongdoing before re-embodiment, one started each new life with a clean slate.

Reincarnation beliefs were quite common throughout the ancient world in the last centuries before Christ and the first centuries after. They are attested for the Jews as well as the Egyptians, although reincarnation vied with a belief in spiritual or bodily resurrection after death, and scholars disagree over which is meant in some circumstances. When the Jewish historian, Josephus, wrote in the 1st century CE that the Pharisees "say that all souls are incorruptible, but that the souls of good men only are removed into other bodies" (*The Wars of the Jews* II.8.14, trans. Whiston), he could have meant resurrection bodies rather than mortal ones.

There are other indications of reincarnation in Jewish teachings during the same period, though. The Hellenistic Jewish philosopher Philo wrote about reincarnation in the 1st century. Although he was influenced by Plato, it seems likely that he was also drawing on the Jewish traditions of his day. Reincarnation figures in the Bahir were first written down in 12th century France, but popularly attributed to the Rabbi Nehunya ben HaKanah, a Talmudic scholar of the 1st century. We find Jewish reincarnation beliefs in the 8th century Karaite movement, and then, from the Bahir on, in various Kabbalistic texts. Today reincarnation is important to the Ultra-Orthodox Hasidim, who esteem the Kabbalah.

It is very possible that the Pharisees and other Jews believed in reincarnation around the time of Christ. Other Middle Eastern groups, including those that developed into the Shia Islamic sects like the Druze, likely believed in reincarnation during that period also. Interestingly, the tenets of the Shia sects include some beliefs—that women do not reincarnate or, if they do, there can be no change of sex between lives; that reincarnation occurs immediately upon death, the soul passing at once into the body of a newborn child—that one also finds in the Kabbalah, but nowhere else. The similarities between the Jewish and Shia beliefs hint at some mutual influence but, if so, it must have been at an early date, because the authors of Kabbalist books such as the *Bahir* and *Zohar* resided in Europe, not the Middle East.

Karmic retribution is not a feature of either the Jewish or Shia systems, but neither is the concept of penance before rebirth. Instead, God decides where to send souls to be reborn and judges them at the end of time, on the basis of the deeds of all their lives together. There are differences between the faiths at this point, due partly to the Islamic influence on the Shia sects. Orthodox Islam does not countenance reincarnation, and neither does Christianity. These religions could have chosen to embrace reincarnation, going with either the Greek model of penance between lives or the Shia deferral of the Day of Judgment to the end of a series of lives, but instead they adopted the resurrection alternative.

Some people in the early Christian church, notably Origen and members of Gnostic sects, believed that the soul existed in a discarnate state before it came to be associated with a body at conception. Some of them taught that it was reborn after death. However, most of the early church fathers inveighed against pre-existence and reincarnation. Reincarnation was never formally declared anathema by the Church, although all overt references to it were excised by the time that the Bible was codified at the First Council of Nicaea in 325 and pre-existence was condemned along with Origen at the Second Council of Constantinople in 553.

After the Edict of Milan legalized Christian worship in the Roman Empire in 313, soldiers and settlers carried the faith into central and Western Europe, as far as the British Isles. With the spread of Christianity came the suppression of reincarnation beliefs in Europe. The rise of Islam in the 600s led to their suppression in the Middle East. Although studies like the Human Values Survey, which Erlendur described in Chapter 16, have shown that many people in Western countries believe in reincarnation today, even while identifying themselves as Christian, while most of their churches continue to oppose it. Sunni Islam and much of Shia Islam also steadfastly reject it. Where the belief has been retained, as among the heterodox Shia sects, or has resurged, as it has in Western countries in recent years, it is typically related to experiences with signs and cases that undermine the doctrinal positions.

21

FIVE EARLY MEMORIES

Pythagoras was not the only person in antiquity who believed he had lived before. Empedocles thought he had been a boy and a girl, a laurel bush, a bird, and a fish. Apollonius of Tyana remembered being a Mediterranean ship's pilot whose boat was boarded by pirates.[3] However, the first good examples of the sorts of reincarnation experiences we hear about today were 12 cases from first millennium China culled by De Groot (1901) from Chinese documents of that era. I summarize one of his accounts next, followed by later cases from India, Syria, Burma, and Japan.

Unnamed Girl (China)

De Groot (1901) relates the story of a man named Chang Khoh-khin who took up with a concubine while he was studying at the university. He treated her well, but she remained childless after a year, so his mother, who wanted a grandchild, made sacrifices to the God of Mount Hwa. The concubine became pregnant and in due course gave birth to a boy, Tsu-lin.

---

[3] Empedocles' memories are related by Diogenes Laertius in his *Lives and Opinions of Eminent Philosophers*, VIII.2.77. Apollonius's memories are described by Philostratus in Apollonius of Tyana, III.23-24.

Five years later, after taking his degree, Khoh-khin married a different woman. She too remained childless for the first year, so his mother again appealed to the God of Mount Hwa for assistance. Soon Khoh-khin's wife became pregnant, but Tsu-lin fell ill. Khoh-khin's mother once more prayed to the God of Mount Hwa. That night she dreamed of a man holding a document with gilt characters and a seal affixed to it. The man explained that it was he who had aided in the conception of Tsu-lin but, because Khoh-khin's wife now also was to bear a boy, Tsu-lin "had necessarily to become incomplete." Unfortunately, the man said, he was powerless to stop this from happening. He thanked Khoh-khin's mother for her sacrifices and vanished.

Tsu-lin died, but before his burial, his family made a red mark on his upper arm and black marks over his eyebrows. The following year Khoh-khin accepted a position in a different city. There he visited a house where he was approached by a young girl who curtsied before him. He was struck by how closely she resembled Tsu-lin and when he got home told his mother about it. She had the girl brought to them and she too was impressed by the similarities. She and Khoh-khin looked for the painted marks on the girl's arm and above her eyes and found them, exactly as they had been made on Tsu-lin.[4] For her part, the girl appeared to recognize Khoh-khin and his mother. She developed an intense affection for them and when her family sent for her, she refused to be parted from them.

Ramdas (India)

Similar features appear in a brief account of a case that came to the attention of Aurangzeb, a Mughal Emperor of India, at the end of the 17th century. It was written first in Persian, then retold in Urdu and translated from that language into English for Ian Stevenson.[5]

In 1699, Rawat Subharam, headman of the village of Bhakar, was overpowered and wounded in his back and at the base of an ear. Rawat died as a consequence, but a few months later his daughter gave birth

---

[4] These marks are examples of "experimental birthmarks," marks on a body near to or shortly after death with the purpose of stimulating a birthmark and thus tracking a spirit into its next incarnation.

[5] A copy of the Urdu and the translation are preserved along with related correspondence at the Division of Perceptual Studies of the University of Virginia Medical Center. I include this text in Matlock (in prep.)

to a son who had birthmarks in the same places as his fatal injuries. The boy was named Ramdas.

When Ramdas grew old enough to speak he said that he had been Rawat Subharam in his previous life. He said things about this man that were checked and found to be accurate. News about Ramdas spread until it came to the attention of Emperor Aurangzeb, who summoned the boy to his court and personally questioned him, satisfying himself that about the authenticity of the case.

Druze Boy (Syria)

In his *Researches into the Religions of Syria* the physician John Wortabet (1860) recounted a case he heard among the Syrian Druze. It involves a five year old boy from a mountain village who recalled having lived before as a rich man in Damascus.

The boy so insisted on visiting Damascus that his relatives took him there. Along the way he astonished them by his knowledge of the names of the places they passed. When they reached the city he led the way through the streets to what he said was his former home. He knocked, and called the woman who answered the door by name. She admitted the party and the boy identified himself as her husband reborn. He asked about their children, other relatives, and acquaintances. He told her things he remembered about his life with them, his property, and the debts he had left.

All was verified as correct, except for a small sum he said a certain weaver owed him. This man was summoned and acknowledged it to be true, but pleaded his poverty as an excuse for not having repaid the debt to the man's heirs. The boy then asked the man's widow whether she had found the money he had buried in the cellar. She had not, so he led the way to the place and dug it up. It was found to be exactly as he had described. The man's widow and children then gave the boy some of the money and accompanied him back to his home to meet the rest of his family.

Maung Gyi and Maung Nge (Burma)

In *The Soul of a People*, Harold Fielding Hall (1898) tells the story of twin boys, Maung Gyi and Maung Nge, who were identified as the reincarnations of a married couple, Maung San Nyein and Ma Gwin.

Maung San Nyein and Ma Gwin were born about 1848, on the same day in neighboring houses in the Burmese village of Okshitgon. They grew up playing together, fell in love, and married. They were devoted to each other and died on the same day in 1886, of the same disease.

This was at the beginning of the British occupation of Burma, which lasted from 1885 until 1948. There was unrest throughout the country and especially in the area around Okshitgon. Many residents fled to safer areas, among them a young couple and their newly born twins, Maung Gyi and Maung Nge. The twins grew up in the village of Kabyu. When they started talking they called themselves Maung San Nyein and Ma Gwin. Their parents recognized these as the names of the couple who had died in Okshitgon and they took them back there. Although they had never been to the town before, the twins were familiar with everything they saw.

They knew the roads and the houses and the people, and they recognized the clothes they used to wear in a former life; there was no doubt about it. One of them, the younger, remembered too, how she had borrowed two rupees from a woman, Ma Thet, unknown to her husband, and left the debt unpaid. Ma Thet was still living, and so they asked her, and she recollected that it was true she had lent the money long ago. (Fielding Hall, 1898, p. 340)

Fielding Hall met the boys when they were just over six years old. The elder, identified as the reincarnation of Maung Gyi, was a "chubby little fellow," but the younger twin was smaller. He had a "curious dreamy look in his face, more like a girl than a boy" (Fielding Hall, 1898, p. 340). The boys told Fielding Hall many things about their former lives, including what had happened between their deaths and rebirths. They had existed for some time without bodies, wandering in the air and hiding in trees, then after some months they were born again as twin brothers. Their memories of the past used to be clearer but had begun to fade, they said.

Katsugoro (Japan)

The case of Katsugoro is a classic reincarnation case from Japan. It was first presented in English by Lafcadio Hearn (Hearn, 1898).

Katsugoro recalled the life of a boy named Tozo, the son of Kyubei, a farmer in the village of Hodokubo, and his wife, Shidzu. Kyubei died at age 48 in 1809, when Tozo was five, and Shidzu re-married a man named Hanshiro. Tozo himself contracted smallpox and died a year later. He was buried in a graveyard on a hill overlooking the village.

Katsugoro was born in 1815, five years after Tozo's death, in Nakano, a village in the same district and province as Hodokubo, but ruled by a different feudal lord. His father, Genzo, was a farmer and basket-weaver. Katsugoro recalled being Tozo from an early age but did not say anything about his memories until he was eight, when he asked his elder sister Fusa where she had been before coming into their household. How could she know that, Fusa retorted. Surprised, Katsugoro told her that he remembered being Tozo, but asked her not to say anything about it to their parents. Fusa promised not to tell them but threatened to do so the next time Katsugoro did something he shouldn't.

From then on whenever there was a dispute between the children, Fusa would threaten to tell their parents, and Katsugoro would back down. Then one day their parents overheard Fusa's threat. They wanted to know what Katsugoro had done. Fusa told the story and Katsugoro added some additional details. He said that he used to be the son of Kyubei San of Hodokubo. His mother was named Shidzu. When he was five, his father had died, and a man named Hanshiro had taken his place. The next year, he said, he had died of smallpox, and three years later (actually, it had been five years) he was reborn to his present mother.

Katsugoro often slept with his grandmother, Tsuya, leaving his mother free to suckle a younger brother. One night Tsuya asked him what had happened after he died. He told her that he recalled that his body had been put in a jar (large earthenware jars were regularly used for burials during this period in Japan) and the jar buried on a hill. After that he returned to his house, where he met an elderly man who took him away. In his travels with this man he always was able to hear people talking at Tozo's house and was aware of rituals performed in his honor. The man led him to his present home and told him this is where he was to be reborn.

After recounting this to Tsuya, Katsugoro was less reticent with his parents. They in turn allowed Tsuya to take him to Hodokubo. When they reached there, Katsugoro led the way through the streets to Tozo's former home, where Tsuya was able to confirm the things he had been saying. Before they left Hodokubo, they visited Tozo's father's tomb, as Katsugoro wished to do.

It did not take long for word about Katsugoro to get around his village and beyond it. He came to be known as Hodokubo-Kozo, the Acolyte of Hodokubo, and people came to Nakano to visit him. On these occasions he would become shy and retire to an inner room of his house. He regarded himself as a spirit of the dead and asked that people be kind to him. Katsugoro's case became well known in Japan and there were two investigations of it after the one Hearn wrote about. In 2015 it was the subject of an exhibit in Tokyo marking the 200th anniversary of Katsugoro's birth. Katsugoro became a farmer and died in 1869 at age 55 (Kito, 2015).

What These Early Cases Tell Us

I think it remarkable how closely these cases resemble those that Erlendur and others have studied in recent years. It is easy to understand how events like these might have suggested the idea of reincarnation to begin with and helped maintain it over time.

The experimental birthmark in the Chinese case is particularly noteworthy. As we shall see, although many birthmarks result from death wounds, by no means do all. Experimental birthmarks are a good example of ones that have a non-violent source. Moreover, the practice of marking the body of a dying or recently deceased person in the hope of stimulating a birthmark upon reincarnation would have come from observations of the transfer of physical scars over many generations. De Groot (1901, p. 144) describes another case with an experimental birthmark. The custom is not confined to China but has been reported from throughout South Asia, so it may actually be quite ancient. Tucker and Keil (2013) provide an overview and describe several recent cases from Myanmar (Burma).

These old accounts have other features that figure in more recent investigated cases. One is what researchers since Stevenson have called "unfinished business." Ma Gwin had left a debt unpaid and the Druze boy wanted to tell his widow where he had hidden money. Katsugoro wanted to visit his father's grave. These things could have provided a motive for reincarnating or they could have helped the memory surface in a child's conscious awareness after rebirth.

Although the five cases described in this chapter all occurred before 1900, most did not become known to the English-speaking world until the end of the 19th century and it took several decades more for psychical researchers to take notice of them. The French Spiritist Gabriel Delanne (1924) produced one of the first compilations of Western past-life memories. Ralph Shirley (1936) and Arthur Osborn (1937) drew attention to British reincarnation experiences in the 1930s. R.B.S. Sunderlal (1924) and K.K.N. Sahay (1927) between them reported eleven Indian cases they investigated themselves. However, it was only after Ian Stevenson published his essay, "The Evidence for Survival from Claimed Memories of Former Incarnations," in the *Journal of the American Society for Psychical Research* in 1960, that systematic field research with reincarnation experiences began.

22

FOUR CASES FROM TRIBAL SOCIETIES

Anthropologists have reported birthmarks, announcing dreams and other reincarnation-related phenomena from many parts of the world since Tylor drew attention to them in *Primitive Culture*, but they have rarely taken them seriously enough to describe them at length, much less to investigate them in the style of psychical research. An exception is Antonia Mills, who has worked for years with Canadian native peoples. I describe one of her reincarnation cases in this chapter.

Ian Stevenson investigated cases in tribal societies in Alaska and British Columbia and in West Africa beginning in 1963, although he was less interested in them than in cases from Asia and the Middle East. His principal reports of tribal cases are in *Twenty Cases Suggestive of Reincarnation* (Stevenson, 1974a) and *Reincarnation and Biology* (Stevenson, 1997). Following Mills' case, I summarize three cases from the latter work.

Nathan

Mills (2010) introduced the story of Nathan in an article published in *Anthropology and Humanism*. My summary of the case includes additional details she supplied in response to queries from me. She plans a more extensive report for her forthcoming book, *That's MY Chair: Rebirth Experience of the Gitxsan and Witsuwit'en.*

Nathan is a member of the Gitxsan nation of British Columbia. As a boy, he recalled the life of his great-grandfather, Mark Peters, Sr., who had suffered a serious accident at a railroad loading site. The mishap was witnessed by his teenage son, Mark Peters, Jr., who later told Mills:

> I was there, working with him. He must have had 70—80 poles—big cedar poles that he was trying to load on the railroad car—something went wrong with the hitch or the way they were being lifted and he was up on top of the railway car. The logs dropped and he fell face down. They thought he'd died. There was blood coming out of his chest-puncture ... I don't know exactly what went into his chest, it broke through the skin and bruised his chest—cracked the rib cage a little. This was in 1955—56; I was 15 or 16. (Mills, 2010, pp. 177-178)

Mark Sr. was taken to a nearby hospital, where he recovered. He lived for many more years, eventually dying in his 80s, but the healed wound from the logging accident left a permanent scar on his chest. After his death, Mark Jr. had a dream in which his father's spirit appeared and told him, "I'll stay with you guys by Karen." This was taken to mean that he would be reborn in their family, to Mark Jr.'s daughter Karen, of whom he had been fond. In 2000, Karen gave birth to a boy she named Nathan. It was immediately noticed that he had a birthmark on his chest in the same place that Mark Sr. had had his scar.

Nathan himself was aware of the birthmark and would point to it even before he could crawl. When he first met Mills, at age four, he proudly displayed it to her. After Mills took a picture of him, he picked up her camera and snapped another photo. When Mark Jr. returned to the house a little later, Nathan told him, "I took a picture." Mills remarked that it was fantastic that he knew how to work a camera, to which Mark Jr. responded that he was "really gifted, that boy. He went to town and could spell 'café'" (Mills, 2010, p. 178). This was considered especially impressive because Mark Sr. had never gone to school and had been illiterate until he was taught to read and write by his wife.

Nathan demonstrated his giftedness—and his identification with his great-grandfather—in many other ways. He knew the old and best fishing sites and how to hang and salt fish. He knew proper berry-picking techniques. He was sad that Mark Sr.'s smokehouse had been neglected, and recognized Mark Sr.'s fishing boots there. When he saw a helicopter flying overhead, he said he had ridden in one, which was true of Mark Sr. Mark Sr. had liked Mark Jr.'s wife and, from the time Nathan was two, he would run up to her and say, "That's my favorite." On one occasion Nathan instructed Mark Jr. on how to respond to a bear attack. Mark Jr. recounted:

> "Ya'ah [grandfather]," he said, "You know how to do it when the bear runs after you?" and I said, "No." "Don't throw your pack away—if you fall down put it behind your head," he said, "the bear will eat the bag, not your neck. . . . But the best way," he says, "is don't run. You stay there. Make your eyes really big and jump around like a monkey." He was really demonstrating how he was going to do it. . . . Yeah, he was telling me how to survive a bear attack. "Don't run away, just stay there." . . ."I'm driving the car. I'm not going to walk," I'm telling him, but he said, "No, no, you got to know," he tells me. (Mills, 2010, p. 180)

"You remember the road was slippery and your tire was flattened? You went in the ditch," Nathan reminded Mark Jr. later that day, evoking an incident that had occurred the week before, when Mark Jr. had had to change a flat tire. Nathan was concerned lest his grandfather run into the same trouble again and a bear appear. He demonstrated the appropriate response to a bear attack to Mills as well.

Alan Gamble

The case of Alan Gamble comes from the Tsimshian, relatives and neighbors of the Gitxsan. Alan was recognized at birth as being the reincarnation of his father's adopted brother, Walter Wilson. Stevenson describes the case in the first volume of *Reincarnation and Biology*.

Walter Wilson died at 21 of complications from gangrene that set in after an accidental gunshot. He was fishing with his brother-in-law, Leonard Davidson. At one point their boat passed close enough to shore for Walter to see a mink running near the bank and he decided to try to take it. He grasped his shotgun by the barrel with his left hand but the gun slipped and discharged, shooting him through the palm and wrist.

Bone protruded through Walter's wound and he bled profusely. Leonard applied a tourniquet to his upper arm and started for the nearest hospital, which unfortunately was several hours away on the water. During the long journey, Walter lost consciousness and never regained it. By the time he reached the hospital, the tourniquet had been on his arm for ten hours, Leonard not having realized that it should have been loosened occasionally to permit blood to circulate. Gangrene developed below the place the tourniquet had been tied, necessitating the amputation of the lower third of Walter's arm. Unfortunately, the stump became infected, and he died on February 18, 1942, only a few days after admission to the hospital.

Alan was born about three years later, on February 5, 1945. Shortly before his birth, his father dreamed that Walter came to him and said that he was returning to the family. He also stated that he would have to go to the hospital once more before his arm was healed. Two birthmarks were noticed on Alan's left hand, one in the palm and the other on the back of the wrist, marking the places the gunshot had entered and exited. Shortly after birth Alan's left arm began to swell below his elbow, beginning at the site of the amputation of Walter's arm. The swelling travelled down to his hand and, true to the prediction of the announcing dream, he was admitted to the hospital.

Alan remained under treatment in the hospital for two weeks. From time to time after being released his left forearm became swollen again. The occasional swelling persisted into adulthood and once he had to leave work because of it. His mother thought she saw similarities in appearance and behavior between him and Walter. As a young child, Alan spoke often about Walter's life, especially when he happened to see shotgun shells or pictures of them. He would say that they were the cause of his having a sore hand. He also seemed afraid of the shells, so his parents hid those in his house from him. When he was six or seven years old, he described to Leonard Davidson how Walter had shot himself accidentally. He recognized at least one other of Walters' friends, correctly associating him with the girlfriend whom the friend had had during Walter's life.

Alan's memories faded as he grew older, yet when he visited fishing camps Walter had frequented, he felt a sense of familiarity with them. He told Stevenson in 1979, when he was 34, that his memories of these places were like memories of a dream one has awoken from, but he no longer had memories of incidents that had occurred at any of them.

Bruce Peck

Another of the many Canadian tribal groups whose reincarnation cases have been studied is the Haida, whose main territory lies on a group of islands off the coast of northern British Columbia. Stevenson reported the case of Bruce Peck, a Haida man who was identified as the reincarnation of his paternal grandfather on the basis of a birth defect, in the second volume of *Reincarnation and Biology*.

Richard Peck, the grandfather, was born on April 23, 1894. He was a fisherman, at which work he was successful but found hard and uncongenial. Many of the fishing lines then used off the coast of Alaska and British Columbia had to be let out and hauled in by hand, a task requiring great strength and endurance. Richard told many people that he wanted to be reborn without an arm or hand, so that he wouldn't have to work so hard in his next life. He died on April 12, 1949, shortly before his 55th birthday, of a heart-attack while fishing. He fell into the water but was pulled out half-drowned and died in the boat.

Richard's son's wife was two months' pregnant at the time of his death. Bruce Peck was born seven months later, missing the last two thirds of his right arm and his right hand. He was identified as Richard's reincarnation on the basis of this defect. He never spoke about memories of Richard but, in his early years, he showed a marked fear of water and of boats. He did not learn to swim until he was 22. When he finally tried fishing, he found that he liked it and wondered why he had not taken it up years before.

Bruce did not allow himself to be limited by having only one arm. He enjoyed playing sports with other boys and, as an adult, found jobs on land in clerical positions. Although he wore a prosthesis for two years in his teens he did not care for it, and when Stevenson met him as an adult he was not using one.

Ngozu Uduji

Ngozu Uduji is an Igbo born in 1969 or 1970 in Awgu, Anambra, Nigeria. Her left arm was severely defective, ending shortly past the elbow. Largely on this basis, confirmed by an oracle, she was identified as the reincarnation of her father's cousin, Ogbonna Iregbu. Stevenson describes this case in the second volume of *Reincarnation and Biology*.

Ogbonna Iregbu, the owner of a bicycle-repair shop, was killed in 1968 during the Nigerian Civil War, when the Igbo were trying to secede from Nigeria and establish their own state, Biafra. The Nigerian government bombed Igbo territory, including, on at least one occasion, the market in which Ogbonna had his shop. He suffered multiple injuries, the most serious being to his left arm, which was so badly damaged that the lower part was left dangling. It was removed before his body was buried.

Ngozu's father believed that her birth defect exactly matched what had happened to Ogbonna, although the girl gave little direct evidence of recalling his life. The most significant event occurred when she was about two years old. She told her paternal grandfather that she was Ogbonna and in order to test her he asked her where Ogbanna's tools were. She led him to a no-longer-used corner of an old house in the family's possession, showed him the tools, and handled them as if she were accustomed to doing so.

For the first two years of her life, Ngozu would run to her mother or hide in their house when she heard airplanes. She also had a phobia of guns, reacting to either the sight of sound of one. This phobia persisted until she was 12. As a young child, Ngozu gave her father the impression that she wanted to be treated like a man. She preferred to play with boys and acted boyishly up to about age four. Sometimes she urinated from a standing position. However, unlike some subjects of sex-change cases, she never tried to dress as a boy, and the masculine behavior gradually became less pronounced.

Common Features of Tribal Cases

Reincarnation experiences from tribal societies closely resemble other reincarnation experiences in important respects. Everywhere we see the same signs: the announcing dreams; distinguishing physical marks and behaviors; memories of having lived before; recognitions of people, places, and things from the previous life, and so on.

At the same time, there are some distinctive things about the cases of tribal societies. In tribal societies, physical marks are especially common, and are looked to in identifying a newborn with a deceased forebear. The congenital marks are not only birthmarks, but, as we see in the cases of Bruce Peck and Ngozu Uduji, may be birth defects also. Bruce Peck's deformed arm is especially interesting, because it appears to have resulted from his grandfather's desire to be born without a hand so that he would not have to work so hard the next time around.

There are fewer cases with conscious memories in tribal societies than in most of the Sri Lankan and Lebanese ones, which Erlendur wrote about in the first part of this book, and the interlocking network of signs is less pronounced overall. Announcing dreams with stated intentions to be reborn to certain women are common, and stated intentions to be reborn to particular women appear with some frequency.

Tribal societies also have an especially high proportion of cases within the same lineage or clan, if not the same nuclear or extended family. Return in the same family line allows a person to inherit and enjoy again the rights, privileges, and other tangible and intangible property he possessed before. It is therefore desired as well as expected. From the evidential point of view, family cases are not so good, however. When the families of the previous and present persons knew each other, a child naturally has more ways of learning about the earlier life by normal means, and this is the main reason that Stevenson stayed away from these cases. He preferred to study cases that demonstrated reincarnation more convincingly to a culture resistant to the idea.

23

TWO CASES FROM INDIA

Many reincarnation experiences have been reported from India since the case studied by Emperor Aurangzeb at the end of the 1600s. In fact, there are more published cases from India than from any other country. No doubt this has to do with the emphasis on research there but, for reasons we do not understand, Indian and other Asian cases tend to be much better developed than tribal (or for that matter, Western) cases. The first of my two examples was investigated by Antonia Mills in the 1980s. The second case has not been described before, although it was investigated in the 1970s and 1980s by Ian Stevenson and Satwant Pasricha.

Toran (Titu) Singh

Antonia Mills studied this case between 1987 and 1989 as part of the same project to "replicate" Stevenson's findings that brought Erlendur to reincarnation research. My summary follows her report (Mills, 1989).[6]

When he was young, Toran spoke about having been Suresh Verme, the son of a teacher in Agra, a city in the northern Indian state of Uttar

---

[6] This case is featured in two YouTube videos, https://www.youtube.com/ watch?v=1sxA2xHHStg and https://www.youtube.com/watch?v=Of2O-_aZR-g.

Pradesh. Suresh was the owner and proprietor of Suresh Radio, a vendor of transistor radios, in Agra's Sadar Bazaar District. He had a modern house and his wife wore handsome chiffon saris. He was active and intrepid and could be hot-tempered.

Alongside his legitimate business, Suresh was a player in the regional black market. These activities led to his abduction by eight *goonda* (hooligans, thugs) in 1975, when he was 22. The goonda got Suresh into their car but, before they were able to kill him, he kicked one and jumped through the window into the Yamuna River, swam across it, and escaped. Around 1981, his white Fiat was stolen, and then two other cars. He got his Fiat back, but, when he went to recover the other cars, the thieves shot at him. Undaunted, he leapt from the car he was driving and caught one of the gunmen by the neck before escaping again.

Finally, on August 28, 1983, when he was 30 years old, Suresh's luck ran out. Not far from his house, his car was stopped by three men, one of whom shot him in the right temple, wounding him fatally. He was declared dead at the Agra hospital. The post-mortem report, which Mills later saw, recorded the bullet as exiting his head "behind" his right ear. Suresh left a wife and two children, together with a large extended family. His four brothers and three sisters were all married and had families also residing in Agra. His murderers were never brought to justice.

Toran (nicknamed Titu) was the youngest of six children. His family was of the Vaishya caste, the same as Suresh's. Like Suresh's father, Titu's father was a teacher, although he also owned and farmed extensive agricultural land. The family lived in a single-story cement house in the village of Bad, 11.5 kilometers (7 miles) east of Agra. Although they were in the same socioeconomic bracket as Suresh's family, they lived more modestly, having a rural rather than an urban lifestyle.

Titu's mother had an uncomplicated pregnancy until the last trimester, but fell ill during the final three months. About a week before Titu's birth she checked into the Military Hospital in Agra, posing as the wife of a family friend who was in uniform and therefore eligible for treatment there. However, her stay and Titu's birth may not have been recorded in the hospital register. The only entry Mills could find with the names of the army man and Titu's mother places the birth on December 11, 1982, nine months before Suresh's death. This seems unlikely and, as Mills notes (1989, p. 157), it is possible that Titu's birth was not registered and that the December 11, 1982, date relates to a different child.[7]

Titu's parents were unsure of his date of birth. Birthdays have only recently become celebrated in India, under Western influence. Traditionally, records of births were not kept and they were often not remembered, unless a horoscope was constructed, but this was not done for Titu or his siblings. Titu's father told Mills that he thought Titu had been born on December 10, 1983, which would mean that he was born a little more than three months after Suresh's death instead of nine months before it.

Titu started to speak coherently at 18 months, earlier than his siblings. Shortly thereafter he said to his mother, "Tell my grandfather to look after my children and my wife. I am having my meals here and I am worried about them." "Who are you?" his mother asked. "I am from Agra. I don't know how I came here," he replied (Mills, 1989, p. 157). Titu began complaining about the size of his family's house and the quality of his mother's cotton saris. When he was expected to walk or travel on a bus, he would say he used to go by car and refused to go anywhere by foot or in a bus. Once, when he accompanied his family to a wedding in Agra, he announced that he had a shop in Sadar Bazaar, although they went nowhere near that district.

As he grew older, Titu cried almost daily, pleading to "go home." He resented his father going to Agra (where he lectured) without taking him. One day in April, 1987, when, according to his father's reckoning he would have been about three years and four months old, he was crying especially bitterly. A friend of his eldest brothers took Titu on his lap and Titu said to him, "My father doesn't take me [to Agra]. Can you take me there? I have a shop of transistor radios and I was a big smuggler and goonda. I am the owner of Suresh Radio" (Mills, 1989, p. 158).

Titu's brother and his friend did not take him to Agra but they did go themselves and sought out Suresh Radio. They found the shop in the Sadar Bazaar District, met Suresh's widow, and confirmed the basics of what Titu had been saying. When they left, the widow alerted Suresh's birth family and a few days later a party consisting

---

[7] The man who took Titu's mother to the hospital would be able to clear up this issue, but he was away from Agra during Mills' three visits to the area and she was never able to contact him (personal communication from Mills). It is not known if he is still living or where he resides at present.

of Suresh's widow, his parents, and three of his four brothers set out for Bad to meet Titu.

When he saw them approaching his house, Titu became very energized. He recognized Suresh's widow, his parents, and two of his three brothers. In the ensuing excitement he failed to acknowledge the third brother but he talked about many events in Suresh's life. He wanted to know why his children had not been brought to see him. He accurately described the layout of Suresh's house and its furnishings. When asked how Suresh had died, he correctly described the murder as it had been reconstructed and added additional details. As Suresh's relatives departed, he accompanied them to the road, and observed that they had not brought his car, which he noted was white in color. After they had gone, he threw his shoes at his mother, saying, "I am not yours. You are not my mother" (Mills, 1989, p. 158).

Later that morning one of Suresh's brothers returned with Suresh's two younger sisters, one of whom Titu called "sister." Asked which was his elder sister, he replied that neither was. In the afternoon of the same day, Titu was taken to Suresh's brother's radio and TV shop in Agra. Again he dispelled the attempt to mislead him, insisting that this was not his shop. At Suresh Radio, he commented on a newly constructed showcase. He identified a photograph of Suresh as himself and called the manager of the shop by name. Titu had a parallel set of reactions when taken to Suresh's father's house and then to what had been Suresh's own house in Agra.

When they first met him, Suresh's relatives noticed several apparent birthmarks on Titu's head. He had a small round birthmark on his right temple at the place the fatal bullet had struck Suresh, and three marks on the back of his head Suresh's widow thought represented sites where fragments of it had exited. Titu also had a mark on the top of his head that corresponded to a mark Suresh had had at birth and retained until his death. Apparently no one noticed that he also had a minor birth defect, a circular bony protrusion at the back of his right ear but, after Mills saw the post-mortem report on Suresh, she examined Titu and found it there. If this bony protrusion commemorates the bullet's exit wound, the three small marks on the back of Titu's head are unexplained.

These anomalies have an important bearing on the question of Titu's birth date. The possibility that he was born nine months before Suresh's death cannot be dismissed summarily because there are well-described cases of what may be termed replacement reincarnation[8] after birth. One

---

[8] "Replacement reincarnation" is my term. Stevenson referred to this phenomenon as "possession" or by the Hindi term parakaya pravesh, which

of these cases, that of Sumitra Singh, was studied by Stevenson (Stevenson, Pasricha, and MacLean-Rice, 1989) and later by Mills and Dr. Kuldip Kumar Dhiman (Mills and Dhiman, 2011). However, none have congenital marks or defects related to the person whose life is recalled by the subject of the case. When birthmarks and birth defects appear in replacement cases, they have no relation to the previous person (Mills, 2003, p. 86 n20; Stevenson, 1997, vol. 1, p. 1068).

Titu's birthmarks corresponding to Suresh are more consistent with a death during the gestation period than one coming nine months after birth. Perhaps we are looking at a prenatal rather than a postnatal replacement here, Suresh's spirit having forced another spirit out of Titu's fetus in a rush to get back to avenge himself for his murder. If so, the three unexplained birthmarks on the back of Titu's head might be related to the original reincarnating spirit. A prenatal replacement could also explain Titu's mother's illness in her last trimester, if her body reacted to the sudden change in her womb. This theory is conjectural but I think it fits the evidence of the case better than the theory of postnatal replacement reincarnation does.

Mills became involved in the case four months after Suresh's relatives met Titu, when he was still strongly identifying himself with Suresh. She observed how he behaved with Suresh's family and employees and how he acted in Suresh's shop. The intense identification was still apparent when she visited in September, 1987, and again in January, 1989. It extended beyond memories to encompass temperament, personality, and habitual behaviors. Titu was as active, intrepid, and hot-tempered as Suresh had been, and he had the same macho streak. He often gave the impression of being a man in charge. Once, when he visited Suresh's father and found that he was sick, he gave orders for a doctor to be fetched and medicine administered.

Toran has changed as he has grown up and has chosen a career path quite different from Suresh's. He studied yoga and in 2012 received his M.D. in Yoga and Naturopathy from Techno Global University in Shillong, Meghalaya. Since 2012 he has been an Assistant Professor at Banaras Hindu University in Varanasi, Uttar Pradesh.[9]

---

denotes the entry of a wandering spirit into a body. This phenomenon is similar to what is often called "walk-in." I cite and discuss several documented cases in Signs of Reincarnation (Matlock, in prep.).

9   I have taken these last details from Toran's curriculum vitae, which he kindly shared with me.

Mridula Sharma

I became acquainted with Mridula Sharma on Facebook in 2014. When she learned that I was a researcher, she asked if I knew why Ian Stevenson had never written about her case after the investigations he and Satwant Pasricha conducted in the 1970s and 1980s. I can only speculate about the answer. Stevenson did not issue detailed reports of many cases he investigated and he may have thought this one not worth probing thoroughly, for evidential reasons. It was already old by the time he and Pasricha began to work on it and Mridula's mother was acquainted with the woman whose life Mridula recalls. The case has interesting features, though, which makes it worth presenting here, even at this late date.

Besides Mridula's recollections, I draw on transcripts of Pasricha's interviews in 1975 and 1985. In addition, Kuldip Dhiman has shared with me his interviews with Mridula in 2013 and with Mr. Vinay Kumar Gupta in 2016.[10] Vinay Gupta is one of the previous person's cousins and the last surviving witness to Mridula's childhood experiences.

As a child, Mridula recalled the life of a woman named Medha (Munnu) Kishore, born in September or October, 1920, in Dehradun, the capital of the present north Indian state of Uttarakhand. Munnu's father was a landed aristocrat with inherited wealth and her mother had received a Vidylankar degree from the Kanya Gurukul girl's school and women's college in Hathras, Uttar Pradesh.[11] She had one sibling, a sister two years her junior.

In the 1930s and early 1940s, India was caught up in the struggle for independence from British rule. Munnu had little interest in politics but she was devoted to social work. She drove a car but dressed simply, as befitted an unmarried Hindu woman. After completing college, she entered a Master's program in Hindi at Banares Hindu University.

When she was 24, Munnu developed throat cancer and was forced to withdraw from the university. Munnu's mother recalled in 1975 that

---

[10] My thanks first of all to Mridula Sharma for answering my many questions. Satwant Pasricha gave permission to use her interviews and Jim Tucker sent me the materials from the DOPS files. I am indebted also to Kuldip Dhiman for sharing his interviews and for discussions about the case. Photo 11 is courtesy of Kuldip Dhiman.

[11] Kanya Gurukul programs are designed to educate girls and young women according to traditional methods and emphasize the study of the Vedas and other religious texts. The Vidylankar degree is attained at the end of the twelfth year, or the conclusion of secondary school.

as Munnu was dying, she said to her, "You are going away; you must come back." Munnu's illness was too advanced to allow her to speak, but she nodded in agreement. Her mother added, "Not just come back, but remember us as well." Mridula credits her recall of Munnu's life to this injunction from her mother. Munnu died in Dehradun on March 30, 1945, shortly before India achieved independence.[12]

Mridula was born four and a half years later, on September 6, 1949, in Nasik, Maharashtra, in west-central India, about 3,000 kilometers (2,000 miles) from Dehradun. Her father was a legal document expert, one of only three in India at the time. He practiced in Delhi but when he became terminally ill the family retired to Nasik, where Mridula's mother's family lived. Mridula's father died 40 days after her birth, at the age of 38. In keeping with Indian social practice, her mother never remarried, but was supported by her father, a businessman of means.

Mridula started to speak in a coherent way at 15 months and shortly thereafter began to say she wanted to go home to Dehradun, where she had a *kothi* (substantial house, mansion). Her mother recalled in 1985 that her first mention of the previous life came about when a visitor asked for something she did not have. Mridula heard her say this, and contradicted her. Her mother asked where this article was and Mridula said that it was at her house in Dehradun. She added that she had another mother as well as a father and sister there. Mridula's mother, a follower of Mahatma Gandhi, had studied at the Kanya Gurukul school in Dehradun. She had obtained a Shastri degree, awarded at the conclusion of seven years of study beyond the Vidylankar level. She realized later that she had seen Munnu in Dehradun, when she came to teach at the school. She left Dehradun in 1943, before Munnu's throat cancer was diagnosed. She did not know that Munnu had died and when Mridula started talking about her life had no reason to connect what Mridula was saying to her.

Mridula's mother told Pasricha in 1985 that she had gone back to Dehradun to attend the opening ceremony of her alma mater in July, 1951, taking the infant Mridula with her. They had seen Munnu's mother at that time but learned nothing about Munnu's death. This was before Mridula first spoke about the previous life, but coming into contact with places and people familiar to Munnu may have awoken something in her subconscious mind.

---

[12] India was granted independence on July 18, 1947.

Everything changed on July 1, 1952, when Mridula and her mother returned to Dehradun for the school's annual ceremony. Mridula was then two years and nine months old. She had been given two garlands, but when she spied two girls about her age she took the garlands off and placed them around their necks. The girls' mother saw her do this, and asked her if she knew her. Mridula replied yes, she was Chotu, using the nickname of Munnu's sister.

Then she saw a car arriving and screamed that it was hers. She announced that the woman who got out was her mother. Later, during the ceremony, she sat next to this woman, Munnu and Chotu's mother, placed her head on her lap, and stroked her sari. When asked who she was, she replied, "I am Munnu." She answered various questions about Munnu. She observed that Chotu's husband, whom Chotu had married after Munnu's death, "does not belong to our family."

Mridula was eager to return to her *kothi* (below) and after the ceremony it was decided that she would go home with Munnu's family. They stopped to pick up Munnu's father, whom Mridula recognized immediately from inside the car. At first she did not recognize the house because of alterations, but as they came closer to it, she realized that it indeed was the house she remembered. Once inside, she excitedly ran all over. She came to the room that had been Munnu's and asked that it be opened for her. She commented that a fan that previously had been in the drawing room was now there. She was tested with photographs from an album and recognized all she was shown, despite attempts to confuse her.

11. Munnu's family home in Dehradun.

In the wake of these developments, Mridula's grandfather decided it would be best if she and her mother stayed in Dehradun. He purchased a house for them there, permitting Mridula to maintain contact with Munnu's family. She visited them frequently, often staying over for a few days, until 1961, when Munnu's father died.

Vinay Gupta (Munnu's cousin) recalls an old wooden box that was locked. Mridula said that the key to it was in a certain book. The book was located and although no key was found in it, there was an impression from where it had been. The key was later discovered lying on the bookshelf and when tried on the box, opened it. Gupta also remembers being in the car with Munnu's father and Mridula when they met some friends of Munnu's father, whom Mridula recognized.

Thanks to her dramatic public recognition of Munnu's mother and sister, Mridula's case was well known in Dehradun. People would throng around her, call her a goddess, bow down and touch her feet, or place garlands around her neck, all of which she found very distressing. "I am not an exhibit (*tamasha*)!" she protested on one occasion, and Munnu's family set a day for people to come see her.[13]

Satwant Pasricha, who is from Dehradun, started working with Stevenson as a research assistant and interpreter in 1973. Mridula remembers meeting with her several times, in her home and that of friends. She met Stevenson once, in 1977, when he visited her to see if her birthmarks related to Munnu.

Mridula had read about birthmarks in reincarnation cases the year before and had mentioned them to Munnu's mother, who told her that a dimple on her shoulder noticed at birth matched one that Munnu had had. Mridula also has birthmarks in the places that Munnu wore earrings. The one on the left ear lobe is more prominent and Munnu's cousins teased her about it. When Mridula mentioned this birthmark to Stevenson in 1977, he took out a flashlight and examined the lobe of her right ear, where he discerned a similar mark.

Mridula's connection to Munnu's family did not end in 1961, when she stopped visiting their house. Munnu's mother came to her, sometimes

---

[13] This is an extreme example of the attention some Asian children with past-life memories receive. They are considered auspicious and merely being in their presence is thought to bring luck. When Rajiv Khanna, whose case is described by Dhiman (2002), was leaving the town of his past-life family after meeting them, so many people gathered at the railway station to see him that his train was delayed for over an hour (personal communication from Kuldip Dhiman). Katsugoro (Chapter 21) was the recipient of similar attention in Japan.

spending a few days. The two mothers became fast friends, due not only to their mutual connection to Mridula, but from their association with Kanya Gurukul and common beliefs, spirituality, and ideologies. The acceptance of Mridula as Munnu reborn extended to other members of both families and has lasted. Mridula's grandfather treated Munnu's mother like a daughter and sent her money, clothes, and other items when her husband died, following the custom of gifts to a daughter on a husband's death. Three of Munnu's cousins attended Mridula's son's wedding in 2013. In 2016, Mridula was invited to the wedding of one of Munnu's nephews.

Mridula spoke actively about Munnu until she was nine, and after that less frequently. Today she does not remember things from Munnu's life, but has retained clear memories of meeting with Munnu's family in July, 1952. She was educated at the Convent of Jesus and Mary High School in Dehradun and received a Master's degree in Political Science from the DAV (Dayanand Anglo-Vedic) College in Chandigarh in 1969. She married that year and has four children, the afore-mentioned son and three daughters. After her husband's death in 2008, she began to write and self-publish books. She has produced four so far and plans one telling the story of her life. She wants to publish another that was written by Munnu and is now in her possession. Mridula, Kuldip Dhiman, and I had some discussion on Facebook as to what to call a work written in one life and published in a later one, and decided to call it a work published reduxly.

Mridula continues to identify with Munnu, even without conscious memories of her life, but she recognizes that she has changed. When she was four, she told her mother that she was not going to live as simply as she did. She likes fine things and she feels that she is more materialistic than Munnu was. Mridula married and had children, whereas Munnu did not want to be married. Mridula received an M.A. in Political Science, whereas Munnu was studying Hindi when she died. Mridula attributes some of these differences to astrology, as many Indians do, as well as to differences in upbringing during different eras. Nevertheless, she believes that as Munnu she chose to come to her present mother, drawn by the spiritual commitment expressed by the dedication to Kanya Gurukul and the ideals of Mahatma Gandhi, and that the changes have been evolutionary ones.

24

TWO CASES FROM BRAZIL

B razil is predominately Catholic and may seem a surprising
place to find receptivity to reincarnation, but Brazilian popular culture is heavily influenced by the traditions of slaves
imported from West Africa and by the French Spiritism of Alan
Kardec. Unlike Anglo-American Spiritualism, which emphasizes
persistence in the afterlife, Spiritism allows for reincarnation after
a period of time.

Ian Stevenson studied two cases in one Brazilian family in the 1960s
and others were studied later by Hernani Andrade, an engineer who
turned to Spiritism at the close of his professional career. I summarize
one of Stevenson's cases below, followed by one of Andrade's.

Marta Lorenz

Ian Stevenson investigated this case initially in 1962, returning to
it in 1972. My summary follows his account in the second edition of
Twenty Cases Suggestive of Reincarnation (Stevenson, 1974a).

Maria Januaria de Oliveiro (known as Sinhá) was born about 1890
into the family of a well-to-do rancher in the southern Brazilian state
of Rio Grande do Sul. She had an older sister and younger brother, but
her family's property was somewhat isolated. It was 12 miles from the

village of Dom Feliciano and 100 miles from the state's largest city, its capital, Porto Alegre.

Although Sinhá liked the rural lifestyle, she suffered from loneliness and occasional depression. She went often to Dom Feliciano, where she had a good friend, Ida Lorenz, the wife of a school teacher. Ida had a large family and Sinhá enjoyed playing with her children. She was god-mother to one of them, a boy named Carlos.

Sinhá's father twice refused to allow her to marry men with whom she had fallen in love. The second of these suitors, a man named Florzinho, killed himself in response, and Sinhá decided to take her own life. During carnival in a coastal city she exhausted herself physically and made herself ill by going out into the cool, wet climate without adequate clothing. As a result, her larynx became infected and her voice got hoarse. The infection spread to her lungs and she contracted tuberculosis. She died some months later, in October, 1917, when she was about 28 years old.

Her friend Ida was with Sinhá the day before she died. Sinhá confessed to Ida that she had intentionally set out to become sick so as to end her life. She also told Ida that she would be reborn as her daughter and that when she was old enough to talk she would relate many things about her life as Sinhá so that her identity would be known.

Ida became pregnant soon thereafter and on August 14, 1918, gave birth to a daughter she named Marta. At some point in Marta's infancy an attempt was made to contact Sinhá through a medium. She responded, "Don't call me up. I have reincarnated!"[14]

When Marta was less than a year old she recognized Sinhá's father on a visit to her house. She went to him, caressed his beard, and said "Hello, papa." He gave no sign of welcoming her affections and she said nothing more about Sinhá until she was two and a half, when one day she asked an elder sister to carry her on her back. The sister declined, saying she could walk just fine by herself. Marta responded that when she had been big and her sister small, she had often carried her on her back, as had been true of Sinhá.

Marta went on to tell her family many things about Sinhá and life at the ranch. She said that she had been called Sinhá, Maria, and one other name she could not remember. She repeated Sinhá's dying declaration

---

[14] Stevenson does not mention this detail in *Twenty Cases*. It comes from a later book (Stevenson, 1980, p. 256). He does not say that the attempt was made by Sinhá's family, although that seems likely.

to Ida, mimicking the manner in which she had spoken. She recounted events that had transpired after Sinhá's death, including arrangements at her funeral, and the fact that two cows, which she had given to her godson Carlos, had borne calves.

Marta's father carefully compiled a list of all of her statements in a German shorthand that another member of the family threw away by mistake. At the time the list was lost, it included 120 items, an unusually large number. Many were about things known to Marta's family, but some were not. For instance, she noted that Sinhá had sat by her father at meals and she talked about her father's mistreatment of a servant boy.

Marta recognized several people whom Sinhá had known, including the first of her fiancés. Although she often asked to be taken to the ranch when she was young, she was not allowed to go until she was 12, when she was no longer talking much about her former life. However, while there she recognized a clock that Sinhá had owned and correctly stated that her name was inscribed on its back.

Marta was thought to resemble Sinhá physically and she suffered from upper respiratory problems, particularly in her early years, but lasting until Stevenson's second meeting with her in 1972. Her voice would become harsh and she frequently developed laryngitis, progressing to bronchitis. During these episodes she experienced herself as having a larger body and felt that she was going to die. There were similarities in personality also. Both Sinhá and Marta enjoyed dancing, liked cats, and were afraid of rain and of blood. Both possessed unusual psychic ability. Sinhá would know when Ida was about to visit and would set up a phonograph to play music for the occasion. Marta awoke one night from a dream about one of Sinhá's friends who, it turned out, had died at just that time, and she was aware of the title and subject of a book, which she was given as a present, without opening it.

Marta carried forward Sinhá's temperament and emotions. She was especially fond of Carlos and would get upset when she thought he was being mistreated. She was greatly affected by his death and that of her younger brother Paulo, who committed suicide when he was 44. She had to be hospitalized for three weeks following Paulo's death. She acknowledged to Stevenson that she had sometimes contemplated killing herself, although she had never reached the point of actually trying. She was convinced that her sweetheart Florzinho had returned as the first two of her sons, both of whom had died in infancy, largely on the basis of birthmarks on their heads that resembled one on Florzinho's head.

Marta was 44 when Stevenson met her in Porto Alegre in 1962 and 54 when he saw her in 1972. She had not had any further contact with Sinhá's family, whose ranch was far from where she lived and most of whom were deceased or dispersed in any event. She still spontaneously thought of Sinhá, however, especially at night when she was praying or going to sleep. She continued to suffer from bronchitis and she continued to be afraid of rain and of blood and to be fond of cats. She had outlived Sinhá and had been able to marry and raise a family, but she still experienced a continuity of identity with her. She judged their lives to have had about equal shares of pleasure and pain. Stevenson commented that the changes looked like changes along a stream of continuous development, something we have seen in other reincarnation cases.

Kilden Alexandre Waterloo

This is another case in which the previous person was known to the subject's mother and seemingly decided to return to her. Andrade wrote about it in *Renasceu por Amor* (2003), translated into English as *Reborn for Love* (2010b). He considered it to be the most important of the 75 cases he learned about.

In 1968, 44-year-old Salesian Father Jonathan, became the chaplain of the Catholic boarding school attended by Marine Waterloo, who would become Kilden's mother. Father Jonathan was from a poor family, unlike the popular chaplain he replaced. Many of the girls disliked him from the outset. Those from his home parish were especially opposed to him. Gradually it emerged that they knew he had been transferred from there for kissing a girl. He had been sent to a larger parish but suddenly was made to leave there as well, and now was at Marine's school.

Marine, then in her sophomore year, was undisturbed by the rumors. She struck up a friendship with Father Jonathan, but before it could progress to anything serious, her school stopped accepting boarders and she had to go elsewhere to finish high school. She and Alexandre (as she had come to call him, after Portuguese novelist Alexandre Herculano) exchanged letters for a while, but then lost contact. She last heard from him in July, 1970.

Marine married in February, 1971, and had her first child early in 1972. One day at the end of May, when she was alone in her house with the baby, preparing his bottle in the kitchen, she heard Father Jonathan's voice behind her. She turned quickly to see the string curtain that separated the kitchen from the living room moving as if someone had passed through it, but she did not see Father Jonathan or anyone else.

That night Marine dreamed that Father Jonathan was reaching out to her across a large lily pond. Her arm extended towards his, but their hands were far apart. She took a step in his direction, but her feet sank in the mud. His arms grew longer and he said, "Come on, it's better over here! Come with me, Marine! Everything out there is so sad . . ." (Andrade, 2010, p. 65). Then she woke up.

The next day Marine again heard Father Jonathan's voice and not long after that was told that the radio had reported that he had been in a car accident. He had died that morning in the hospital. The news hit her hard. She began praying for another contact with her friend. There were no more disembodied voices or dreams, though, and in time, she stopped thinking about him so much.

Marine became pregnant with her fourth child in the fall of 1979, more than seven years after Father Jonathan's death. During her pregnancy, she wanted to eat potato salad and salads with lettuce, tomato, and cucumbers. It didn't occur to her to connect the craving to Father Jonathan until she learned (much later) that it coincided with his food preferences.[15] Nevertheless, she gave her private name for him, Alexandre, to her new son as a middle name.

Kilden Alexandre was born on May 25, 1980. At 24 months he started to say his name was not Kilden, but Alexandre. Since Alexandre was his middle name, Marine did not make the association with Father Jonathan, and Kilden would get frustrated trying to explain the situation to her. Once he even said, "I'm not Kilden, you silly! I am the priest! I am Alexandre!" (Andrade, 2010, p. 74).

Early in 1983, after giving Kilden a bath, Marine playfully asked him where she had found him, and he said:

"You know! I was on a motorcycle. Then a truck came and hit the motorcycle. It fell over, and I hit my head on the ground, and I died, and went down there . . . and then you got another me!"

"When did this happen?" Marine asked.

---

[15] Pregnancy cravings matching the food preferences of the previous person figure in some reincarnation cases. Sometimes the foods are ones that the subject also likes after he is born.

"When I was a priest! My motorcycle fell over and I went down into the hole . . . and you got another me" (Andrade, 2010, p. 76).

Marine had always believed that Father Jonathan had died in a car accident, as the radio news had reported. If Kilden was indeed Father Jonathan reborn, why was he saying something different? Realizing the potential significance of his words, she immediately wrote them down, beginning her documentation of the case. She consulted a Spiritist center for advice and a month later started attending meetings there. Still, she resisted the idea of reincarnation, which was contrary to her Catholic upbringing. She had resumed praying for Father Jonathan to contact her, but when she noticed that her prayers coincided with anxiety attacks Kilden experienced in his sleep, she quit.

One day in 1985, Kilden saw a picture postcard fall to the floor and recognized the boarding school at which Father Jonathan had ministered to Marine. He pointed out the Priests' school in which he had lived as Father Jonathan and the Nuns' school where Marine had resided. Marine asked him what he had done there, and he said he had played soccer with the boys, something Father Jonathan had enjoyed doing.

Not long after this, Kilden's father brought home a record album by the popular Brazilian singer, Paulo Sérgio. Kilden was strongly affected by the first song on the album, Última Canção, which happened to be playing on the radio one of the last times Father Jonathan and Marine were together. When Marine asked him why he was crying, he told her again that he was Alexandre.

This was finally enough for Marine. She needed more information about Father Jonathan. She wrote to his last parish and was sent biographical information that included a description of how he had died. He had been riding his motorcycle when he had been struck by a truck. He had fallen on his head and had been hospitalized in a coma, dying the next day. Not only was Kilden right about Father Jonathan's accident, the disembodied voice Marine had heard coincided with the period he was in the coma.

Kilden stopped speaking as much about Father Jonathan when he was about five years old but, as he grew older, Marine noticed personality traits, behaviors, and interests the two had in common. Both were extroverted and both were pranksters. Father Jonathan had the habit of joking using rhyming words, and Kilden did the same thing. Father Jonathan had established many soccer teams, and Kilden was good at soccer. Kilden was much attached to Saint John Bosco, the founder of the Salesian order. When he was 11, he joined a church officiated by

Salesians so that he could become an altar boy, and enrolled in cate-
chism classes there.

In one area there was a marked difference; Father Jonathan had
taught many people to read and write, but Kilden had trouble learning
to read and did poorly in school. This was puzzling to Marine until she
realized that it might be a result of Father Jonathan's having fallen on
his head after the accident. His concussion might have transferred to
Kilden as a neurological disorder.

In 1990, when Kilden was 10 years old, the Spiritist center contacted
Andrade and put him in touch with Marine. She provided a long account of the case, reproduced in his book, and from then on sent him
notices of developments as they occurred.

When he was 12, Kilden recognized a fruit common in the areas
Father Jonathan had lived, but unknown where he himself had grown
up. He also recognized photographs of the school where he and Marine had met. He indicated a shortcut between the buildings that Father Jonathan had used, and reminded his mother about something she
had forgotten. He referred to a "cave" beside a certain tree. Although
there was no cave or grotto near the tree, there was a small enclosure
formed partly by roots that held an image of Saint John Bosco.

Also at 12, Kilden panicked at the sound of an ambulance, a reaction
that suggests awareness of Father Jonathan's experience while coma-
tose. Even more interesting and significant was Kilden's response the
following year to hearing about a man who had died after falling from
a ladder. Notice the shift in tense from present to past and perspective
from third to first person in the account that Marine sent to Andrade:

It is like this: "The person who suffered the accident arrives and is put
in a room full of instruments. The doctors connect them . . . . Then the
equipment is connected to the chest and the head, and the doctors
keep trying to save the life of the person. At this point the person flies
into a corner of the ceiling, watching the doctors' fight to save him.
Then a big hole like a funnel appeared in the corner of the wall near
me, trying to suck me . . ."

"Suck you, or the person who suffered the accident?" I asked him.

Very surprised, he said:

"Well, I think it was me. I saw my body and the doctors trying to save me."

"Anyway, what happened to the person who suffered the accident?" I asked.

"When he was sucked through the hole into the tunnel, he saw a strong light at the end, so strong that I turned my head to one side. The light was very bright, and the hole closed behind him, near the wall. At that moment the doctors saw the screen on their machine stop. Then all the machines stopped working."

"When did you dream all this?"

"I didn't dream it. I'm afraid of hurting my head . . . but we can see the doctors. . . Ah! When the hole was sucking the person in, the two most important doctors went over to the patient." (Andrade, 2010, pp. 130-131)

Kilden drew a picture of the hospital room and the scene he described. From Andrade's account it does not appear that the details of Father Jonathan's hospitalization were ever established and so the veridicality of Kilden's memories is not known with certainty, but they seem plausible. His experience is similar to what is described in many near-death experiences, but here it is from the point of view of someone who actually died.

25

TWO NORTH
AMERICAN CASES

Reincarnation experiences from around the world have very similar characteristics but some are more developed than others. Like cases from tribal societies, those from culturally Western societies tend to be weaker, often much weaker, than the average Asian ones, both in the strength of penetration of the past-life memories and in their evidential value. Western cases as strong as the best Asian ones do appear, but they are rare. In this chapter I summarize two North American cases. One is weak, the other strong. The first involves a man who reincarnated in his grandson; the second, a man who returned in a family to whom he had no known connection.

Craig Mitchell

Craig Mitchell is a high-functioning autistic boy whose personality and behavior are reminiscent of his mother's father, Michael Mitchell. Craig's autism is one of the noteworthy features of this case. Another is the relationship between his grandfather and his mother, Katherine. Michael sexually abused Katherine throughout her teenage years. His apparent reincarnation as her son has allowed for a forgiveness and reconciliation that was not possible to achieve before his death.

I investigated this case in 2015 and spoke about it at a conference in October of that year. My summary follows the expanded version of the presentation I subsequently made available on my web site (Matlock, 2015). All the personal names are pseudonyms; other details are unaltered.[16]

Michael Mitchell was born in 1923 into a devout Roman Catholic family in Lviv (Lwów), Poland, in an area that since World War II has been part of Ukraine. His father was employed in the Polish government service. His parents were cold and distant and his closest relationships were with the household servants. In 1939, when he was 16, Germany invaded Poland from the west. When the Soviets attacked from the east later that year, Michael's father was arrested, and Michael himself was confined in a Soviet concentration camp. He spent the next two years in the camp but was released to help fight the Germans after Hitler invaded the Soviet Union in 1941, breaking the non-aggression pact he had made with Stalin.

At the end of the war, when he was 22 or 23, Michael left Ukraine. He anglicized his name, met Katherine's mother, and married her. The marriage was increasingly unhappy, but the couple agreed to stay together until the last of their four children were grown. They had two sons and two daughters. Katherine was their youngest child. Michael sexually molested his elder daughter, although this did not become known in the family until some years later. She agreed not to say anything if he stayed away from Katherine, which he promised to do, although he had already begun molesting her at the time. The incest continued until Katherine was 19, in 1980, when he left the home and she finally felt strong enough to put a stop to it.

Katherine and Michael continued to meet occasionally for the next three years, but he never again pressured her for sex. When Michael's divorce was finalized in 1983, Katherine told her mother about what her father had done. This led to her siblings and others learning about

---

[16] I am indebted first of all to Katherine Mitchell for sharing her story with me so openly, and for collecting supporting documents at my request. Katherine also put me in touch with other witnesses—her former partner Gail Paterson; their friend Sarah Jones, who went to the trouble of tracking down the emails I cite; and Sister Mary Rose, who taught and observed Craig at an annual summer retreat for children with neurological disorders.

it, and Katherine's sister disclosed that she had been abused as well. As a result, Michael became estranged from all of his children, Katherine included. He tried to resume contact with her immediately following her mother's death in 1991, blaming her mother for their falling out, but she rebuffed him.

Katherine's mother had urged her to sue Michael for sexual assault in 1983, but she held off acting on the suggestion until 1992. She keenly wished for an apology from Michael, but did not want to ask for it outright, remembering the broken promise to her sister. Michael never openly acknowledged or apologized for his actions, but he settled the suit out of court for a five-figure sum, giving Katherine a sense of satisfaction.

Michael picked up smoking in the concentration camp and never quit. He died on May 11, 1997, of lung cancer, after a period of hospitalization. He was 74.

An engineer by trade, Michael was mechanically inclined and enjoyed building and doing things with his hands, although he was multi-talented and possessed considerable musical ability as well. He could pick up a tune by ear and create harmony in singing. He was a perfectionist, who worked at things until he was satisfied that he had them right. He did not like to leave tasks undone and would carry on until the job was complete. He had a knack for color-coordinating his wardrobe, and dressed well.

Katherine was in a same-sex relationship at the time of Michael's death. She and her partner Gail had decided to have children and had arranged to become impregnated by a man of their acquaintance. Gail had gone first and already had her son. Katherine received the settlement from the lawsuit against Michael on December 31, 1996, and used the funds as support during her pregnancy. She had intercourse twice during each of her monthly fertile periods. She became pregnant in February, 1997, but miscarried in March, skipped April, then became pregnant again in May. Because of a scheduling issue, only one attempt was made that month, on May 21, 1997, but it was successful. Craig was born on March 1, 1998.

Due to their estrangement Katherine was not notified when Michael died. She was not aware that he had passed only ten days before she conceived Craig. She learned about his death later from a family friend, while she was pregnant. The thought that her father might return as her child occurred to her as a "horrific" possibility, which she voiced to friends at the time. It continued to concern her after Craig's birth, and in January, 2001, she sought answers through precision muscle testing, a biofeedback procedure used to bypass conscious belief systems, thus helping to identify and clear traumas.

On the assumption that Katherine was subconsciously aware of whether or not Craig was Michael reincarnated, Gail took her through a series of questions that led to determining that it was true. Katherine was devastated. She emailed friends that she felt like Craig was no longer her child. The friends helped bring her to the view that Craig and her father were different people, even if Craig embodied something of her father, and a week later she was able to understand the situation as an opportunity for healing. Nonetheless, it continued to trouble her.

In November, 2001, when Craig was three years and eight months old, Gail decided to try to help relieve Katherine's persisting anger at Michael with shiatsu finger massage. Katherine reacted by releasing her emotions, as usual. Normally Craig avoided being with her as she was experiencing these crises, but on this occasion he settled beside her on the mat, Katherine related to friends in an email written no more than thirty minutes after the event.

Craig was looking at her more than usual and he started putting his hands on her, telling her over and over, "It's okay." Then he looked at her and said, "I'm sorry! I'm sorry! I'm sorry!" Astonished, Katherine asked Gail, "Do you think he means 'I'm sorry' for what I think he means?" Gail said yes, she thought so. "And [Craig] said, a little mushily as he usually speaks, but clear enough to understand, 'I never said so,'" Katherine wrote in her email.

That Craig was developmentally delayed became apparent by 30 months. He was officially diagnosed with "autism, mild" in September, 2001, when he was 42 months (three and a half years) old. His half-brother was diagnosed with "Pervasive Developmental Disorder Not Otherwise Specified," another condition on the autism spectrum. Their biological father sired a neurotypical child before Craig and his brother, but with two children by the same father on the spectrum, it seems likely that Craig's condition is hereditary and not specific to him.

Craig has never again said anything that suggests that he recalls having been Michael, but he has several character traits that remind Katherine of him. Craig is mechanically inclined and enjoys molding clay and working with his hands, as Michael did, yet he also is multi-talented and possesses strong musical abilities. He picks up tunes easily and knows the lyrics of his favorite songs. He is a perfectionist, as Michael was, and has the same tenacity. When he was young, Craig had trouble with fine motor skills, but his creative drive and his perfectionistic side mean that it is now one of his strengths, as it was for Michael. Craig reminds Katherine of her father too in his facility for color-coordinating his clothing, something in which Michael took pride.

Craig has shown an eagerness to attend church and has demonstrated an untaught knowledge of Catholic rituals, prayers, and songs. When he was eight, he began to spend two weeks each summer at a camp for children with neurological disorders. On Sundays, the children were asked if they would like to go to a Catholic Mass, and Craig would raise his hand immediately each time. Neither Katherine nor Gail took him to a church of any kind and he has no model for this activity in his family.

At the same time, there are aspects of Michael's personality that do not match Craig's, and vice versa. Craig is less distant and more demonstrative than Michael was. He is more extroverted than Michael and enjoys going out, to parties, to the theater, et cetera. These differences may be attributable to differences in the way he has been brought up. Katherine has made a point of being affectionate to Craig, correcting the way both she and Michael were raised. Other differences are more likely due to heredity. Craig is very gentle, like his biological father, but unlike Michael, who could be very rough. The traits stemming from his autism clearly have a genetic origin as well.

One difference is significant. Michael smoked heavily for decades and died of lung cancer. Craig has a dislike for smoking that is so intense that Katherine describes him as "rabid about it, like a reformed smoker." At 13, he would march up to strangers he saw smoking and tell them, "You shouldn't smoke!" When Katherine asked him why he said that, he explained, "Cause it's bad for them." "What's it going to do to them?" she pressed. "Kill them!" he replied. "How?" she wanted to know. "Burn them," he said, and then, "by giving them cancer." "He said it very definitely," Katherine told me.

Is Michael reincarnated in Craig? Katherine definitely believes that he is. Craig's apology during the shiatsu session is very meaningful to her and allowed her to work through her residual anger about what Michael took from her as she was growing up.

This case is weak evidentially but it has elements we see in stronger cases. Craig was three when he said he was sorry, the age at which most past-life memories surface for the first time. Craig's personality is in some ways like Michael's, he has some of Michael's skills, and he has evinced strong feelings regarding the cause of Michael's death.

Interestingly, however, there is no physical resemblance between Michael and Craig, something that is so common that its absence may be significant here.

If we regard this as a case of reincarnation, it is another that shows a strong motive on the part of the previous person for returning in the family he did. We see a man utterly obsessed with his daughter. Not only did he force himself on her repeatedly during her teen years, he blamed her mother for their eventual falling out and doubtless also for the lawsuit brought against him. He settled that lawsuit out of court shortly before his death and was reborn in a body conceived only ten days after he died. This case also is a nice example of how we change from life to life and how our differing relationships to each other allow us to work out emotional conflicts over successive lives.

Ryan Hammons

Most solved Western cases develop in the same family or among acquaintances. Ryan Hammons recalls having been a dancer, actor, and owner of a Hollywood talent agency who went by the name Marty Martyn, a man his parents had never heard of. Ryan's case is one of the most important Western—and more specifically, American—reincarnation cases to come to the attention of researchers, partly for that reason, but also owing to the extensiveness of Ryan's memories of Martyn's life. The case was studied by Jim Tucker and reported in *Return to Life* (Tucker, 2013). My summary follows Tucker's account, augmented by information supplied by Ryan's mother, Cyndi.[17]

Marty Martyn was born Morris Kolinsky in Philadelphia, Pennsylvania, on May 19, 1903.[18] His parents were Ukrainian Jews recently settled in the United States. He had two sisters, one of whom died young. He and his surviving sister went to New York in the 1920s to become dancers and he tap-danced on Broadway as Marty Kolinsky. He then moved to Los Angeles, where he took the name Marty Martyn and tried to make it in movies. He appeared in a non-speaking role in the

---

[17] I am grateful to Cyndi Hammons for answering my many questions about this case.

[18] These details come from Martyn's IMDb biography, posted online at http://www.imdb.com/name/nm0554421/bio?ref_=nm_ov_bio_sm, but not available when Tucker wrote his account.

1932 drama *Night After Night*, starring George Raft, but was unable to obtain other parts. His talent agency, the Marty Martyn Agency, was more successful, and he became wealthy later in life.

Politically, Martyn was a Republican. He was a flashy dresser. He was partial to Chinese food and went often to a Chinese restaurant in Beverly Hills. He had an extensive collection of sunglasses and enjoyed the beach, although he regularly suffered from sunburn. He was married four times. He had one biological daughter but also five stepchildren. He adopted the last three, all boys, when he married his fourth wife, but had a difficult relationship with them. The family lived in a large house with an outdoor swimming pool on Roxbury Drive in Beverly Hills. Martyn travelled to Europe on an ocean liner, the *Queen Mary*, and visited Paris more than once. He was stricken with leukemia and died in a Los Angeles hospital of a cerebral hemorrhage on December 25, 1964, at the age of 61.

Ryan was born in Muskogee, Oklahoma, in 2004. Due to recurring problems with his adenoids, which became enlarged and affected his ability to hear, he was slow to begin talking. He only started speaking in complete sentences when he was four years old, after his adenoids were removed, but then began to say he wanted to go home to Hollywood and pleaded with his mother to take him there so that he could see his "other family." His first comments about the other life concerned three adopted sons to whom he had given his name. He would tell stories about Hollywood at home and in kindergarten, where he would play at directing movies.

Ryan sometimes had nightmares and would wake up grabbing his chest, saying he couldn't breathe. He said he had died in Hollywood when his heart exploded.[19] One night, he described for his mother what it was like to die. He said that there is an awesome light that you should go towards, but that everyone came back to live again. He told his mother he had seen her from heaven. He had known her from a previous life and had chosen to be with her again, so that he could take care of her. He said that he remembered being in her womb and asked why she had wanted him to be a girl. He recalled that when she learned that the baby she was carrying would be a boy, she had cried

---

[19] It is not unusual for the subjects of reincarnation cases to make mistakes in recalling the circumstances of the previous person's death, as Ryan apparently did. Because Martyn's death was not witnessed, we don't know precisely what happened, though.

for a long time, a reaction Cyndi had soon regretted and had never mentioned in his presence.

Ryan spoke spontaneously about the previous life most often after his nightly bath, when he was preparing for bed, although he made many statements in response to things he saw or heard at other times of day. The peak of his memories and the greatest intensity of his identification with Martyn came at age four, well before Martyn was known to be the person he was referring to.

Ryan spoke a lot about working for an "agency" at which people changed their names. At times he behaved arrogantly, saying things like, "Do you know who I am? If you mess with me you won't ever work in this town again." He expressed disdain for Franklin Delano Roosevelt. He said he had a big house with a swimming pool located on a street that had "rock" in its name. He talked about travelling on ships, visiting Paris and seeing the Eiffel Tower. From a young age he was fascinated with sunglasses, and he remembered having gotten sunburnt many times. He recalled having been scratched badly by a cat; he hated cats and was afraid of them. He referred to China, Chinatown, and Chinese food, and when his parents took him to a Chinese restaurant, he proved adept at using chopsticks, without being taught how. He liked to dance and demonstrated tap dance routines.

Ryan recounted things about Martyn's birth family as well as his marital ones. He recalled that Martyn's mother had curly brown hair and said that he had two sisters, one three years younger than he was. He talked about dancing on Broadway, which Martyn had done as a young man. He spoke about having only one natural child, a daughter, from his last marriage, in addition to his adopted sons. He had worked so hard in that life that he had forgotten that love was the most important thing, he said. He had not spent enough time with his family, and that's why he had returned.

Wanting to help Ryan come to terms with his memories, Cyndi borrowed some books about Hollywood movies from her town's public library. In one of them they came across a still from *Night After Night* and Ryan recognized a man as himself, as well as another man he called George, and a third he said was a friend who was a cowboy and a star in cigarette commercials. George was George Raft. The cowboy was Gordon Nance (Wild Bill Elliot), who had made Westerns and was a spokesman for Viceroy cigarettes. Unfortunately, the name of the actor Ryan identified as himself was not given in the book, nor was it clear from the movie credits.

When Ryan was five, Cyndi started keeping a journal of what he said about his life in Hollywood. She wrote to Jim Tucker, who went to Oklahoma to interview Ryan and his family. Tucker also involved a television production company wanting to make a documentary on children with past-life memories, and this turned out to be key in solving the case. At first the production company hired a film crew that made an identification based on perceived facial resemblance. They flew Ryan to Los Angeles and drove him around. Ryan did not recognize houses owned by the actor they had in mind, but he did recognize the home of Wild Bill Elliot. The production company then hired a film archivist who determined that the actor Ryan had pointed to in the photograph was Marty Martyn. Ryan was already six by this time.

On a later trip to California Ryan met Martyn's daughter. She had been eight when Martyn died and was 57 then, so naturally she had changed much in the interim. Although he recognized her face, Ryan felt that her "energy" was different. He complained that she had not "waited" for him and he showed no interest in seeing her again. He regretted that he had not gotten to see one of Martyn's adopted sons, with whom he had hoped to make amends.

Ryan's story, *The UneXplained: A Life in the Movies,* premiered on the Biography Channel on April 20, 2011, by which time Ryan was moving away from his identification with Martyn. He told Cyndi, "Mommy, I just want to be me, not the old me" (Tucker, 2013, p. 107). Six months after the show aired, Cyndi walked into Ryan's room to find that he had taken down all of his wall decorations, including his pictures of New York and his iron Eiffel Tower.

Ryan talks much less about Martyn now, but his memories have not faded entirely. As of March, 2016, Cyndi's list of his statements contained some 230 different items, not all of which it has been possible to check. By Tucker's count, 55 (24%) are correct for Marty Martyn and 15 (6.5%) are incorrect, while the status of 140 (69.5%) remain undetermined (personal communication from Jim Tucker).

Cyndi reports that Ryan is in honor classes in school this year. He has a very mature vocabulary. He is a very social child and has always been able to make friends easily. He does well in leadership roles. The impact of Martyn on Ryan's personality persists, even though the memories are less prominent. At 11, Ryan loves music from the 1950s. He wants to return to New York, where Martyn lived in the 1920s, and visited thereafter. He is still fascinated with sunglasses and favors bow ties and button-up dress shirts. He follows politics and is aligned with the Republican Party. He wants to study Judaism, a source of friction in his Christian family. In one respect there has been a marked change from when he was younger: He is no longer afraid of cats. Although not a huge fan of the creatures, he now tolerates them without anxiety.

26

CULTURAL PATTERNS: BELIEFS AND EXPERIENCES

E rlendur and I have described reincarnation experiences from several different countries and periods of time. We have done this purposefully, partly to make it clear that past-life memory is a universal human phenomenon, but also so that you can see what these experiences have in common and where they diverge. In this chapter I examine the patterns more systematically. I begin with characteristics that are found in cases globally and then discuss some features that are culture-linked. I conclude with thoughts on how beliefs about reincarnation might affect the process of reincarnation, producing the variations that we see.

Universal Features of the Reincarnation Experience

Several elements of the reincarnation experience appear over and over, in cases from all parts of the world. These include birthmarks and distinctive behaviors that match a deceased person, phobias for things concerning that person's death, and memories of his or her life. Along with the memories come recognitions of people and places and emotional reactions to them. There may also be memories of the period between death and birth. Quite a few children describe choosing their parents.

Some people decide before they die where they want to be reborn. Some common case elements, like announcing dreams and pregnancy cravings, involve the child's mother or other adult rather than the child himself.

In addition to these and other basic elements there are universal features relating to the process of reincarnation or past-life memory. Everywhere, children who talk about previous lives begin to do so between two and five years. A few begin earlier, at around 18 months, or as soon as they start to speak coherently. After a while, children stop recounting their memories and, in most cases, they fade completely from conscious awareness by age eight. Thanks to the studies Erlendur described in Chapter 11, we know that many children retain some of their memories into adulthood, but fading is the norm for most children.

Curiously, more boys than girls talk about past lives. In 1986 Ian Stevenson reported that about two thirds of the subjects in his case collection were boys. There were more boys than girls in all the countries in which he had studied cases, except Sri Lanka, where about 51% of the case subjects were girls (Stevenson, 1986).[20]

Solved and Unsolved Cases

Cases vary a lot in how developed and how evidential they are, even when the previous persons are identified and the cases solved. Many reincarnation experiences are too vague to permit investigation, but not all those that are investigated lead to the identification of a previous person. Cases may remain unsolved for many reasons. Some may contain memory distortions or fantasy intrusions; others may refer to events and people in places that investigators cannot reach or lie further back in time than they are able to check. Erlendur and I are emphasizing solved cases in our reports and summaries but these solved cases should be considered in the context of all cases, solved and unsolved.

Interestingly, among cases that are well enough developed to be investigated, the percentage of cases that are solved varies from place to place. The figures in Table 26-1 come from a 1983 journal paper by Emily Williams Cook (now Kelly) and colleagues (Cook et al., 1983b), with the addition of Brazil.[21] As of 2013, there were a total of 2,500 cases in the main collection

---

[20] In Erlendur's Sri Lankan cases, investigated between 1988 and 2006, an even greater percentage (55%) of subjects were girls.

[21] Brazilian numbers are based on the research of Hernani Andrade and Ian

at the Division of Perceptual Studies, 68% or 1,700 of them solved (Mills and Tucker, 2013), but we have no breakdowns by culture for that data.

Although the numbers in Table 26-1 are out of date, the story they tell is unlikely to have changed appreciably. Notice that there is a far higher percentage of solved cases in Asian countries than in the United States and Brazil.

Table 26-1. Solved vs. Unsolved Cases in Seven Countries

Country	Percent Solved	Percent Unsolved	Number of Cases
Thailand[a]	92	8	38
Burma[a]	80	20	230
Lebanon[a]	79	21	51
India[a]	77	23	266
Sri Lanka[a]	32	68	117
United States (nontribal)[a]	20	80	79
Brazil[b]	9	91	78

[a] Cook et al. (1983b). [b] The Brazilian data include all of Andrade's cases, as confirmed by Suzuco Hashizume, plus three cases published by Stevenson (1974a, 1997).

Cultural Variation in the Incidence of Violent Death

Stevenson (2001) reported that violent death figured in 61% of the reincarnation cases he investigated, based on the data of Cook et al. (1983b), but this includes both solved and unsolved cases. In unsolved cases, the cause of death is not known for sure, so the counts are based on memory alone. The same study showed that violent deaths were recalled in unsolved cases more often than in solved cases to a statistically significant extent. When we look just at solved cases, where the cause of death is known for sure, we find that only 51% of the cases featured violent death.

Although the number of solved cases in Brazil is small I have included them in Table 26-2 to provide a comparison with other countries. As the table shows, there is cultural variation in the percentage of violent deaths. The highest proportion of violent deaths occurred in

Stevenson. I am a grateful to Suzuco Hashizume and Guy Lyon Playfair for assistance in compiling them.

Brazil (71%), Lebanon (69%) and Sri Lanka (54%). These were also the only countries in which violent deaths outnumbered natural deaths in the solved cases. Still, everywhere violent deaths are far more common in reincarnation cases than in the general population. Interestingly, as Erlendur pointed out in Chapters 16 and 17, violent deaths also figure in many veridical apparition and mediumship cases.

The greater number of boys with past-life memories is sometimes thought to be associated with the tendency of the remembered lives to conclude in violence, but the figures in Table 26-2 belie that inference. More girls than boys recall previous lives in Sri Lanka, which has one of the highest incidences of violent death in reincarnation cases.

Table 26-2. Violent vs. Natural Death in
the Solved Cases of Seven Countries

Country	Percentage of Violent Deaths	Percentage of Natural Deaths	Number of Cases
Brazil[a]	71	29	7
Lebanon[b]	69	31	94
Sri Lanka[b]	54	46	35
India[b]	49	51	193
Burma[b]	45	55	168
United States (nontribal)[b]	43	57	14
Thailand[b]	41	59	32
[a] Includes all solved cases published by Andrade (1988, 2010) and Stevenson (1974a, 1997). [b] Cook et al. (1983b).			

Relationship Status

The relationship between the previous person and the subject's family is strongly culture-linked. The relationship may be classified in one of three ways: as a family connection, as an acquaintance connection, or as no connection. Where there is no connection, the subject's family is completely unknown to the previous person. We call these "stranger cases." Acquaintance includes chance encounters as well as close friendships. Family connections cover any sort of traceable genetic relationship, including extended families and, in tribal societies, lineages or descent groups. Family or "same-family" returns are not necessarily in the same nuclear family, although they may be.

Table 26-3 shows the relationship status for solved reincarnation cases in 12 countries or ethnic groups, ordered by percentage of family cases. Data on relationship are available from more places than data on solved and unsolved cases and violent and natural death, but they are almost as old. The last systematic reporting from Stevenson's collection was in 1986 (Stevenson, 1986). The Gitxsan data are from 1994 (Mills, 1994). Although the number of solved cases in Brazil is small, I have included them in order to provide a comparison with other countries. The figures for the United States are based on those reported by Stevenson in 1983 (Stevenson, 1983), with the addition of cases described by Jim Tucker, in *Return to Life*, and me, in this book.

Table 26-3 Percentages of Family, Acquaintance and
Stranger Cases in 12 Countries or Ethnic Groups

Country or Ethnic Group	Percentage of Family Cases	Percentage of Acquaintance Cases	Percentage of Stranger Cases	Number of Cases
India[a]	16	41	43	183
Sri Lanka[a]	19	29	52	31
Lebanon[a]	24	46	30	80
Turkey[a]	29	54	17	63
Burma (Myanmar)[a]	54	31	15	154
Brazil[b]	58	28	14	7
Thailand[a]	69	9	22	32
U. S. (nontribal)[c]	70	9	21	23
Haida[a]	87	13	0	23
Igbo[a]	92	6	2	53
Tlingit[a]	96	4	0	67
Gitxsan[d]	100	0	0	67

[a] Stevenson (1986). [b] Includes all cases of Andrade and all published cases from Stevenson.
[c] Stevenson (1986) + more recent cases from Tucker (2013) and present book. [d] Mills (1994).

Intermission Length

Table 26-4 shows the median intermission length for cases of the same 12 countries or ethnic groups, ordered by length of time, from shortest to longest. With the exception of the Gitxsan and Brazil, the figures come from Stevenson (1986).[22] The number of cases for individual societies differ from Table 26-3 due to variations in the data available.

Some of the shortest intermissions are found in Lebanon and Turkey. The Druze religion holds that reincarnation occurs immediately upon death and directly into a child being born. Although the cases do not match that ideal, they come closer to it than cases from most other places. Cases from Buddhist societies (Sri Lanka, Thailand and Burma) all have intermissions longer than nine months, in accord with the Buddhist belief that reincarnation occurs at conception. Intermissions in Western societies (the United States and Brazil) are among the longest, perhaps because many Westerners expect to be around to meet their loved ones when they die. Westerners generally do not expect to be reborn and, if they do, many imagine that it will be a long time before they come back.

Table 26-4: Median Intermission Length in
12 Countries or Ethnic Groups

Country or Ethnic Group	Median Intermission Length (in months)	Number of Cases
Haida[a]	4	17
Lebanon[a]	8	79
Turkey[a]	8.5	64
India[a]	12	170
Gitxsan[b]	16	22
Sri Lanka[a]	16	35
Thailand[a]	18	33
Burma (Myanmar)[a]	21	125

[22] Without the original figures, it is impossible to adjust the median intermission length to accommodate more recent cases. For the six solved American cases that have been investigated and reported in print since 1986 (by Tucker, 2013, and me, in this book), the median is 420 months (35 years).

Tlingit[a]	24	41
Igbo[a]	34	35
Brazil[c]	69	7
U. S. (nontribal)[a]	141	25

[a] Stevenson (1986). [b] Mills (1994). [c] Includes all of Andrade's cases, and all cases published by Stevenson.

Sex Change

Ideas about whether it is possible to change sex between lives vary. The Druze and Alevi and some other people deny that it is possible but other cultures allow for it. So what do the cases tell us? Again, the cases conform to cultural precepts.

The percentage of sex-change cases in our 12 countries or ethnic groups is shown in Table 26-5. The data come from Stevenson (1986), with the addition of the Gitxsan and Brazil.

No sex-change cases have been reported from Lebanon and Turkey. Like the Druze and Alevi, the Tlingit Indians with whom Stevenson worked thought that one could not change sex between lives, and he found no sex-change cases among them. The Haida, neighbors of the Tlingit, allow for sex changes, but have no reported sex-change cases. In other places, the possibility of changing sex is not denied, and cases occur. In Burma, about a third of Stevenson's cases involve a change of sex between lives.

Table 26-5: Percentage of Sex-Change Cases
in 12 Countries or Ethnic Groups

Country or Ethnic Group	Percentage of Sex-Change Cases	Number of Cases
Lebanon[a]	0	77
Turkey[a]	0	133
Haida[a]	0	24
Tlingit[a]	0	65
Gitxsan[b]	1	67
India[a]	3	261

Sri Lanka[a]	10	114
Thailand[a]	13	32
United States (nontribal)[a]	15	60
Igbo[a]	18	56
Brazil[c]	28	7
Burma (Myanmar)[a]	33	154

[a] Stevenson (1986). [b] Mills (1994). [c] Includes all published cases from Stevenson and Andrade.

Belief and Experience

For some critics, correlations between beliefs about reincarnation and experiences of reincarnation prove that the experiences are products of the beliefs. According to this way of thinking, parents shape their children's behavior or selectively remember things in line with their prior conceptions. This position is hard to sustain when the previous person was unknown to the family, yet the child is correct about what he remembers, as in solved stranger cases like many of Erlendur's and Stevenson's.

Another possibility is that cases with features contrary to the beliefs never come to the attention of investigators, so the statistics give a misleading picture of what actually happens. Indeed, investigators have heard of cases that were dismissed by witnesses or interpreters simply because they had characteristics they believed impossible. However, one must wonder whether all anomalous cases could have been suppressed in the countries where there has been a concentrated research effort over several decades.

Where does this leave us? If cases of reincarnation conform to beliefs about reincarnation, why is that? I believe the answer is that the ideas we hold in life continue with us into death and help to determine what we do next. In Asian societies, karma is thought to dictate the circumstances under which one reincarnates, and for the Druze and Alevi it is God who makes the determination. Personal responsibility is downplayed in these belief systems and general religious tenets take over. By contrast, in animistic tribal societies like the Gitxsan, Haida, Tlingit, and Igbo, the decision is believed to lie with the individual, and we see many more family cases in those societies. Not only that, in matrilineal societies like the Gitxsan, Haida, and Tlingit, the reincarnation is on the mother's side, but in patrilineal societies like the Igbo, it is on the father's side (Stevenson, 1986).

In the next chapters, I supply other evidence of personal control over the reincarnation process. In Chapter 32 I deal with the issue of why that control is not always apparent, as in the majority of stranger cases.

27

REINCARNATION ACROSS BORDERS: INTERNATIONAL CASES

I n children's reincarnation cases, the place of death usually is not far from the place of rebirth. Longer distances appear in larger countries like the United States and India. Marty Martyn died in Los Angeles but Ryan Hammons was born in Muskogee, Oklahoma, about 1,500 miles away along Interstate 40. Munnu died in Dehradun, Uttarakhand, but Mridula was born in Nasik, Maharashtra, 2,000 miles away on the other side of India. Cases of reincarnation across international borders are less common, and not many are solved. In Chapter 6, Erlendur wrote about Wael Kiwan, who killed himself in Los Angeles and was reborn in Lebanon. Below I briefly describe other "international cases" that have been solved and discuss what they have to teach us.

Fourteen Solved International Cases

The Druze believe that Druze are always reborn as Druze, not necessarily in the Druze communities of Lebanon, Syria, and Israel, but somewhere in the world. In two cases, Druze who died in the United States were reborn in Lebanon. One is Wael Kiwan (Chapter 6); the other is Suzanne Ghanem, who recalled being a woman who died during cardiac surgery in Richmond, Virginia. Stevenson mentions Suzanne in *Children Who Remember Previous Lives,* but her case is treated at greater length in *Old Souls,* a book by *Washington Post* journalist Tom Shroder. Shroder met Suzanne when he accompanied Stevenson on a research trip to Lebanon in 1997.

Warriors killed overseas may return to their native countries. We see this with James Leininger, who recalled having died when his fighter plane was downed off Iwo Jima during World War II. James told his parents he found them when they were vacationing in Hawaii and gave accurate details of the hotel at which they had stayed there (Leininger and Leininger, with Gross, 2008; Tucker, 2013). Another example of a fallen fighter returning home is Adnan Kelleçi, a Turkish boy who remembered being a Turkish soldier killed in Korea during the Korean War (Stevenson, 2001).

Sometimes there is a familial or acquaintance link between the previous person and the subject's family. Yvonne Ehrlich, born in Brazil in 1953, was identified as the reincarnation of her maternal grandmother's sister, who had been killed in Austria during Allied bombing in 1944 (Stevenson, 1997). Yvonne was born two weeks after her due date, on her grandmother's sister's birthday. She had birthmarks on her head in the same places that the woman had been injured in the fatal explosion. She behaved like her and had a phobia of airplanes. Only once did she say anything that suggested memories of her life, but that was to tell her grandmother that she was her sister.

A Burmese girl, Ma Win Myint, never said anything about a previous life, yet a dream her mother had while pregnant along with her appearance and behavior linked her to Paul Taylor, an English friend of her mother who had spent much of his life in Burma (Stevenson, 1997). Paul had been a pipe smoker and had developed cancer of the tongue. He had returned to England for treatment and had died there. He had a ruddy complexion, freckles, a patch of white hair, and was color blind. Before he died, his throat become sore and his neck thickened. Ma Win had an unusual ruddy complexion, freckles, a patch of white hair, and was color blind. She often suffered from sore throats and her neck was unusually thick, although it became more normal as she entered her teens.

Jenny Cockell, born in England, remembers events from several lives and has been able to trace the person she was before in the two most recent. She remembers in greatest detail the life of Mary Sutton, an Irish woman (Cockell, 1993). Mary was reborn as an English boy, Charles S., who died after being run over by a truck (Cockell, 2008). The international link is between Mary and Charles. Cockell refrained for years from contacting Charles's family, but finally got in touch with his surviving brother and learned that their grandfather was born in Ireland to an Irish family.[23] We do not know of an association between Mary and Charles's grandfather, but the Irish connection is suggestive.

Tibetan Buddhist lamas figure as previous persons in several international cases. The present Dalai Lama was discovered in China, born into a house his predecessor, who died in Tibet, had seen and admired (Wangdu, Gould, and Richardson, 2000). British journalist, Vicky Mackenzie, tracked down the reincarnations of Buddhist monks who were reborn in Western countries, with the intention of spreading their faith to the West. Osel Hita Torres was recognized as the reincarnation of an esteemed leader, Lama Yeshe, who had died when his heart gave out on a visit to California in March, 1984, at age 49. Osel was born in February, 1985, in a Spanish Buddhist retreat familiar to Lama Yeshe. He was taken to India and in March, 1987, when he was not quite three, was enthroned in Lama Yeshe's place (Mackenzie, 1988).

In her book *Reborn in the West: The Reincarnation Masters*, Mackenzie (1996) describes similar cases. One is a Canadian boy named Elija Ary, born to a Protestant Christian mother and Jewish father who ran a Buddhist center in Vancouver before moving to Montreal. From birth Elija was unusually serene, quiet, and observant, but also outgoing and engaged with people. After hearing a Buddhist lecturer at his parents' center when he was three, he started talking about a past life in Tibet. He spoke about it for the next four years. When he was seven the Dalai Lama recognized him as the return of Geshe Jatse, a Tibetan sage who had died while meditating in his cave 30 years before, and gave him the name Tenzin Sherab. Much of what Tenzin had said when he was younger turned out to fit Geshe Jatse.

Two other cases reported by Mackenzie are less well developed but no less compelling. Trinley Tulku was born in 1975 to a French father and American mother who were followers of Tibetan Buddhism. As a small child he was eager to visit Buddhist monasteries and liked

---

[23] Cockell noted this in my Signs of Reincarnation Facebook group on May 8, 2016, and supplied further information in a personal communication. She is writing a book about Charles's life, now in preparation.

dressing in monks' robes. Trinley was ordained at age three, spent seven years traveling with a lama, and at 10 started formal training at a monastery in France. Trinley was identified as the reincarnation of Khashap Rinpoche, who had died in India of tuberculosis. He recalled that Khashap had wanted to be reborn in the West, but apparently nothing else about his life.

Another French boy, Pierre, remembered having been a woman named Zina Rachevsky, a cousin of his father's grandmother. Zina grew up in California but became interested in Buddhism and travelled to India to seek guidance there. She was the first Western woman to become a Buddhist nun. At 42 she fell ill, from either food poisoning or cholera, and died while meditating in a Himalayan cave.

The well-known case of Barbro Karlén is a solved international case, if we accept that she was Anne Frank, as she claims (Karlén, 2000). It differs from the cases described above, though, not only in involving a famous person, but in there being no apparent reason for Anne to be reborn in Sweden or into Barbro's family. We see the same lack of connection between the past and present lives in another Holocaust narrative, the powerful story of Yael Shahar, a Texas-born woman who recalls being a Greek Jew transported to Auschwitz-Birkenau in Poland, where he was killed in 1944 (ben Malka and Shahar, 2015). With these cases we may wonder whether the desire to get out of Nazi-controlled Europe was the reason for going elsewhere for the next life.

What the Patterns Tell Us

With only 14 cases, we cannot draw firm conclusions, and yet the patterns are striking. In Chapter 26 we saw that the connection between past and present lives may be classified in terms of family, acquaintance, and stranger relationships. When we focus on international cases, we find that the situation is more complicated.

Reincarnating internationally does not seem to come about by accident, but rather to be the result of a deliberate act. These 14 cases reveal several motives for being reborn abroad, summarized in Table 27-1. In the Dalai Lama's case, his predecessor chose to go to a familiar house that he liked. In the cases of Yvonne Ehrlich, Ma Win Myint, Pierre, and Jenny Cockell, it was to join a family, friend, or compatriot. In the cases of Wael Kiwan, Suzanne Ghanem, James Leininger, and Adnan Kelleçi, the motive was to return from overseas to one's native country. In the cases of Osel Hita Torres, Tenzin Sherab (Elija Ary), and Trinley Tulku, it was to spread the word about Buddhism. In the cases of Barbro Karlén and Yael Shahar it seems to have been to escape an intolerable situation.

Table 27-1: Motives for Reincarnating Abroad in
14 Solved International Cases

Motive for Reincarnation Abroad	Number of Cases
Go to family, friend, compatriot	5
Return to homeland	4
Spread the word	3
Leave homeland	2
No known motive	0

The majority of unsolved international cases lack the information required to determine the presence or absence of motive, but there are suggestions of a motive in some of them. Two unsolved Brazilian international cases have past lives set in Europe (Andrade, 1988; Playfair, 2006). Like Yvonne Ehrich's grandmother's sister, the previous persons could have followed the (embodied) migration stream to Brazil. Also, a large number of Holocaust memories have been reported from the United States and parts of Europe outside the area in which the Nazi atrocities took place (Gershom, 1992, 1996), consistent with fleeing that part of Europe we see suggested in the cases of Barbro Karlén and Yael Shahar.

There are relatively few international cases, solved or unsolved, in our dataset, however. Most reincarnations take place within the same country, generally within the same region. In a great many of Stevenson's cases, rebirth occurred within 25 kilometers (15.5 miles) of the place of death. What the solved international cases seem to be telling us is that we need to have a specific reason to reincarnate beyond that radius and outside our native countries and comfort zones. I will return to this topic in Chapter 32, but meanwhile I want to draw attention to another issue: the impact on reincarnation of the nature of death.

Typically in reincarnation research, deaths are classified as either natural or violent, but these international cases should make us wonder whether that is the correct contrast. The data presented in Table 27-2 suggests a different way of thinking about death: Deaths that are expected and may be prepared for mentally, versus deaths that are sudden and unexpected.

The category of natural death includes illness as well as the body wearing out in old age. The category of violent death includes accidents, murders, suicides, executions, and deaths in wartime. When we look at the causes of death in our 14 solved international cases, we find eight of them were natural, whereas six were violent. There is nothing interesting there. However, if we subdivide our categories and examine the data more closely, we see something quite different.

Table 27-2: Cause and Nature of Death in 14 Solved International Cases

Cause of Death	Nature of Death	Number of Cases
Natural-Age	Expected	1
Natural-Illness	Expected	6
Natural-Unknown	Expected	1
Violent-War	Expected	5
Violent-Suicide	Expected	1
Violent-Accident	Unexpected	0
Violent-Murder	Unexpected	0

Only one case involved a natural death in old age (the Dalai Lama). In six cases, the previous person died of some sort of illness, usually a protracted one (Susanne Ghanem, Ma Ma Myint, Osel Hita Torres, Pierre, Jenny Cockell). In the case of Tenzin Sherab (Elija Ary), the death was natural, but the exact cause is unclear. Of our five violent death cases, four occurred during wars, when death would not have been unexpected (James Leininger, Adnan Kelleçi, Yvonne Ehrlich, Barbro Karlén, Yael Shahar). In the sixth violent death case, Wael Kiwan intentionally took his own life. There are no examples of accidents or murders among these solved international cases.

Accidents and murder are more likely to produce a sudden, unexpected death, leaving a person unprepared for what comes next. That, I think, is the key to this finding. It is as if the impact on the psyche of a sudden, unexpected death reduces the control it has to determine its fate. These 14 cases suggest that it is not only a desire to go abroad that is important in reincarnating internationally, but that the psyche must retain sufficient mastery of itself to pull it off.

28

SPEAKING IN FOREIGN TONGUES: XENOGLOSSY

S urprisingly, some children who remember having lived before use languages they have not been taught or even come into contact with in their present lives. The use of language unlearned in the present life is called xenoglossy. The ability to interact in an unlearned language is known as "responsive xenoglossy." The use of an unlearned language in a rote, uncomprehending way is "recitative xenoglossy." The unconscious impact of an unlearned language on speech, reading, or writing is "passive xenoglossy."

Xenoglossy is common in international cases. Xenoglossy also appears in cases in which the previous and present persons are from different regions of the same country or when they are of different ethnicities or language groups. In this chapter I give examples of the three types of xenoglossy in children's reincarnation cases.

Responsive Xenoglossy

I must start by acknowledging that because researchers have not yet been able to study a child while he or she was actively speaking an unlearned foreign language, we cannot say how proficient they are in using it. Nevertheless, reports of this kind are frequent in cases where there are language differences between lives and there can be no doubt that xenoglossy is a real phenomenon.

A Thai boy named Bongkuch Promsin remembered being a Laotian youth who had been murdered at 18, eight years before he was born. Laos borders Thailand to the north and west and there are many Laotians living in Thailand. Bongkuch spoke about being a member of one of those expatriate families, so this is not an international case, although it is an inter-ethnic one. Bongkuch behaved in many ways out of keeping with his family. He ate with his hands rather than with a spoon and washed his hands by immersion in a bowl rather than running water over them, following the custom of the previous life. He spoke Thai with a Laotian accent and referred to certain fruits and vegetables with words his mother didn't use and came to find out were Laotian. Most significantly, he was able to converse in Laotian with his past-life family and friends (Stevenson, 1983).

We see something similar in the case of Tutkhorn Chitpricha, another Thai boy. Tutkhorn identified himself as the reincarnation of his father's elder brother, who had owned a company that supplied construction vehicles. He had died in an automobile accident the year before Tutkhorn was born. Tutkhorn's family lived in Bangkok but his uncle was from a distant part of Thailand, where a different dialect was spoken. When he was between 18 and 27 months old, Tutkhorn recognized two drivers who had been his uncle's employees. He called them by their nicknames and spoke to them in their dialect, using a linguistic form appropriate for a man addressing an inferior. He understood them when they spoke to him and replied appropriately, although his vocabulary was limited (Keil, 1991).

Another child who spoke a language unintelligible to her parents is Nawal Daw, a Lebanese Druze girl who refused to learn Arabic and babbled away in a strange language for her first five years. She was drawn to Indian music and favored Indian styles of dress. Once, when she was four, she saw some Sikh tourists from India, ran to them, and carried on a conversation with them in their language. Stevenson investigated this case when Nawal was nine, by which time she was speaking Arabic and gave no sign of understanding either Hindi or Punjabi (Stevenson, 1974b).

There are many other reports of xenoglossy in unsolved inter-ethnic and international cases but, without speakers of the foreign languages around them, the children have no one to interact with and their responsive command of the language cannot be demonstrated. The identity of the language is not always confirmed, although it may be inferred. Several Burmese children who recalled being Japanese soldiers killed in Burma during World War II spoke in a language that presumably was Japanese. Like Nawal, they were slow to learn the language of their parents, but gradually adopted it (Stevenson and Keil, 2005).

Recitative Xenoglossy

Two of the three Sri Lankan boys who remembered being Buddhist monks (described by Erlendur in Chapter 3) employed recitative xenoglossy. Duminda Ratnayake and Gamage Ruvan Tharanga Perera behaved in many ways like the monks they said they had been and both recited religious stanzas in Pali, the extinct Buddhist ritual language that in Sri Lanka is used only by monks. Duminda recited the stanzas holding a fan in front of his face, as monks do. In addition to stanzas, Ruvan recited part of the Buddha's first sermon. Unlike children who speak languages responsively, Duminda and Ruvan did not demonstrate a capability for conversing in Pali. In their previous lives, they would not have spoken it either, apart from the stanzas and other passages they had memorized.

A recitative xenoglossy was displayed also by Tomo, a Japanese child who recalled having lived in Scotland in a previous life. Tomo was not yet three when he heard the song "Top of the World" for the first time and surprised his mother by singing along to it (Ohkado, 2013). An Indian girl, Swarnlata Mishra, sang songs and performed dances she said she had learned in a previous life in Bengal, in an area that this now part of Bangladesh. The Bengali life fell between her present life and an Indian life she also recalled. The Indian life was confirmed but the Bengali life was not, although Swarnlata described the environment accurately and sang the songs well enough for them to be transcribed and identified as traditional Bengali folk tunes (Stevenson, 1974a).

Passive Xenoglossy

For people reborn into families that speak the same language as they did before, the past acquaintance with the language can help to master it again. Children with past-life memories sometimes start speaking earlier than their siblings and peers. They may even start speaking with an adult vocabulary and syntax. The processes that allow for this rapid acquisition of one's native language no doubt underlie xenoglossy, too; with xenoglossy, they just relate to a language to which one has had no exposure in one's present life.

Passive xenoglossy manifests in many ways. It may be expressed as a resistance to learning the language of one's parents, as it was for Naw-al Daw and the Japanese soldiers reborn in Burma, or it may help with learning the previous language later in life. Two of the international cases summarized in Chapter 27 illustrate this. Trinley Tulku was fortunate to have a Tibetan nanny and by 18 months was already speaking Tibetan. Tenzin Sherab (Elija Ary) became proficient in Tibetan very quickly once he reached a group that spoke it, when he was in his teens (Mackenzie, 1996).

Passive xenoglossy may be reflected in accents, like Bongkuch Promsin's Laotian-accented Thai, and it may show up in reading and writing as well as speaking. An Indian boy, Bishen Chand Kapoor, recalled having been a man who had learned Urdu. Bishen Chand used some Urdu words and as a young child was able to read that language without being taught it (Stevenson, 1975). Tomo learned to read Latin letters before Japanese characters and wrote his name in Latin letters for the first time when he was about 34 months old (Ohkado, 2013).

Passive xenoglossy is a central feature of an American case I learned about through my Facebook group in October, 2015. This is an international case with a past life in Mexico. It is unsolved, but it comes close to being solved, because the death recalled was during an historic event, the siege of the Alamo in February and March, 1836. The subject, Stephen Stein, was born in March, 1984, meaning that there is an intermission here of 148 years. There is no known connection between the past and present lives.

A New Case with Passive Xenoglossy: Stephen Stein

Stephen (Steve) was born in Philadelphia, Pennsylvania. He is the oldest of three brothers. Shortly before she became pregnant with him, his mother, Patricia, dreamed about a boy. At the time she knew nothing about reincarnation or announcing dreams but accepted this dream as a sign she would bear a son. After becoming pregnant she was determined to name the baby Stephen, even though this was not a name she and her husband had been considering before that.[24]

When he was born, Steve resembled the child Patricia had dreamed about (Photo 12). He looked distinctly different from his younger brothers in infancy and those differences are still apparent in adulthood (Photo 13). Patricia noticed a small round mark on the lobe of Steve's left ear at birth, at the spot an earring would have been worn. The birthmark has now faded somewhat, but is still visible.

12. Steve two hours after birth

13. Steve (far left) and his brothers in 2015

[24] My information for this case comes from Patricia Stein and Steve Stein. Photo 12 is used with the permission of Patricia and Steve and Photo 13 with the permission of Steve and his younger brothers.

During her pregnancy with Steve, Patricia craved hot, spicy food, especially traditional Mexican dishes. She had not eaten these foods before the pregnancy and did not like them very much, yet she felt she must have them. After she gave birth, the craving went away. Since neither she nor her husband liked hot foods, they did not serve them at home. Steve had no opportunity to sample them, even after he began to eat "adult" foods, but when he was three, it turned out that he loved them. The discovery came about by chance.

Patricia and her sister were in the habit of going out to restaurants in the evening when Patricia's husband worked late, and they took Steve along on these occasions. One night they went to a Mexican restaurant they had not patronized before. Patricia recalls not being happy with the choice, but since it was close to her sister's house, she agreed to go. Steve clearly relished the food and thereafter the family took him to Mexican restaurants on birthdays and other special occasions.

A fondness for Mexican food was not the only thing Steve revealed on that occasion. The group was seated at a table in the back of the restaurant, where a framed map of Mexico decorated the wall. It was yellowish in color, made to look old. Steve was standing, absorbed in the map, while his mother and aunt were chatting in the booth. When their waitress came up he pointed to a town in north-central Mexico, read the name, and announced that that is where he was from.

The waitress, a Spanish major in college, was impressed with his accent. She wanted to know whether Patricia was teaching him Spanish, but she was not. She had studied German and her sister French. Patricia told her husband about this curious incident, but thought little of it. Steve had been precocious in learning to read, excelled at word games, and was fascinated with maps, but up until then had not shown an affinity for the Spanish language or Mexico.

The next incident came shortly after the restaurant visit, when Steve was still three. He and Patricia were watching a TV documentary about Davy Crockett, who died at the Alamo. For Patricia, it recalled a Disney production starring Fess Parker she had watched as a child but Steve was much more engaged with the Alamo compound, the surrounding area, and the Mexicans, than with the beleaguered Texians. He got up and moved close to the television set. He drew his finger around the screen and described what it had "really" been like at the time. He told Patricia, "I had boots, gold buttons, and I fell down," pointing to a spot in front of the compound.

Patricia later researched the Alamo siege and found that what Steve had told her was true. Unfortunately, though, she didn't write this down, and does not now remember the details. She has not yet identified the man Steve was talking about but, if we can locate a list of Mexican casualties, it may be possible to do so. Only about 70 Mexicans lost their lives in the campaign. From Steve's early interest in maps and his ability to find and read the name of the town on the map in the restaurant, we may infer that the soldier was well educated. Perhaps he was an officer. Steve's birthmark suggests that he wore an earring. Steve remembers dying outside the compound. These clues may be enough to single out a specific individual, if we can find the records we need.

Steve said nothing more about the Mexican soldier and has had no other memories of his life that he recalls. Now in his 30s, he continues to like Mexican food. He has a strong interest in Mexican music, particularly classic ranchera and corridos norteños. Although he has never studied Spanish, he appears to those around him to have an inborn sense of the language. When Patricia decided to try to learn it recently, he stood by her shoulder and corrected her pronunciation as she muddled through. His girlfriend, a flight attendant who speaks some Spanish, has been impressed by the words he knows. Steve acknowledges that he sometimes is able to decipher the meaning of words by recognizing Latin or Greek roots or picking up on contextual or emotional cues. "But once in a while it just 'comes to me,'" he says.

There are obvious problems with this case from the researcher's point of view. Even if we are able to solve it, without contemporary records of what Steve said and did when he was three, we have only his mother's memory to go on. Patricia's sister is now deceased and the restaurant with the map is no longer in business. Steve's subliminal acquaintance with Spanish seems real enough, but it is has never been assessed by a native Spanish speaker. I gave some thought to arranging to have this done but realized that it would have little value at this late date. Steve has had too much exposure to Spanish over the years for tests to have much meaning now. We will have to wait for other children with similar capabilities to appear, but meanwhile Steve's experience shows the impact that passive xenoglossy and unconsciously-felt past-life memories can have on our lives.

Steve's case comes close to being a solved international case with no known connection between the past and present lives. Notably, however, the death was during a military skirmish, and may therefore be counted as expected. Moreover, we don't know the meaning of the name "Stephen" that impressed itself on Patricia's mind during her pregnancy. Had her subconscious mind recognized Steve as someone she knew in the past? Is there a link to a previous life they shared together? We will likely never know.

29

THE EFFECTS OF SELF-KILLING: SUICIDE CASES

At the conclusion of Chapter 27, I commented on the need to look beyond the labels "natural death" and "violent death" to ask whether a death was expected or unexpected. When a death is expected, the psyche has time to prepare for it. That preparation may confer a degree of control that is not available when death comes suddenly and unexpectedly.

In this chapter, I look at suicide cases. Ending one's life is a deliberate act and death is expected. Wael Kiwan (Chapter 8) and Marta Lorenz (Chapter 24) remembered being people who killed themselves. Rabih Assaf acted out of frustration in not being able to return to his people in Lebanon, where Wael was born. Sinhá made herself fatally ill and Marta was born the daughter of the friend Sinhá had pledged to return to. The previous person's will is key in both of these cases. Do we see the same in other suicide cases?

There are other questions too. How do suicide cases compare with other reincarnation cases in their main features? Does it make a difference whether the self-killing was accidental or intentional? Does it make a difference if it was done to avoid having to deal with the effects of a failing body, or to escape money problems, or conflicts stemming from the feeling of being in a body of the wrong sex, or simply a deep depression? Is the time before reincarnation after suicide longer or shorter than with other types of death? What is the effect on the next life of committing suicide? There are many ideas about the spiritual consequences of suicide and how this might impact the reincarnation process, but what do the cases tell us?

Nine Suicide Cases

A Turkish boy, Cemil Fahrici, recalled the life of a bandit who had shot himself rather than allowing himself to be taken captive (Stevenson, 1997). He was about 23 at the time. Cemil was born within two days of the bandit's death, into the family of one of his distant relatives. Cemil had two birthmarks, one under his chin and the other on the top of his head, in the places the bullet had entered and exited. He had a strong phobia of blood and experienced headaches whenever he saw blood. He showed no tendency toward banditry, though, and as an adult started a bakery and went into business for himself.

When he was three years old, Faruq Andary, another Turkish boy, began recalling the life of a hot-tempered and impetuous youth who had killed himself at 16 by ingesting insect poison following an argument with his mother over his missing cigarette lighter (Stevenson, 1980). Faruq was born four weeks later into the family of relatives. As a child he also had a temper and was afraid of poisons. He expressed a strong but ambivalent desire to return to the previous family.

Navalkishore Yadev of India was identified as the reincarnation of his father's second cousin on the basis of his stated intention to be reborn into the family, announcing dreams, and a birthmark on the back of his neck (Stevenson, 1997). In the previous life he had hung himself at 17 to avoid an arranged marriage to a woman he did not like, one or two months before his birth. Navalkishore's birthmark matched the place the knot on the noose had rested. He had not yet spoken about the previous life at two years, when Stevenson investigated this case.

Rajani Singh, also of India, was recognized by birthmarks as being the reincarnation of her father's cousin, Mithilesh (Pasricha, 2008). Mithilesh had been staying with Rajani's family while she prepared for a high school exam. She got involved with a boy her family did not approve, became depressed, poured kerosene on her head, and set herself on fire. She was rushed to the hospital, but died there, at age 16. Rajani's mother was pregnant at the time and Rajani was born about five weeks later. She had red marks all over her body, but especially on her head. As she grew older, she was observed to behave in many ways like Mithilesh.

Wael Kiwan (Chapter 8) was four years old when he began talking about the previous life and recognized a photograph of Rabih Assaf as himself. Rabih had been 24 when he hung himself. He was unhappy with his life in Los Angeles and saw no other way out. Wael was born in Lebanon about eight weeks later, into a Druze family to whom Rabih had no connection.

Marta Lorenz (Chapter 24) was about two and a half when she started talking about her memories of having been Sinhá, who had gotten herself infected with tuberculosis at 28, after her father had forbidden her to marry for the second time (Stevenson, 1974a). Marta was born 10 months after Sinhá's death into the family of Sinhá's best friend, as she had promised to do. Marta was very susceptible to upper respiratory infections and when she caught a cold, her voice would become hoarse or she would contract laryngitis—things Sinhá had to endure before her death.

In Chapter 9, Erlendur summarized the German case of Rolf Wolf, reported by Dieter Hassler (2013). Rolf recalled the life of a young man who apparently set out to kill himself, first by driving his car off the road and then running onto an autobahn high-speed highway. Rolf's mother stopped to help him and he died her in her arms. He then negotiated his return as her child in a series of dreams. Rolf was born about 17 months after the young man was killed.

Paulo Lorenz was one of Marta's brothers (Stevenson, 1974a). When he was three and a half he started talking about being the reincarnation of an older sister, Emilia, who had killed herself at 19—just 18 months before he was born. Emilia had never felt comfortable as a girl and had ended her life with the intention of becoming male the next time around. Paulo identified with her behaviorally as well as in his memories and before he was 4 demonstrated how to thread and operate her sewing machine. He was not happy as a man, however, and at 43, took his own life.

Another Brazilian, Jacira Silva, was precocious in speaking and by 11 months was talking about having been her mother's brother, who had killed himself at 28 by drinking insecticide mixed in a red soft drink, for no apparent reason (Andrade, 2010). He had died about five years and nine months before Jacira's birth. Jacira was tomboyish as a child, although she didn't mind being a girl. She had a phobia of red liquids. She disliked the notion of suicide and, as she got older, began to speak out against it.

A Tenth Suicide Case: Cruz Moscinski

I learned about this case through Facebook late in 2015 and began investigating it immediately through instant messaging and email. Cruz Moscinski was born on October 16, 2014 and, as of April, 2016, is only about 18 months old. The case is still developing; the following represents only a preliminary account of it.[25]

Cruz Moscinski (little Cruz) is thought to be the reincarnation of his father's best friend, Cruz Rodriguez (big Cruz). Big Cruz was born on October 7, 1991. He was smart and charismatic, a natural leader. He enjoyed hanging out with his friends, chief among them Derek Moscinski. His sister, Bianca, two years his junior, is best friends with Derek's fiancée, Brittany. Bianca's boyfriend at the time was another member of big Cruz's circle.

Only his immediate family knew that big Cruz had a troubled side. He was diagnosed with oppositional defiant disorder at eight, depression at 12, and manic depressive or bipolar disorder at 15. Medications were prescribed but he thought they were making him worse and often missed taking them on schedule. His problem behaviors were most often displayed at home, in the form of anger directed at his mother, Ronni.

Big Cruz's depressions were aggravated in the last months of his life by a series of deaths around him. First Derek's father died of prostate cancer, then a cousin to whom he was close killed himself. The cousin's death came the day after a night he had spent with big Cruz's family. It was a shock from which big Cruz never fully recovered. A month later, in February, a childhood friend took his life. The immediate cause of his own suicide was a fight with his girlfriend, following his discovery that she had been unfaithful to him yet again. He hung himself in his family's garage just after midnight on June 13, 2014, when he was 22.

Brittany was pregnant at the time. She and Derek stopped by the Rodriguez house, the morning after big Cruz's death, to share the results of their latest ultrasound, which showed the baby to be a boy. That night Derek dreamed that he and big Cruz walked into work to find big Cruz's girlfriend and Bianca's boyfriend 'all over each other.' "I know in dreams everything seems like reality, even the oddest of

---

[25] My information for this case comes from the subject's father, Derek Moscinski, and the previous person's mother, Ronni Tepp-Rodriguez, and sister, Bianca Rodriguez. Photo 14 is used courtesy of Ronni Tepp-Rodriguez and Photo 15 courtesy of Derek Moscinski.

things, but this was different because I knew it wasn't right," Derek told me. "I looked at Cruz and he responded to me, 'just let it go, it's nothing.'" A couple of weeks later Bianca and her boyfriend broke up and he started dating big Cruz's girlfriend.

When he was born a little less than four months later, Derek and Brittany named the baby Cruz Jeffrey James Moscinski in honor of big Cruz, Derek's father, and another man in Derek's life who had died earlier that year. The name was decided upon before little Cruz's birth, but it quickly became apparent that it was a highly appropriate choice. Little Cruz has a prominent cleft chin, matching one big Cruz had (Photo 14 and Photo 15). Cleft chins have a genetic basis and can be inherited, but they are unknown in either Derek's or Brittany's families. Big Cruz's great-grandfather (Ronni's paternal grandfather) had a similar cleft chin but, given the absence of a biological relationship between Derek and Brittany and the Rodriguez family, we might consider little Cruz's "butt chin" a birth defect or birthmark of the sort seen in many reincarnation cases.

14. Cruz Moscinski (little Cruz) at 10 months

15. Cruz Rodriguez (big Cruz) at 15.

Little Cruz is as outgoing and active as big Cruz was. The only time he sits still on Derek's lap is when Derek plays video games, something he and big Cruz enjoyed doing together. In fact, Derek and big Cruz were the most avid gamers among their friends. Big Cruz had a contagious giggle and little Cruz has as well. Little Cruz laughs at the same things big Cruz did and gives people the same looks. Derek has noticed that little Cruz is a very open baby who warms to people quickly, just as big Cruz did, but he acts differently with those who were close to big Cruz.

Shortly before Christmas, 2014, when he was about nine weeks old, Derek and Brittany took little Cruz to the Rodriguez house for the first time. He was immediately comfortable with the family. When Ronni held him, she felt a strong connection to him, but noticed that he continuously looked around her head rather than at her face. He fixed his gaze on a framed picture of big Cruz that rested on a shelf and stared at it for a long time. He looked up at the ceiling and smiled. On later occasions, he was more demonstrative with Ronni. Once when she held him he cuddled up to her and caressed her cheek with his hand. He has behaved similarly with Bianca and, on the few occasions he has seen big Cruz's father, has seemed to smile more than usual. He also responds to the family dog, a pit bull that big Cruz had brought home as a young puppy. At 110 pounds, the dog is now quite large, but little Cruz has no fear of him and wants to be near him.

On a visit to the Rodriguez house in the summer of 2015, when he was around eight months old, little Cruz kept looking up the stairs and trying to crawl up them. Big Cruz's bedroom was on the second floor. Derek had not been in that room since his death and felt nervous about going there, but eventually was persuaded to take little Cruz to it to observe his response. At the top of the landing there is a window and on each side of the window are pictures, cartoonish caricatures of big Cruz and Bianca done on a visit to Disney World when they were young. These pictures are visible from the stairs and as Derek walked up the stairs little Cruz fixated on the one of big Cruz, much as he had done earlier with his picture on the shelf.

They came to the landing and were about to enter big Cruz's room when Bianca called up to say that the light was out. With little Cruz in his arms Derek was unable to reach an alternative switch and used his cell phone to light the room from the doorway. As he panned from left to right, he was suddenly hit by a gust of hot air, "hard enough actually to move my hair while, at the same moment, I became super light headed and very very fatigued as if I had just got done working out extensively," he wrote. When his light reached the bed, he saw big Cruz lying there on his stomach, his hand supporting his chin, smiling at him. Derek hurried back downstairs, shaking so hard that Bianca took little Cruz from him. "I was not ready for that, I was not ready for that," Ronni recalls him saying repeatedly.[26]

Little Cruz's recognitions of people familiar to big Cruz have not been confined to the Rodriguez home. Whenever Bianca visits Derek and Brittany, he smiles broadly and gives her all of his attention until she leaves. He has also seemingly recognized two of big Cruz and Derek's friends. Their friend Kyle offered to watch him while Derek and Brittany attended a meeting. Derek had the impression that little Cruz wanted to say something to Kyle but, since he was not yet talking, no words emerged. They left him in his big sister's walker so that he could move around but, uncharacteristically, he stood staring at Kyle for the 45 minutes they were away. When little Cruz met another of big Cruz's friends, Dylan, he immediately stuck out his arms to be picked up, something he had not done before with his parents or anyone else.

---

[26] When Ronni first described this event on Facebook, she asked whether it was consistent with big Cruz having been reincarnated in little Cruz. I think it is. There are accounts of out-of-body experiences from all ages. They may be especially common before birth and shortly after, when the spirit is less securely bound to the body. Little Cruz's spirit could have left his body and gone to the bed but appeared as big Cruz to Derek because that was still his self-identity.

The most recent event of this sort came in December, 2015, when little Cruz was 14 months old. Ronni had had big Cruz's remains cremated and his ashes placed in urns. She preserved the largest urn in her house but gave several smaller ones to big Cruz's relatives and friends. Derek placed his on a shelf six feet off the floor. He does not recall ever talking about it in front of little Cruz, but one day the boy repeatedly pointed to the shelf, so Derek picked him up. He continued pointing toward the urn. At first, Derek thought it was an alligator head that had drawn his attention, but little Cruz indicated no. Finally understanding, Derek let him hold the urn, but "all he wanted was to give it a kiss then gave it right back to me."

Bianca later witnessed something similar. "Derek and Brittany told me the story of little Cruz reaching for and kissing big Cruz's little urn of ashes," she related, "but I hadn't seen it until they told me to grab the urn from the shelf and put it by little Cruz when he was being fussy one day. I grabbed the urn and as I turned around and it caught Cruz's eye, he got silent and his eyes got wide and excited, and he kissed and tried to grab the urn right out of my hands."

Little Cruz has been speaking for some months now but there are no reports yet of his having said anything about big Cruz's life. His behaviors have been more suggestive of memories than they are for most preverbal children, however, and we may well hear from him at some point.

What the Patterns Tell Us

The reasons for the self-killing vary a lot, but these ten suicide cases are similar to other cases in their main features. The children begin to speak of their memories at about the same age as other children. Many have behavioral traits and birthmarks that relate to the deceased persons whose lives they recall. Most have not been followed for long enough to draw any conclusions about the long-term effect of their suicides, however.

How about the role of will in these cases? Do we see evidence of greater control over reincarnation in them? Yes, we do, and not just with Wael Kiwan and Marta Lorenz. The data are summarized in Table 29-1. In no fewer than six of the nine cases, the reincarnation was into the same nuclear or extended family. In three cases the previous person was acquainted with the new family and, in one case, the relationship was to an ethnic group. There are no reincarnations into random, stranger families among them. This finding is especially noteworthy given that two of the countries involved (Turkey and India) are ones with a relatively low percentage of same-family cases.

Table 29-1: Country, Relationship, and Intermission Length in Ten Suicide Cases

Case	Country	Relationship	Intermission Length
Cemil Fahrici	Turkey	Family	2 days
Faruq Andary	Turkey	Family	4 weeks
Rajani Singh	India	Family	5 weeks
Navalkishore Yadev	India	Family	4-8 weeks
Wael Kiwan	Lebanon	Ethnic group	8 weeks
Cruz Moscinski	United States	Acquaintance	4 mos.
Marta Lorenz	Brazil	Acquaintance	10 mos.
Rolf Wolf	Germany	Acquaintance	17 mos.
Paulo Lorenz	Brazil	Family	18 mos.
Jacira Silva	Brazil	Family	5 yrs. 9 mos.

The data tell us something else too, something unexpected. The intermissions in all these cases are unusually short. The median intermission length of the 1,700 solved cases in the Division of Perceptual Studies database is 16 months (Tucker, 2013), but the median for the 10 suicide cases is only three months. Moreover, all the cases with intermissions longer than the median are Western cases, but even the longest intermission, the five years and nine months for Jacira Silva, is much shorter than is usual for Western cases. There is no obvious reason for this and with so small a sample it would be unwise to make much of it. Nonetheless, coupled with the tendency for suicides to be reborn among family and friends, it adds to the impression that reincarnation is not a random process, or one decided by forces beyond our control, but rather something over which we can have some say under certain conditions.

30

APPEARANCES CAN BE DECEIVING: SPURIOUS CASES

S keptics have many ways of explaining away the evidence for reincarnation. One of their most common charges is that facts are being overlooked, misremembered, or misinterpreted in order to make a child's recollections fit a specific deceased person, when really they do not. Investigators try hard to rule out this possibility, but sometimes it does seem to be the answer.

Ian Stevenson, along with Satwant Pasricha and Godwin Samararatne (Stevenson, Pasricha and Samararatne, 1988), reported several instances of self-deception in Asia. Titus Rivas (1991) described one from Holland. In Rivas' case, a retired engineer thought that he had been an infant who survived the *Titanic*'s sinking. He recalled a partial name, which he had linked to a name on the passenger manifest but, when Rivas looked more closely at the situation, he found that none of the man's apparent memories matched either this child or the conditions on the ship.

Another charge skeptics make is that parents impose past-life identities on their children and, again, there are examples of this. Stevenson, Pasricha, and Samararatne (1988) have a case in which parents believed their child was Mahatma Gandhi reborn and another in which they thought he was John F. Kennedy. The children grew up hearing that they were these people and came to believe that they were, although they never had memories or behaviors that would suggest it to be true.

Less common than self-delusion and parental imposition of identity is willful deception, but this too can, and does, occur. An example is the case of David Morris, published in *Fate* magazine in 1968. David was supposed to be an Israeli boy who spoke an ancient form of Hebrew at age three. His utterances were consistent with legends about King David, who had lived 3,000 years before. The story was full of named people in prominent positions and seemed to be well substantiated.

There were two investigations of this case, one by a newspaper that was considering reprinting the story but thought it wise to check it out first. The second was by Stevenson, who wrote about it in his paper with Pasricha and Samararatne in 1988. Neither investigation turned anything up to support the story and *Fate* printed a retraction to it in 1969. This was enough to put the case to rest for some years, but it may be making a comeback. The German regression therapist and writer, Trutz Hardo, treats it in his *Children Who Have Lived Before* (Hardo, 2005) as if there were no question about its authenticity.

Stevenson (in Stevenson, Pasricha, and Samararatne, 1988) says that he exposed several journalistic hoaxes in India. A common denominator of the cases is that they are in some way atypical and slightly too good to be true, as the David Morris case was. Next I consider two other cases that have received a lot of attention recently. The first is thanks to another write-up by Hardo (2005).

The Druze Boy Who Exposed his Murderer

In *Children Who Have Lived Before,* Hardo told the story of a three-year-old Israeli Druze boy from the Golan Heights who identified his murderer and forced a confession from him. Hardo said he heard the story from Eli Lasch, an Israeli physician. Lasch (1998), however, does not mention it in his autobiography, *The Light Came over Me: My Journey from Medical Doctor to Spiritual Healer,* and it has been impossible to verify.

According to Hardo, the Druze boy was born with a linear birthmark that stretched from his "upper forehead" to "the center of his head." When he was about three years old, he said that he had been murdered with an axe. On the assumption that he had been killed nearby, a party of 15 men, including his father and other relatives, set out with him on a tour of the area a few months later. Dr. Lasch, Hardo says, was invited to accompany the group.

When they came to a certain village, the boy said this was where he had lived. He suddenly recalled his name from the past life and also that of the man who had murdered him. A villager recognized the name he gave for his past self as that of a man who had disappeared four years before. The boy then led the way to his former home. He went up to a man in the crowd that had gathered around them, identified him as his former neighbor, and accused him of having murdered him with an axe. The man blanched as if guilty.

The boy added, "I even know where you buried my body." A little while later, the group followed him into the fields, where he pointed to a pile of rocks and said that his body would be found beneath it. The rocks were moved, and sure enough, there was a skeleton under them. On seeing the body dug up, the murderer, who had been persuaded to accompany the group, confessed to the crime. The boy then pointed out where the axe was buried and it, too, was found where he said it was. Hardo relates that Dr. Lasch asked the villagers if they would turn the murderer over to the police but was told no, they would handle the punishment themselves.

This story was first picked up from Hardo's book by the *Epoch Times* on May 17, 2014. The online version, which has gone through several revisions,[27] has been spread around the internet since then. Another version, purporting to be a scan of a newspaper article dated "Golan Heights, May 21" and credited to "Agencies," made its first appearance on Facebook on May 22, 2014, less than a week after the *Epoch Times* story but at least 15 years after the events were supposed to have taken place. [28] It was illustrated with the same stock photo of a boy pointing used by *Epoch Times*.

This story has become quite well known and several web pages are devoted to it. Erlendur and I learned about this story on Facebook in 2014. We determined that Eli Lasch had died in 2009, so could no longer be questioned about it. We contacted Hardo, but he was unable to provide any substantiating information.

Erlendur asked an Israeli Druze friend who follows these cases if he knew about this one. The man did not recognize it, made further

---

[27] For the latest version, see http://www.theepochtimes.com/n3/681034-3-year-old-remembers-past-life-identifies-murderer-and-location-of-body/

[28] See https://www.facebook.com/photo.php?fbid=764911416882702&set=a.457829557590891.104793.100000915517086&type=3&theater.

inquiries, and found it to be without foundation. In reporting these findings to my Facebook group, Erlendur noted that this case shows how cases can get embellished or fabricated. It also shows how they can get picked up by the media and spread around without appropriate scrutiny.

In retrospect, one can see several reasons to be suspicious of this story. The boy said very little about the previous life spontaneously, but when he reached the past-life village, he recalled both his name and that of his murderer. Even stranger is the boy's reaction to seeing the murderer. He showed no fear, but marched up to him and accused him of the crime, evidently quite dispassionately. It also does not ring true, but is quite convenient for the narrative, that the villagers decided to take justice into their own hands, rather than turning the boy over to the justice system, which would have kept a record of the proceedings.

It is possible that there was a case of some sort here, but that Hardo either did not understand or remember well what Lasch had told him. In any event, it is remarkable that this story has attracted so much attention when it has so little substance.

Did Carl Edon Live Before as Heinrich Richter?

This last case returns us to the issue of the will to believe uncritically. Peter and Mary Harrison wrote about Carl Edon in a 1983 book, republished in 1991 as *The Children that Time Forgot* (Harrison and Harrison, 1991). Ian Stevenson independently studied the case and included it in *European Cases of the Reincarnation Type* (Stevenson, 2003).

Carl was born in Middlesbrough, North Yorkshire, England, on December 29, 1972. From the age of two years he talked about having been a Nazi pilot shot down over England during World War II. When he first began to speak coherently he said, "I crashed a plane through a window." He repeated this often, gradually adding other details. His plane had been a Messerschmitt, he said. He gave the number as 101 or 104, but his mother later could not remember which. He had been on a bombing mission when he blacked out and accidentally flew into the building. He had lost his right leg in the crash. He had been 23 at the time.

Carl said his name had been Robert. His father's name was Fritz and he had a brother named Peter. When he became able to draw he made sketches of swastikas with eagles on them. At five or six he drew a sketch of the panel of a pilot's cockpit. He answered questions about his past life from his father and others. His father borrowed books from the local library and was able to confirm many details of things Carl talked about and drew.

Unlike other members of his family, Carl had blond hair and looked more German than English. He preferred drinking coffee to tea and liked thick soups with sausages. When he first talked about the German life, he spontaneously demonstrated the Nazi salute and goose-stepped. When he saw photographs of Hitler, he responded in the same way. He wanted to go to Germany and live there.

After his case was reported in a local newspaper, Carl was teased and bullied at school, which caused him to stop talking about his memories by the age of 10 or 11. His life came to a tragic end in 1995 when he was stabbed to death by a co-worker.

The person Carl remembered has never been satisfactorily identified. For a while his family thought he might have been the father of Carl's uncle's wife, a German woman whose father had been a Nazi pilot killed in England during World War II. This would be consistent with the tendency of international cases to involve some sort of personal link. Unfortunately, this woman's mother (the pilot's widow), who had remarried and also moved to England, rejected the case and refused to speak about it with anyone.

When the wreckage of a Dornier bomber that had crashed in 1942 after hitting the cable of a barrage balloon was unearthed near Middlesbrough in 1997, Carl's family came to believe that he had been either the pilot of this plane, Joachim Lehnis, or its bombardier, Heinrich Richter, although few of his memories fit either of these men (Table 30-1). Carl said his name had been Robert, not Joachim or Heinrich. He said his plane had been a Messerschmitt, not a Dornier, and that he had crashed through a window, not hit a balloon cable. The only point of agreement with Carl's statements besides the very general one that he had died during a bombing mission over England is that Richter had lost a leg in the accident, but he had been the plane's bombardier, not its pilot.

In 2013, an historian located a picture of Richter, which Carl's mother believes bears a "chilling resemble" to Carl. That, and the fact that Carl spent his last hours traversing the same route flown by Richter's plane and was killed in the same town Richter had bombed before he died, impressed her as beyond coincidence. The newspaper that first reported Carl's story updated it and posted it online, without noting the lack of correspondence between Carl's memories and Richter's death. That posting and a 2015 YouTube video about the case leave the impression that it is now solved—no doubt a major part of the reason these links have spread so widely around the web. Far from providing proof of reincarnation, however, they show how identifications can be made on the weakest of grounds; and, for skeptics, they do nothing but confirm that there is nothing of substance to cases of past-life memory.[29]

Table 30-1. Comparison of Carl Edon's Statements to Joachim Lehnis and Heinrich Richter

Statement	Source	Joachim Lehnis	Heinrich Richter
He was a Nazi pilot	Stevenson, Harrisons	Yes	No—he was a bombardier
His name was Robert	Stevenson	No	No
He died during a bombing mission over England	Stevenson, Harrisons	Yes	Yes
His plane was a Messerschmitt 101 or 104	Stevenson	No—it was a Dornier 217E	No—it was a Dornier 217E
He crashed his plane through the window of a building	Stevenson, Harrisons	No—it hit a balloon cable	No—it hit a balloon cable
He lost a leg in the crash	Stevenson, Harrisons	No	Yes
It was his right leg	Stevenson, Harrisons	—	?
He was 23 when this happened	Stevenson	?	No, he was 24

---

[29] The newspaper account may be found at http://www.gazettelive.co.uk/news/local-news/uncanny-case-carl-edon-3857619. The YouTube video is at https://www.youtube.com/ watch?v= CLnpazQBhfo& feature=youtu.be. See also https://exemplore.com/paranormal/The-Reincarnation-Of-Carl-Edon-And-His-Nazi-Airman-Past, where it is declared that "there can be no doubt" that Carl was Heinrich Richter.

31

WHY DO ONLY SOME REMEMBER?

The problem of why—if reincarnation occurs—we do not recall our past lives has been around for a long time. The Christian church father, Tertullian, made a big deal about it early in the Common Era and the issue has been brought up repeatedly since then. As it has become clear that some people do remember having lived before, the arguments have changed, though. Skeptics of reincarnation no longer assert that no one remembers previous lives, but contend that the reported memories are not what they appear to be. The question we have to ask nowadays is not, why do people not remember previous lives?, but rather, why do only some remember?

Memory, Brain, and Mind

Before we can tackle this important question, we must address a more fundamental one—How is it possible to remember past lives at all? Materialist neuroscientists assume that memories are stored in the brain, but have not been able to locate the spot in decades of research. As more and more of a rat's brain is removed, the rat still remembers. Recent studies have found that different types of memory—imaged episodic memory, semantic or verbal memory, emotional memory, memory for actions and behaviors—are handled by different parts of the brain, but that does not tell us anything about where they are stored. It merely says that different regions and sub-regions of the brain are involved in the retrieval of different types of memories.

If memories are not contained in the brain, where could they be? Many people, including a good number of parapsychologists, believe that they are preserved in the Akashic Records, or a subquantum Akashic field, and accessed via extrasensory perception.[30] However, there are problems with this concept. The biggest one is that our memories are personal. If memories are retrieved from an Akashic field, what keeps us from getting our memories confused with those of other people? Why do we zero in on one life, rather than remembering bits of several? (This is a separate issue from remembering things from more than one past life in sequence, as some people do). True, psychics sometimes say they are getting information from the Akashic Records, but their intuition that this is what is going on does not actually make it so.

Another possibility—the one I favor—is that our memories are preserved in the subconscious portion of our minds. This would explain why our memories are personal to us, and we know from laboratory tests, as well as everyday experience, that our minds are not off limits to psychics. The persistence of consciousness after death is suggested by near-death experiences, communications through mediums, apparitions, announcing dreams, and intermission memories. If memories are preserved in our minds, this information would survive death along with our minds, and would be available to us after our minds became associated with new bodies in reincarnation.

Mental Blocks

We can now consider the main questions of this chapter. If memories of our past lives are preserved in our subconscious minds, why do they so rarely present themselves to our conscious awareness? What makes them come to those who have them when they do?

The cases we have studied furnish some clues. The things children remember are frequently not very nice and may be quite traumatic.

---

[30] See, for example, Ervin Lazlo's *The Akashic Experience: Science and the Cosmic Memory Field* (2009).

Erlendur's psychological studies in Sri Lanka and Lebanon found that children with past-life memories had many more psychological and behavioral problems than their peers did. Many previous persons died violently and children who remember their lives often have phobias of people, places, and articles related to their deaths. The children's problems are similar to those seen in post traumatic stress disorder, although they stop short of being pathological (Chapter 9).

Even when deaths are nonviolent and peaceful, there can be difficulties. The tendency for natural death to lead to reincarnation in the same family or among friends means that we are constantly returning to varying relationships with one another, and this can be confusing to those who remember. When the previous families are strangers, children who retain ties to them beyond their early years may come to regret it. Reena Kulshreshtha, an Indian girl studied by Antonia Mills, continued to be so attached to her past-life husband that she was unable to form bonds with other men and refused marriages arranged in her twenties (Mills, 1989). I have heard from Usa Wongsangkul that a Thai man, Chanai Choomalaiwong, whose case was documented by Stevenson in *Reincarnation and Biology* (Stevenson, 1997), has broken off relations with the previous family and stopped speaking of the previous life so that he can devote himself to his present family and present life.

It may be that our psyches act to keep memories of previous lives from entering our conscious awareness in order to protect us emotionally and to allow us to adapt more easily to our present circumstances. This would explain why most of us do not remember having lived before. It also suggests that, rather than asking why we do not generally remember previous lives, we should be asking why we ever do? What is the value of past-life memory? What purpose does it serve? The answer seems to vary from person to person, but we should not forget that remembering may have positive as well as negative consequences. The psychological studies by Erlendur and Jim Tucker (Chapter 8) found that children with past-life memories as a group are more intelligent and better adjusted socially than their peers. Erlendur's studies found that teachers reported fewer problem behaviors than parents because teachers engaged with the children when they were older. This fact may indicate that the problems had receded over time, leaving longer term benefits.

Factors in Past-Life Remembering

Associational cues or triggers are as important in retrieving memories of past lives as they are in retrieving memories of present lives. Some children say little without some sort of stimulus, while for others stimuli are most evident in bringing forth the initial memories. Mridula Sharma (Chapter 23) first spoke about the previous life in response to a request of a visitor to her home for an item Munnu had possessed in Dehradun. Similar names and familiar people may have played a role with Kilden Alexandre Waterloo (Chapter 24) and Cruz Moscinski (Chapter 29). Younger children may begin to speak about the previous life without cuing, however. Ryan Hammons (Chapter 25) made his first reference to Marty Martyn without any apparent stimulus. Some years ago I made a study of the relationship of the subject's age to the presence of triggers to the initial memories in 95 solved cases, and this confirmed my impression that the older the subject was when first speaking about the previous life, the more likely the memories were to be cued (Matlock, 1989).

Other factors influencing past life memory retrieval relate to the previous person, rather than the subject. This is not surprising if memories are impressed on our subconscious minds and carried forward from death to birth. If our mental blocks are overcome and memories of past lives reach our conscious awareness, it is in great measure due to the meaningfulness of the remembered things to the deceased person of whom we are the continuation.

A considerable number of remembered lives ended violently, leading to the impression that violence makes past lives memorable, although, as I pointed out in Chapter 26, it may be the incompleteness of the life cut short, rather than the violence itself, that is the real factor here. There are many types of unfinished business besides the major ones of wanting to return to families left behind, the need to collect or repay debts, and the desire to tell widows where valuables are hidden. Suresh Verme (Chapter 23) rushed back to avenge his murder, for instance. Marty Martyn (Chapter 25) felt he had not spent enough time with his family. Munnu (Chapter 23) promised her mother she would remember. The frequency with which some sort of unfinished business is involved in reincarnation cases shows how significant a factor it is in bringing memories to conscious awareness.

Another factor affecting past-life memory is mental characteristics. In a study of 10 reincarnation cases with deaths that ended naturally at age 60 or after, Iris Giesler-Petersen found that in the majority of cases, the previous persons had been "devout" or "pious" Buddhists or were experienced meditators.[31] We see the same factors in cases in which the previous person died at a younger age, for instance, with the Tibetan Buddhist tulkus described by Mackenzie (1996). The reason could be that religious persons and meditators have conditioned their minds in a way that allows past-life memories to penetrate into awareness more easily, and this quality carries over into the new incarnation.[32]

Subconscious Influences on Personality and Behavior

It is not just memories and mental qualities that carry over, of course. So does temperament and other aspects of personality, and these attributes may be as crucial as veridical memories and recognitions in identifying a case subject with a specific previous person. Titu Singh (Chapter 23) was as active, intrepid, and hot-tempered as Suresh Verme had been, and he shared Suresh's machismo. Kilden Alexandre Waterloo (Chapter 24) had Father Jonathan's sense of humor and love of soccer, and he followed him into the Salesian order. Some children continue to develop the held-over personality traits as they grow older, whereas others lose them, but these changes are very much like the changes we all go through over the course of our lives. They are changes along lines of continuous development, not abrupt shifts.

Most children with past-life memories stop talking about them after a few years and their memories fade from their conscious awareness. Often the fading is associated with the start of school, with its new concerns and impressions requiring a new level of social and intellectual adaptation. Some children who speak of their memories at school are subjected to teasing and bullying, as Carl Edon was, and this naturally furthers their suppression. However, we know from Erlendur's studies in Sri Lanka and Lebanon, reviewed in Chapter 11, that a good number of children retain some memories into adulthood, so the complete loss of past-life memories to conscious awareness is not inevitable.

---

[31] Giesler-Petersen reported these findings to our Facebook group on January 2, 2015.

[32] Past-life memories may surface during meditation. Pratomwan Inthanu, a Thai woman of 20, recalled two past lives during meditation in enough detail for them to be verified (Stevenson, 1983).

We do not need to have conscious memories for them to have an impact on us, in any event. Bruce Peck (Chapter 22), identified as the reincarnation of a man who fell into the water after a heart attack, had no conscious memories, but he did have a phobia of water and boats when he was young. Unconscious influences show up in the passive xenoglossy of Stephen Stein (Chapter 28), and they may be present from very early in life. The memories of Nadine Maan (Chapter 6) and Alan Gamble (Chapter 22) were expressed physiologically before they were able to put them into words. Preverbal influences are apparent also with Cruz Moscinski (Chapter 29).

It may be that we all feel the effects of reincarnation subliminally, acting on our personalities and behaviors, even in the absence of conscious memories of previous lives, but do not recognize these influences for what they are. The influences nevertheless help us adapt to the conditions of our new lives when we return in the same ethnic, social, and linguistic groups. They provide the basis for psychological and perhaps spiritual growth. Past-life recall is not required to receive these benefits and may even interfere with them so, when it occurs, it likely has for some psychological purpose best known to the individual psyche.

32

HOW DOES
REINCARNATION WORK?

A more exact title for this chapter would be: "What Do the Rein-carnation Experiences of Children Suggest About How Rein-carnation Works?" Our insights into the reincarnation process come from cases of past-life memory, almost entirely those of young children. As discussed in Chapter 31, those who remember probably do so for a reason and may not be representative of all of us. Nevertheless, if we want to give our understanding of reincarnation an empirical grounding, solved children's cases are what we have to work with. Adults also may recall past lives spontaneously, but their cases are usually less well developed and are much less often solved; the same is true of past-life memories that emerge during age-regression under hypnosis.

The Disembodied Mind

It would be good to begin by asking: "What is it that survives bodily death and reincarnates?" The answer that flows from Chapter 31 is in some ways rather simple: "What survives and reincarnates is the mind, or consciousness." We might call it the spirit or the soul, too, but at a minimum it is a consciousness composed of both supraliminal and subliminal strata. The supraliminal stratum includes our conscious awareness, whereas the subliminal stratum comprises our subconscious minds.

Along with our minds come our memories, but also our personalities and our intellects. We see evidence of this survival in deathbed visions, apparitions, communications through mediums, and memories of the intermission period, womb, and birth (Chapters 13-18).

Our ingrained ideas about how the world works, our deep-set convictions and beliefs, are shaped by the cultures in which we grow up. This is especially true of those who have spent most or all of their lives in the same region, among the same people. These deep-seated beliefs are part of our personalities and it should not be surprising if they are carried over into death, along with other aspects of personality, and continue to influence behavior.

The case material makes clear that the disembodied mind retains its capacity to reason, but that is not all it is able to do. It can communicate telepathically with other discarnate minds and with the minds of incarnate people. It can perceive terrestrial events clairvoyantly and affect the terrestrial world via psychokinesis. An embodied mind possesses the same psi capabilities, but the psi cababilities are overshadowed by physical senses and instrumentality, which take precedence. For the disembodied mind, psi provides the sole means of communication and action.

The Return to Corporeal Life

In earlier chapters I showed that we often return to our families, friends, or compatriots, usually in the same cultural environments. There is cultural variation in the frequency of family, acquaintance, and stranger cases, but even where stranger cases form a major proportion of cases, the subjects almost always reside in the same country as the previous persons. International cases occur, but in all 14 solved international cases known to me, a motive for reincarnating abroad is clearly discernable. These patterns are far from random and could not be due to chance. It is hard to see how they indicate anything other than a discarnate mind choosing where and when to be reborn.

Stevenson (2001) identified two key factors in explaining why one life follows another: 1) a psychic (or psychological) factor and 2) a geographical factor. The cases Erlendur and I have presented include numerous examples of psychological factors. In the Rolf Wolf case (Chapter 9), Mario died in the arms of the woman who would become Rolf's mother. In the case of Kilden Alexandre Waterloo (Chapter 24), Father Jonathan was reborn as the son of Marine, with whom he had once been close. In the case of Craig Mitchell (Chapter 25), Michael Mitchell took the first opportunity—ten days after his death—to return as the son of the daughter he had sexually assaulted throughout her teenage years.

Geographical factors figure in cases in which a person was reborn near to where he died, even if it was different from where he had lived most of his life. The Igbo "enemy case" I mentioned in Chapter 26 is an example of this. The man was from another tribe, but died in Igbo territory during a war. Another type of geographical factor appears in cases in which a pregnant woman (or occasionally her husband or other intermediary) passes by the place the previous person died. A geographical factor of this sort is combined with a psychological factor in the case of Cruz Moscinski (Chapter 29). His mother, Brittany, was pregnant when she visited Cruz Rodriguez's house the day after he hung himself there. Because they bring the mind of the deceased previous person into contact, directly or indirectly, with the subject's mother, geographical factors can account for many stranger cases.

Intermission memories provide another way of examining the reincarnation process. In *Signs of Reincarnation* (Matlock, in prep.), I distinguish between "elective reincarnation" and "assisted reincarnation" in intermission memories. In elective reincarnation, a child recalls having chosen one or both parents. Ryan Hammons (Chapter 25) told his mother that he had known her in an earlier life and had chosen her for that reason. In assisted reincarnation, another discarnate entity encourages rebirth and sometimes determines the choice of parents. Katsugoro (Chapter 21) remembered that Tozo was met after death by an old, bearded man who led him to his parents' house.

Assisted reincarnation often has an elective element, as in the case of Christina studied by Titus Rivas (Rivas, 2004; summarized in Chapter 9). When she was three and a half, Christina dreamed she had died in a house fire. After death, she was met by a woman who showed her several possible mothers and told her to pick one to be her new mother. She chose a woman with blonde hair who was typing in an office, which matched the appearance and occupation of her mother at the time of the fire. This is the mode of rebirth depicted by Plato in the Myth of

Er: Er recounts that he saw souls of the deceased choosing their new lives from an array of possibilities presented to them.

Elective and assisted reincarnation do not cover all contingencies, however. Many children cannot explain how they came to be reborn where they were and there are no external factors to assist us in understanding how it happened. Purnima Ekanayake (Chapter 1) said that after she died she saw a light and the next thing she knew, she had been reborn in another part of Sri Lanka into a family with whom the man she was before, Jinadasa Perera, had not been acquainted. It is not clear in cases like Purnima's whether the children have amnesia for intervening events, if they were guided to their new bodies by a force of some kind, or if the connection was made wholly by chance.[33]

Jinadasa died suddenly, when his bicycle was hit by a bus. Unexpected death may play a role in cases like this by leaving the mind befuddled and reducing its control over its subsequent actions. Entrenched belief is another possible factor in many stranger cases. Stranger cases occur frequently in Sri Lanka and other Asian countries, where karma is thought to be responsible for selecting the circumstances of the new life, and in Lebanon, among the Druze, who believe God makes the arrangements. Stranger cases are also common in Western countries. The expectation that karma or God will make the decision about where one is reborn would naturally lead to not even trying to do so oneself, and this might account for fewer family and acquaintance cases in most Asian countries. In the West, an absence of belief in reincarnation would have the same effect.

Stranger cases appear to be associated with unexpected death, but they do not stand out from other cases in their cultures in length of intermission or frequency of sex-change. This could mean that, although no conscious decision of where to reincarnate is involved in them, the reincarnation nevertheless is driven by the subconscious mind, which has absorbed the cultural precepts.

---

[33] It is possible that not all cases that appear to be stranger cases actually are stranger cases, if there are connections from prior lives we do not know about. We have an indication that this is more than a possibility in the case of Ryan Hammons (Chapter 25) and perhaps also Stephen Stein (Chapter 28).

The Transmission of Physical Traits and Practiced Skills

Traces of imaged, verbal, and emotional memories might be carried in the subliminal mind, but how about physical traits such as fatal wounds, and skills such as the correct pronunciation of foreign words in responsive and recitative xenoglossy (Chapter 28) or Paulo Lorenz's ability to thread and use Emilia's sewing machine (Chapter 29)? In *Twenty Cases Suggestive of Reincarnation* (Stevenson, 1974a), Stevenson described a Tlingit boy born with the ability to repair outboard motors, as the person whose life he recalled had done. Skills at this level are perfected through practice and are neurologically rooted. How can wound residues and skills be transmitted to another body? Unless I can provide a satisfactory answer to these questions, I will not have shown how reincarnation works.

Let's look more closely at what we're dealing with here. Birthmarks commemorate death wounds in many cases. Purnima Ekanayake (Chapter 1), Chatura Karunaratne (Chapter 7), and Toran Singh (Chapter 23) are examples. However, violent deaths do not always result in birthmarks and, when autopsy reports are available, they may show more wounds on the previous person's body than there are birthmarks on the subject's body (Stevenson, 1997). Moreover, birthmarks may correspond to physical scars other than fatal wounds. Nathan, the Gitxsan boy, was born with a mark on his chest where his great-grandfather had a scar from having been hurt in a logging accident decades before his death (Chapter 22). Mridula Sharma (Chapter 23) has a dimple on her shoulder where Munnu had a dimple, and both she and Stephen Stein (Chapter 28) have birthmarks suggesting earring perforations on the lobes of their ears.

Experimental birthmarks reflect marks intentionally made on the previous person's body, sometimes after death. Tsu-lin's grandmother placed a red mark on his upper arm and black marks over his eyebrows and when she and Khoh-khin later discovered similar marks on another child those marks confirmed their sense that she was Tsu-lin reborn (Chapter 21). The girl is said to have resembled Tsu-lin physically, which brings up another issue—it is not just wounds and scars that may be reproduced on new bodies. Other physical features, such as general physique, facial structure, eye form, skin color, etc., may be involved as well (Stevenson, 1997). However, there is nothing automatic about any of this. Craig Mitchell (Chapter 25) bears no physical resemblance to Michael Mitchell, for instance.

The great variability in when and how physical traits carry over in reincarnation suggests to me a psychosomatic role in their transmission. That is, I think that the reincarnating mind is responsible for reproducing the scars on its new body (or in the case of Craig Mitchell, intentionally avoiding them). There is nothing at all outlandish about this idea. An incarnate mind impacts its body in many ways.[34] I am only proposing that the influence begins prenatally, the incoming mind in effect customizing its new body for the life ahead.

This would make sense of some extremely puzzling phenomena in reincarnation cases, such as the left-right reversal of Chatura Karunaratne's birthmarks (Chapter 7)—understandable if they are the result of a mind viewing its old body from the outside and then conveying that perspective to its new body. It would also help to explain birth defects like that of Bruce Peck (Chapter 22), identified as the reincarnation of a man who had stated his intention to be reborn without a hand so that he would not have to work so hard in his next life. Bruce's severe deformity has no model in the previous life but seemingly derives from Richard Peck's desire not to have a hand.

I do not mean to claim that conscious will is involved in every physical carryover. On the contrary, I believe that most effects are driven by the subconscious mind. If a feature is emotionally salient or meaningful to the previous person, that is enough to bring about its impression on the new body. Thus, we see Cruz Moscinski's cleft chin, an aspect of the identity of Cruz Rodriguez (Chapter 29). There is a likely subconscious influence also in the case of Wijeratne, a Sri Lankan boy who remembered the life of an uncle who killed his bride when she tried to back out of her marriage commitment to him and was hung for the crime. Wijeratne did not have a birthmark related to the hanging, but he was born with a shrunken right arm and associated pectoralis muscle (Stevenson, 1974a, 1997). Wijeratne interpreted his birth defects as karmic retribution for knifing his bride to death, but would they not more plausibly stem from the guilt his uncle felt for his action?

I am suggesting that a reincarnating mind, either consciously or unconsciously, employs psychokinesis to affect the genome, epigenome, or tissues of the new body. Skills may be transferred in much the same way, through the laying down of supporting neural pathways in the new brain (Matlock, in prep.).

---

[34] See Stevenson (1997, chaps. 1 & 2) and Kelly (2007) for good treatments of this subject.

So Where Do We Stand?

How valid are the conclusions I have drawn from children's rein-carnation experiences? Can we trust them to give us insight into how reincarnation works for everyone, or are they specific to children who happen to remember previous lives? We can't know at this point be-cause the data from adult spontaneous cases are too meager to provide a check. There are many more regression experiences, but regressions are unsatisfactory for a variety of reasons. Hypnosis is not a reliable memory-enhancer, which is why testimony based on it is not allowed in court. If hypnosis is not good enough for legal proceedings, that is reason enough not to accept regression experiences into our area of inquiry.

Only further research will tell whether the theory I have sketched has any general validity. Meanwhile, my conclusions may serve as hy-potheses for testing against new data.

In summing up, let me state a few things which the present data do not support. Above all, they provide no evidence of karma operating in the way it is popularly conceived. Personality and mental charac-teristics definitely carry over, and people often grapple with the same concerns life after life, but the impulse to do so is an internal psycho-logical one. There is no good evidence of a moral cause and effect con-nection between lives imposed by a grand cosmic law.

With rare exceptions, children's reincarnation experiences provide no evidence of judgment or self-judgment between lives or of planning the next life beyond the choice of the new parents. If life reviews and life-planning occur at all, they appear to be individual and personal activities, not something we all go through as a matter of course.

There is no evidence that we routinely reincarnate in soul groups or even that we have soul mates with whom we become involved re-peatedly. We do come back to be with each other again and again, but in varying relationships. There is some evidence of minds meeting up between lives and returning together as twins, but very rarely for co-ordinating group returns. I suspect that where there seem to be soul groups, it is most often the result of people finding each other after they have reincarnated, not planning their returns in advance.

The data suggest a process of continual development, over the course of one life, through death, and into the next. Subconscious influences ensure that this development progresses even in the absence of con-scious memories of previous lives. I do not believe that reincarnation necessarily entails spiritual advancement, although it may. Its purpose and value, I think, lie with the assist it gives to biological, cultural and social adaptation; mind and body joined in a symbiotic relationship that will never come to an end.

REFERENCES

American Psychiatric Assocaition (2013). Diagnostic and statistical manual of mental disorders (5th ed.). Arlington, VA: American Psychiatric Association.

Andrade, H. G. (1988). *Reencarnação no Brasil.* Matão: Casa Editora O Clarim.

Andrade, H. G. (2003). *Renasceu por amor: Um caso que sugere reencarnação.* (Monograph No. 7.) São Paulo: Instituto Brasileiro de Pesquisas Psicobiofísicas.

Andrade, H. G. (2010a). A case suggestive of reincarnation. In G. L. Playfair (Ed.), *Science and spirit* (pp. 135-184). London: Roundtable. (Originally published 1980 as *A case suggestive of reincarnation: Jacira and Ronaldo.* Monograph No. 3. São Paulo: Brazilian Institute for Psychobiophysical Research).

Andrade, H. G. (2010b). *Reborn for love: A case suggestive of reincarnation.* London: Roundtable.

Barrington, M. R. (2002). The case of Jenny Cockell: Towards a verification of an unusual 'past life' report. *Journal of the Society for Psychical Research, 66,* 106-12.

ben Malka, O., & Shahar, Y. (2015). *A Damaged Mirror: A Story of Memory and Redemption.* St. Paul, Minnesota: Kasva Press.

Brody, E. B. (1979). Review of *Cases of the reincarnation type. Volume II: Ten cases in Sri Lanka* by I. Stevenson. *Journal of Nervous and Mental Disease, 167*, 769-774.

Chamberlain, D. (1988). *Babies remember birth.* New York: Ballantine.

Cockell, J. (1993). *Across time and death: A mother's search for her past life children.* New York: Simon & Schuster.

Cockell, J. (2008). *Journeys through time: Uncovering my past lives.* London: Piatkus.

Cook, E., Pasricha, S., Samararatne, G., Maung, W., & Stevenson, I. (1983a). A review and analysis of "unsolved" cases of the reincarnation type. Part I, Introduction and illustrative case reports. *Journal of the American Society for Psychical Research, 77*, 45-67.

Cook, E., Pasricha, S., Samararatne, G., Maung, W., and Stevenson, I. (1983b). A review and analysis of "unsolved" cases of the reincarnation type. Part II, Comparison of features of solved and unsolved cases. *Journal of the American Society for Psychical Research, 77*, 115-137.

De Groot, J. J. M. (1901). *The religious system of China, Vol. 4.* Leiden, the Netherlands: Brill.

Delanne, G. (1924). *Documents pour sevir a l'étude de la réincarnation.* Paris: Éditions de la B.P.S.

Dhiman, K. K. (2002, Jan. 17). Back from the land of no return. *The Tribune* (Chandigarh, India) Online Edition. http://www.tribuneindia.com/2002/20020112/windows/main1.htm

Edwards, P. (1996). *Reincarnation: A critical examination.* Amherst, NY: Prometheus Books.

Fenwick, P., & Fenwick, E. (1999). *Past lives: An investigation into reincarnation memories.* New York: Berkeley Books.

Fielding [Hall], H. (1898). *The soul of a people.* London: Bentley and Son.

Gershom, Y. (1992). *Beyond the ashes: Cases of reincarnation from the Holocaust.* Virginia Beach, VA: A.R.E. Press.

Gershom, Y. (Ed.) (1996). *From ashes to healing: Mystical encounters with the Holocaust.* Virginia Beach, VA: A.R.E. Press.

Greyson, B. (2000). Dissociation in people who have had near-death experiences: Out of their bodies or out of their minds? *The Lancet, 355,* 460-63.

Greyson, B. (2014). Differentiating spiritual and psychotic experiences: sometimes a cigar is just a cigar. *Journal of Near-Death Studies, 32(3), 123-126.*

Gurney, E., Myers, F. W. H., & Podmore, F. (1886). *Phantasms of the living. (*2 vols.). London: Trübner.

Haraldsson, E. (1991). Children claiming past-life memories: Four cases in Sri Lanka. *Journal of Scientific Exploration, 5,* 233-262.

Haraldsson, E. (1994). Psychodiagnostische Untersuchungen an Kindern mit "Rückerinnerungen" mit Fallbeispielen aus Sri Lanka. *Zeitschrift für Parapsychologie und Grenzgebiete der Psychologie, 36,* 22-38.

Haraldsson, E. (1995). Personality and abilities of children claiming previous-life memories. *Journal of Nervous and Mental Disease, 183,* 445-451.

Haraldsson, E. (1997). Psychological comparison between ordinary children and those who claim previous-life memories. *Journal of Scientific Exploration, 11,* 323-335.

Haraldsson, E. (2000a). Birthmarks and claims of previous life memories I. The case of Purnima Ekanayake. *Journal of the Society for Psychical Research, 64 (858),* 16-25.

Haraldsson, E. (2000b). Birthmarks and claims of previous life memories II. The case of Chatura Karunaratne. *Journal of the Solciety for Psychical Research. 64 (859),* 82-92.

Haraldsson, E. (2003). Children who speak of past-life experiences: Is there a psychological explanation? *Psychology and Psychotherapy: Theory Research and Practice,* 76(1), 55-67.

Haraldsson, E. (2006). Appendix: Three Lebanese cases of children who claim to remember a past life. In G. L. Playfair, *New clothes for old souls: Worldwide evidence for reincarnation* (133-157). London: Druze Heritage Foundation.

Haraldsson, E. (2012). *The departed among the living. An investigative study of afterlife encounters.* Guildford, UK: White Crow Books.

Haraldsson, E., & Abu-Izzeddin, M. (2002). Development of certainty about the correct deceased person in a case of the reincarnation type in Lebanon: The case of Nazih Al-Danaf. *Journal of Scientific Exploration, 16(3),* 363-380.

Haraldsson, E., & Abu-Izzeddin, M. (2004). Three randomly selected Lebanese cases of children who claim memories of a previous life. *Journal of the Society for Psychical Research, 86, 875,* 65-85.

Haraldsson, E., & Abu-Izzeddin, M. (2012). Persistence of "past-life" memories in adults in Lebanon who, in their childhood, claimed memories of a past life. *Journal of Nervous and Mental Disease, 200,* 985-989.

Haraldsson, E., Fowler, P., & Periyannanpillai, V. (2000). Psychological characteristics of children who speak of a previous life: A further field study in Sri Lanka. *Transcultural Psychiatry, 37,* 525-544.

Haraldsson E., Gissurarson, L. R. (2015). *Indridi Indridason: The Icelandic Physical Medium.* Hove, UK: White & Crow Books.

Haraldsson, E., & Houtkooper, J. M. (1991). Psychic experiences in the multinational Human Values Study. *Journal of the American Society for Psychical Research, 85*(2), 145-165.

Haraldsson, E., & Samararatne, G. (1999). Children who speak of memories of a previous life as a Buddhist monk: Three new cases. *Journal of the Society for Psychical Research, 63*(857), 268-291.

Hardo, T. (2005). *Children who have lived before: Reincarnation today.* London: Rider.

Harrison, P., & Harrison, M. (1991). *The children that time forgot.* New York: Berkley Books. (First published 1983 as *Life before birth*)

Hassler, D. (2011) *"...frueher, da war ich mal gross. Und...." Indizienbeweise fuer ein Leben nach dem Tod und die Wiedergeburt.* Achen: Shaker Media.

Hassler, D. (2013). A new European case of the reincarnation type. *Journal of the Society for Psychical Research, 77,* 19-31.

Hearn, L. (1898). *Gleanings in Buddha-fields: Studies of hand and soul in the Far East.* Boston and New York: Houghton Mifflin.

Ikegawa, A. (2005). Investigation by questionnaire regarding fetal/infant memory in the womb and/or at birth. *Journal of Prenatal and Perinatal Psychology and Health, 20*(2), 121-133.

Inglehart R., et al. (2004). *Human beliefs and values. A cross-cultural sourcebook based on the 1999-2002 values surveys.* Buenos Aires: Siglio Veintiuno Editores.

Keil, J. (1991). New cases in Burma, Thailand, and Turkey: A limited field study replication of some aspects of Ian Stevenson's research. *Journal of Scientific Exploration, 5,* 27-59.

Keil, J. (2010) Questions of the reincarnation type. *Journal of Scientific Exploration, 24,* 79-99.

Kelly, E. W. (2007). Psychophysiological influence. In E. F. Kelly, E. W. Kelly, A. Crabtree, A. Gauld, M. Grosso, & B. Greyson, *Irreducible mind: Toward a psychology for the 21st century* (pp. 117-239). Lanham, MD: Rowman & Littlefield.

Kito, K. (2015, October 15). Boy's rebirth claim from 200 years ago featured in exhibition in Tokyo suburb. *The Ashai Shimbun.* http://ajw.asahi.com/article/behind_news/social_affairs/AJ201510150001

Kristjan fra Djupalaek (1962) "Eg var myrtur" [I was murdered]. In *Thvi gleymi eg aldrei* (pp. 97-103). Akureyri: Kvöldutgafan.

Lasch, E. (1998). *Das Licht kam über mich: Mein Weg vom Schulmediziner zum Geistheiler [The light came over me: My journey from medical doctor to spiritual healer].* Freiburg: Hans Nietsch.

Laszlo, E. (Ed.) (2009). *The Akashic experience: Science and the cosmic memory field.* Rochester, VT: Inner Traditions.

Leininger, B., & Leininger, A., with Gross, J. (2009). *Soul survivor: The reincarnation of a World War II fighter pilot.* New York: Grand Central Publishing.

Mackenzie, V. (1988). *Reincarnation: The boy lama.* London: Bloomsbury.

Mackenzie, V. (1996). *Reborn in the West: The reincarnation masters.* New York: Marlowe.

Matlock, J. G. (1989). Age and stimulus in past life memory cases: A study of published cases. *Journal of the American Society for Psychical Research, 83,* 303-316.

Matlock, J. G. (1993). A cross-cultural study of reincarnation ideologies and their social correlates. Unpublished M.A. thesis. Hunter College, City University of New York.

Matlock, J. G. (2015). Evidence of past-life memory in a mildly autistic boy. Paper read at the Third Annual Meeting of the Lithuanian Society for the Study of Religions, Vilnius, October 22-23. (http://jamesgmat-lock.net/wp-content/uploads/2015/11/Past-Life-Memory-in-a-Milldy-Autistic-Boy1.pdf)

Matlock, J. G. (in prep.). *Signs of reincarnation: Lectures and readings for an inter-disciplinary graduate course.*

Mills, A. (1988a). A comparison of Wet'suwet'en cases of the reincarnation type with Gitksan and Beaver. *Journal of Anthropological Research, 44,* 385-415.

Mills, A. (1988b). A preliminary investigation of reincarnation among the Beaver and Gitksan Indians. *Anthropologica, 30,* 23-59.

Mills, A. (1989). A replication study: Three cases of children in northern India who are said to remember a previous life. *Journal of Scientific Exploration, 3,* 133-184.

Mills, A. (1994). Making a scientific investigation of ethnographic cases suggestive of reincarnation. In D. E Young & J.-G. [A.] Goulet (Eds.), *Being changed by cross-cultural encounters: The anthropology of extraordinary experience* (pp. 237-269). Peterborough, ON.

Mills, A. (2003). Are children with imaginary playmates and children said to remember previous lives cross-culturally comparable categories? *Transcultural Psychiatry, 40,* 63-91.

Mills, A. (2006). Back from death: Young adults in northern India who as children were said to remember a previous life, with or without a shift in religion (Hindu to Moslem or vice versa). *Anthropology and Humanism Quarterly, 31,* 141-156.

Mills, A. (2010). Understanding the conundrum of rebirth experience of the Beaver, Gitxsan, and Witsuwit'en. *Anthropology and Humanism, 35,* 172-191.

Mills, A., & Dhiman, K. (2011). Shiva returned in the body of Sumitra: A posthumous longitudinal study of the significance of the Shiva/Sumitra case of the possession type. *Proceedings of the Society for Psychical Research, 59 (223),* 145-193.

Mills, A., Haraldsson, E., & Keil, H. H. J. (1994). Replication studies of cases suggestive of reincarnation by three independent investigators. *Journal of the American Society for Psychical Research, 88,* 207-219.

Mills, A., & Tucker, J. B. (2013). Past-life experiences. In E. Cardeña, S. J. Lynn, & S. Krippner (Eds.), *Varieties of anomalous experience: Examining the scientific evidence* (2nd ed.) (pp. 303-332). Washington, DC: American Psychological Association.

Ohkado, M. (2013). A case of a Japanese child with past-life memories. *Journal of Scientific Exploration 27(4)*, 625-636.

Ohkado, M. (2015). Children's birth, womb, prelife, and past-life memories: Results of an Internet-based survey. *Journal of Prenatal and Perinatal Psychology and Health, 30(1)*, 3-16.

Osborn, A. W. (1937). *The superphysical.* London: Nicholson & Watson.

Osis, K., & Haraldsson, E. (1977, 2012). *At the hour of death.* Guildford, UK: White Crow Books.

Pasricha, S. K. (2008). *Can the mind survive death? Vol. 2: Reincarnation and other anomalous experiences.* New Delhi: Harman Publishing House.

Pasricha, S. K. (2011). Do attitudes of families concerned influence features of children who claim to remember previous lives? *Indian Journal of Psychiatry, 53(1)*, 21–24.

Playfair, G. L. (2006). *New clothes for old souls: Worldwide evidence for reincarnation.* With Appendix by Erlendur Haraldsson. London: Druze Heritage Foundation.

Playfair, G. L. (2011). *The flying cow: Exploring the psychic world of Brazil.* Guildford, Surrey: White Crow Books.

Rawat, K. S., & Rivas, T. (2007). *Reincarnation: The Scientific Evidence is Building.* Vancouver, British Columbia: Writers.

Rivas, T. (1991). Alfred Peacock? Reincarnation fantasies about the *Titanic. Journal of the Society for Psychical Research, 58*, 10-15.

Rivas, T. (2004). Six cases of the reincarnation type in the Netherlands. *Paranormal Review*, No. 29, 17-20.

Sabom, M. (1982). *Recollections of death: A medical investigation.* New York: Harper & Row.

Sahay, K. K. N. [1927]. *Reincarnation: Verified cases of rebirth after death.* Bareilly, India: Gupta.

Shirley, R. [1936]. *The problem of rebirth: An enquiry into the basis of the reincarnationist hypothesis.* London: Rider.

Shroder, T. (1999). *Old souls: The scientific evidence for past lives.* New York: Simon & Schuster.

Stemman, R. (2012). *The big book of reincarnation: Examining the evidence that we have all lived before.* San Antonio: Hierophant Publishing.

Stevenson, I. (1960). The evidence for survival from claimed memories of former incarnations. Part I. Review of the data. *Journal of the American Society for Psychical Research, 54,* 51-71.

Stevenson, I. (1974a). *Twenty cases suggestive of reincarnation* (2nd ed., rev.). Charlottesville: University Press of Virginia.

Stevenson, I. (1974b). *Xenoglossy: A review and report of a case.* Charlottesville: University Press of Virginia.

Stevenson, I. (1980). *Cases of the reincarnation type. Vol. III: Twelve cases in Lebanon and Turkey.* Charlottesville: University Press of Virginia.

Stevenson, I. (1983). American children who claim to remember previous lives. *Journal of Nervous and Mental Disease, 171,* 742-748.

Stevenson, I. (1986). Characteristics of cases of the reincarnation type among the Igbo of Nigeria. *Journal of Asian and African Studies, 21,* 204-216.

Stevenson, I. (1997). *Reincarnation and biology: A contribution to the etiology of birthmarks and birth defects* (2 vols.). Westport, CT: Praeger.

Stevenson, I. (2001). *Children who remember previous lives: A question of reincarnation* (rev. ed.). Jefferson, NC: McFarland.

Stevenson, I. (2003). *European cases of the reincarnation type.* Jefferson, NC: McFarland.

Stevenson, I., & Chadha, N. (1990). Can children be stopped from speaking about previous lives? Some further analyses of features in cases of the reincarnation type. *Journal of the Society for Psychical Research, 56,* 82-90.

Stevenson, I., & Haraldsson, E. (2003). The similarity of features of reincarnation type cases over many years: A third study. *Journal of Scientific Exploration, 17,* 283—289.

Stevenson, I., & Keil, J. (2005). Children of Myanmar who behave like Japanese soldiers: A possible third element in personality. *Journal of Scientific Exploration, 19*, 172-183.

Stevenson, I., Pasricha, S., & McClean-Rice, N. (1989). A case of the possession type in India with evidence of paranormal knowledge. *Journal of Scientific Exploration, 3*, 81-101.

Thordarson, Th. (1942). *Indridi Midill*. Reykjavik: Vikingsutgafan.

Thwaites, R. G. (Ed.) (1897). *The Jesuit relations and allied documents. Vol. 10: Hurons, 1636*. Cleveland: Burrows Brothers.

Tucker, J. B (2005). *Life before life*. New York: St. Martin's Press.

Tucker, J. B. (2013). *Return to life: Extraordinary cases of children who remember past lives*. New York: St. Martin's Press.

Tucker, J. B., & Nidiffer, F. D. (2014). Psychological evaluation of American children who report memories of previous lives. *Journal of Scientific Exploration, 28*, 583—594,

Tylor, E. B. (1920). *Primitive culture: Researches into the development of mythology, philosophy, religion, language, art, and custom* (6th ed., vol. 2). New York: Putnam's.

van Lommel, P. (2010). *Consciousness beyond life*. New York: Harper One.

Veniaminov, I. (1840/1984). *Notes on the islands of the Unalashka District*. Kingston, Ontario: University of Alaska Press.

INDEX

Cases are entered under subjects' first names.

Paperbacks also available from
White Crow Books

Elsa Barker—*Letters from a Living Dead Man*
ISBN 978-1-907355-83-7

Elsa Barker—*War Letters from the Living Dead Man*
ISBN 978-1-907355-85-1

Elsa Barker—*Last Letters from the Living Dead Man*
ISBN 978-1-907355-87-5

Richard Maurice Bucke—
Cosmic Consciousness
ISBN 978-1-907355-10-3

Stafford Betty—
The Imprisoned Splendor
ISBN 978-1-907661-98-3

Stafford Betty—
Heaven and Hell Unveiled: Updates from the World of Spirit.
ISBN 978-1-910121-30-6

Ineke Koedam—
In the Light of Death: Experiences on the threshold between life and death
ISBN 978-1-910121-48-1

Arthur Conan Doyle with Simon Parke—
Conversations with Arthur Conan Doyle
ISBN 978-1-907355-80-6

Meister Eckhart with Simon Parke—
Conversations with Meister Eckhart
ISBN 978-1-907355-18-9

D. D. Home—*Incidents in my Life Part 1*
ISBN 978-1-907355-15-8

Mme. Dunglas Home; edited, with an Introduction, by Sir Arthur Conan Doyle—*D. D. Home: His Life and Mission*
ISBN 978-1-907355-16-5

Edward C. Randall—
Frontiers of the Afterlife
ISBN 978-1-907355-30-1

Rebecca Ruter Springer—
Intra Muros: My Dream of Heaven
ISBN 978-1-907355-11-0

Leo Tolstoy, edited by Simon Parke—*Forbidden Words*
ISBN 978-1-907355-00-4

Erlendur Haraldsson and Loftur Gissurarson—
Indridi Indridason: The Icelandic Physical Medium
ISBN 978-1-910121-50-4

Goerge E. Moss—
Earth's Cosmic Ascendancy: Spirit and Extraterrestrials Guide us through Times of Change
ISBN 978-1-910121-28-3

Steven T. Parsons and Callum E. Cooper—
Paracoustics: Sound & the Paranormal
ISBN 978-1-910121-32-0

L. C. Danby—
The Certainty of Eternity: The Story of Australia's Greatest Medium
ISBN 978-1-910121-34-4

Madelaine Lawrence —
The Death View Revolution: A Guide to Transpersonal Experiences Surrounding Death
ISBN 978-1-910121-37-5

Zofia Weaver—
Other Realities?: The enigma of Franek Kluski's mediumship
ISBN 978-1-910121-39-9

Roy L. Hill—
Psychology and the Near-Death Experience: Searching for God
ISBN 978-1-910121-42-9

Tricia. J. Robertson —
"Things You Can do When You're Dead!: True Accounts of After Death Communication"
ISBN 978-1-908733-60-3

Tricia. J. Robertson —
More Things you Can do When You're Dead: What Can You Truly Believe?
ISBN 978-1-910121-44-3

Jody Long—
God's Fingerprints: Impressions of Near-Death Experiences
ISBN 978-1-910121-05-4

Leo Tolstoy with Simon Parke—
Conversations with Tolstoy
ISBN 978-1-907355-25-7

Howard Williams with an Introduction by Leo Tolstoy—*The Ethics of Diet: An Anthology of Vegetarian Thought*
ISBN 978-1-907355-21-9

Vincent Van Gogh with Simon Parke—*Conversations with Van Gogh*
ISBN 978-1-907355-95-0

Wolfgang Amadeus Mozart with Simon Parke—*Conversations with Mozart*
ISBN 978-1-907661-38-9

Jesus of Nazareth with Simon Parke—*Conversations with Jesus of Nazareth*
ISBN 978-1-907661-41-9

Thomas à Kempis with Simon Parke—*The Imitation of Christ*
ISBN 978-1-907661-58-7

Julian of Norwich with Simon Parke—*Revelations of Divine Love*
ISBN 978-1-907661-88-4

Allan Kardec—*The Spirits Book*
ISBN 978-1-907355-98-1

Allan Kardec—*The Book on Mediums*
ISBN 978-1-907661-75-4

Emanuel Swedenborg—*Heaven and Hell*
ISBN 978-1-907661-55-6

P.D. Ouspensky—*Tertium Organum: The Third Canon of Thought*
ISBN 978-1-907661-47-1

Dwight Goddard—*A Buddhist Bible*
ISBN 978-1-907661-44-0

Michael Tymn—*The Afterlife Revealed*
ISBN 978-1-970661-90-7

Michael Tymn—*Transcending the Titanic: Beyond Death's Door*
ISBN 978-1-908733-02-3

Guy L. Playfair—*If This Be Magic*
ISBN 978-1-907661-84-6

Guy L. Playfair—*The Flying Cow*
ISBN 978-1-907661-94-5

Guy L. Playfair — *This House is Haunted: The True Story of the Enfield Poltergeist*
ISBN 978-1-907661-78-5

Carl Wickland, M.D.—*Thirty Years Among the Dead*
ISBN 978-1-907661-72-3

John E. Mack—*Passport to the Cosmos*
ISBN 978-1-907661-81-5

Peter & Elizabeth Fenwick—*The Truth in the Light*
ISBN 978-1-908733-08-5

Erlendur Haraldsson— *Modern Miracles*
ISBN 978-1-908733-25-2

Erlendur Haraldsson— *At the Hour of Death*
ISBN 978-1-908733-27-6

Erlendur Haraldsson—*The Departed Among the Living*
ISBN 978-1-908733-29-0

Brian Inglis—*Science and Parascience*
ISBN 978-1-908733-18-4

Brian Inglis—*Natural and Supernatural: A History of the Paranormal*
ISBN 978-1-908733-20-7

Ernest Holmes—*The Science of Mind*
ISBN 978-1-908733-10-8

Victor & Wendy Zammit —*A Lawyer Presents the Evidence For the Afterlife*
ISBN 978-1-908733-22-1

Casper S. Yost—*Patience Worth: A Psychic Mystery*
ISBN 978-1-908733-06-1

William Usborne Moore—*Glimpses of the Next State*
ISBN 978-1-907661-01-3

William Usborne Moore—*The Voices*
ISBN 978-1-908733-04-7

John W. White—*The Highest State of Consciousness*
ISBN 978-1-908733-31-3

Lord Dowding—*Many Mansions*
ISBN 978-1-910121-07-8

Paul Pearsall, Ph.D. — *Super Joy*
ISBN 978-1-908733-16-0

All titles available as eBooks, and selected titles available in Hardback and Audiobook formats from www.whitecrowbooks.com

CPSIA information can be obtained
at www.ICGtesting.com
Printed in the USA
LVHW090925270519
619132LV00002B/861/P